Windows® 2000 User Management

Other Books by New Riders Publishing

Windows NT Power Toolkit
Stu Sjouwerman and Ed Tittel, 0-7357-0922-x

Planning for Windows 2000
Eric Cone, Jon Boggs, and Sergio Perez, 0-7357-0048-6

Windows NT DNS
Michael Masterson, Herman Kneif, Scott Vinick, and Eric Roul, 1-56205-943-2

Windows NT Network Management: Reducing Total Cost of Ownership
Anil Desai, 1-56205-946-7

Windows NT Performance Monitoring, Benchmarking and Tuning
Mark Edmead and Paul Hinsburg, 1-56205-942-4

Windows NT Registry: A Settings Reference
Sandra Osborne, 1-56205-941-6

Windows NT TCP/IP
Karanjit Siyan, 1-56205-887-8

Windows NT Terminal Server and Citrix MetaFrame
Ted Harwood, 1-56205-944-0

Cisco Router Configuration and Troubleshooting
Mark Tripod, 0-7357-0024-9

Exchange System Administration
Janice Rice Howd, 0-7357-0081-8

Implementing Exchange Server
Doug Hauger, Marywynne Leon, and William C. Wade III, 1-56205-931-9

Network Intrusion Detection: An Analyst's Handbook
Stephen Northcutt, 0-7357-0868-1

Understanding Data Communications, Sixth Ed.
Gilbert Held, 0-7357-0036-2

Windows NT Power Toolkit
Stu Sjouwerman & Ed Tittel, 0-7357-0922-x

SQL Server Administration
Sean Baird, Chris Miller, et al., 1-56205-955-6

Domino System Administration
Rob Kirkland, 1-56205-948-3

Cisco Router Configuration & Troubleshooting
Mark Tripod, 0-7357-0024-9

Network Intrusion Detection: An Analyst's Handbook
Stephen Northcutt, 0-7357-0868-1

Understanding Directory Services
Doug & Beth Sheresh, 0-7357-0910-6

Understanding the Network
Michael Martin, 0-7357-0977-7

Internet Information Services Administration
Kelli Adam, 0-7357-0022-2

Inside Windows 2000 Server
William Boswell, 1-56205-929-7

Windows 2000 Active Directory
Edgar Brovick, Doug Hauger, William C. Wade III, 0-7357-0870-3

SMS 2 Administration
Darshan Doshi and Michael Lubanski, 0-7357-0082-6

Windows® 2000 User Management

New Riders

201 West 103rd Street,
Indianapolis, Indiana 46290

Lori Sanders

Windows 2000® User Management

Lori Sanders

International Standard Book Number: 1-56205-886-X

Library of Congress Catalog Card Number: 98-84885

Printed in the United States of America

FIRST EDITION: *March, 2000*

04 03 02 01 00 7 6 5 4 3 2 1

Interpretation of the printing code: The rightmost double-digit number is the year of the book's printing; the right-most single-digit number is the number of the book's printing. For example, the printing code 00-1 shows that the first printing of the book occurred in 2000.

Trademarks

All terms mentioned in this book that are known to be trademarks or service marks have been appropriately capitalized. New Riders Publishing cannot attest to the accuracy of this information. Use of a term in this book should not be regarded as affecting the validity of any trademark or service mark. Windows 2000 is a registered trademark of Microsoft Corporation.

Warning and Disclaimer

This book is designed to provide information about Windows 2000 user management. Every effort has been made to make this book as complete and as accurate as possible, but no warranty or fitness is implied. The information is provided on an "as is" basis. The authors and New Riders Publishing shall have neither liability nor responsibility to any person or entity with respect to any loss or damages arising from the information contained in this book or from the use of the discs or programs that may accompany it.

Publisher
David Dwyer

Associate Publisher
Brad Koch

Acquisitions Editor
Leah Williams

Executive Editor
Al Valvano

Managing Editor
Gina Brown

Product Marketing Manager
Stephanie Layton

Development Editor
Katherine Pendergast

Copy Editor
Lunaea Hougland

Indexer
Lisa Stumpf

Manufacturing Coordinator
Jim Conway

Book Designer
Louisa Klucznik

Cover Designer
Aren Howell

Proofreader
Debbie Williams

Composition
Amy Parker

Contents

About the Author

Lori Sanders has recently given up the road warrior's life and has joined the staff of HRchitect as a project manager for one of their Fortune 500 clients in Memphis, Tennessee. Previously, Lori owned iSolve Consulting Group, a company specializing in NT networking, I-net based system design, and technology consulting. Lori is also a technical editor and instructor for Learning Tree International, focusing on the Windows 2000, NT4, and client/server arenas. Lori has been working with Windows 2000 since the first beta release and has implemented the OS in several lab sites for her clients. Her 17-year background in the Information Technology field includes project management, information systems engineering, network administration, and technical support. She also has been a programmer, but you have to promise not to tell anyone about that. Lori is based in Tennessee where she lives most happily with her wonderful husband, Wade, their daughters, beautiful grandchildren, six cats, and two dogs. You can contact Lori at `lsanders@isolveconsulting.com`.

About the Reviewers

Grant Munroe is an MCSE. Grant has been working and playing on computers for the past 15 years. He currently works for the Heritage Group as a Network Administrator specializing in SMS administration. His responsibilities at the Heritage Group include WAN administration, new product testing and development, training, product evaluation, and software/hardware implementation. In addition, Grant has worked as a freelancer and consultant on various projects including technical editing, beta testing, development editing, and building and testing software products. He lives in Indianapolis, Indiana, with his wife and their nine computers.

Steve Crandall is a technology consultant in Cleveland, Ohio. During his 20 years in the industry, Steve has held positions in systems engineering, technical marketing, and technical management. He is currently a graduate student in the history of technology and science at Case Western Reserve University.

This book is dedicated to Sheree H. at AEDC who once asked me
"What else can you do?" A question I have never forgotten
and decided to answer for Sheree…and for myself.
Thanks Sheree.

Acknowledgments

This sounds really trite, but there are so many people to thank for helping me finish this book.

First, let me thank Steve Banach and Gary Ehling for their excellent work on the appendixes. I'm sure you will appreciate their template and scripting examples when you start seriously administering your Windows 2000 environments. Without their help, we never would have been done on time. Great work guys—thanks!

Second, and most naturally, I want to say thanks to my husband and best friend, Wade, for his constant support and patience even during my most tense "creative moments," (in other words, tantrums). For the times he put up with me stealing all the computing resources in the house to make new domains and networks to test theories on—I thank him. For all the late nights and early mornings and missed meals that he has suffered through while I worked on this book, thanks. For taking the kids, friends, visiting relatives, dogs, cats, and other obstacles out of my way when I needed to work, thanks again. I owe you hon.

I also owe my daughters a word of grateful appreciation for all the times when I was typing and only half listening—or couldn't get enough time in a day to do everything. You ladies have been patient and humored me well for the past few months. Thanks Nene and Crissy.

Also, I need to acknowledge the contributions of the whole group of wonderful professionals I've worked with at Learning Tree International who have sat around with me and discussed theories, and who havegraciously let me learn from their vast reservoir of knowledge and experience.

The group at New Riders deserve a medal for their patience and unfailing support throughout this project. Al, Katie, Gina, Leah, and everyone else, thanks for everything you've done to help get this text on the shelves.

And finally, to a small, dedicated Sheltie puppy who has sat so quietly under my desk while I typed and waited so patiently until I could get to a point to stop and go out for a walk. Thanks for the company Dundee.

Tell Us What You Think

As the reader of this book, *you* are our most important critic and commentator. We value your opinion and want to know what we're doing right, what we could do better, what areas you'd like to see us publish in, and any other words of wisdom you're willing to pass our way.

As the Executive Editor for the Networking team at New Riders Publishing, I welcome your comments. You can fax, email, or write me directly to let me know what you did or didn't like about this book—as well as what we can do to make our books stronger.

Please note that I cannot help you with technical problems related to the topic of this book, and that due to the high volume of mail I receive, I might not be able to reply to every message.

When you write, please be sure to include this book's title and author, as well as your name and phone or fax number. Please be sure to include the title of the book in your message, as well as the ten-digit ISBN number, which can be found on the back cover above the bar code. I will carefully review your comments and share them with the author and editors who worked on the book.

Fax: 317-581-4663

Email: `nrfeedback@newriders.com`

Mail: Al Valvano
Executive Editor
New Riders Publishing
201 West 103rd Street
Indianapolis, IN 46290 USA

Introduction

The purpose of this book is to provide a comprehensive, practical guide to managing users and their desktop environments with Windows 2000. The book is currently divided into three sections. The first is an overview of the new capabilities Windows 2000 offers for user and resource management, plus an overview of the Active Directory, domain models, and security mechanisms available. The next section will cover all aspects of user management; creation of users, bulk tools, migrations from other directory structures, groups, and planning for efficient use of groups. The final section deals with managing the user's environment through the use of profiles, group policy objects, and the functions Microsoft has grouped and marketed as IntelliMirror; such as Offline Files, Remote Operating System Installation (ROSI)services and Application Deployment.

With the dawn of Windows 2000, it has become even more difficult to draw a clear line between managing the user and managing the user's environment and desktop. That is one reason that the two topics are grouped together in this book. It was simply too difficult to determine where one subject stopped and the next began. That difficulty is reflected in the framework of this outline. It is difficult, for example, to know precisely where the chapter on group policies should be placed since some functions fall clearly under the user management topic and others are just as clearly environment oriented.

Part I: Windows 2000 Fundamentals

The primary goal of this section is to provide the reader with the background they must have in order to gain the maximum benefit from the rest of the book. It will begin with a high level discussion of the new features of Windows 2000 as they relate to user and desktop management, and proceed to discussions of the Active Directory architectural components, security mechanisms, domain models and mixed verses native mode operation. The collapsing of domains will be addressed from a high level standpoint, to demonstrate the inherent benefits to delegation of administration using Organizational Units (OUs).

Part II: Managing Users and Groups

In this section, the reader is given a step by step guide to creating users and groups in the Active Directory or on local machine SAMs using various tools sets. Creating users and groups from scratch using the User Interface (UI) and Active Directory Services Interface (ADSI) scripting will be discussed as well as tools to load users from databases, spreadsheets, earlier NT versions and NetWare environments. Much use will be made of scenarios and scripting examples.

The reader will be guided through existing groups and planning the creation of new security and distribution efficient use of groups. Other topics that will be included in the group chapter are deep group nesting, downlevel clients, mixed mode operations and token explosion in a multidomain tree. Concerns associated with each of these topics will be reviewed. A scenario that demonstrates the most efficient design of groups to minimize enterprise replication traffic will finish out the section.

Part III: Environment Management

This section will cover all the technologies that an administrator can employ in Windows 2000 to manage users and their day to day computing environments. Using profiles to manage the user's desktop and the types of profiles available for employment are discussed. Chapter 8, "Employing Group Policies," in this section will deal with the topic of group policy objects and the role they can play in user and environment management. Each type of policy object is discussed in detail as well as the way in which policies propagate and can be filtered in a domain tree. Chapter 9, "IntelliMirror Features for Client Management," reviews the remaining IntelliMirror components that deal with client management; Offline Files and ROSI services for example.

Is This the Right Book for You?

A primary objective of this text is to open the reader's eyes to the new possibilities that exist for managing users and their environments with Windows 2000 and to get them excited about those possibilities.

I have made the assumption that most of the readers of this text will be administrators (rather than programmers, for example). With this in mind, war stories and real world examples will be used extensively to drive home the points being made. When scenarios are called for, a single mythical organization will be used. This strategy provides the reader with continuity throughout the text that I feel is beneficial when trying to grasp new concepts. The reader is not trying to decipher a new scenario and naming convention at the same time they are trying to learn the fundamentals of ADSI scripting, for example. This method will be blended throughout the book with the real world experiences mentioned earlier so that the reader gets maximum benefit from the text.

I also assume that the audience will have a fair level of familiarity with administering Microsoft environments. As a result, the level of instruction is a little more abstracted than one might find in a text addressed to new NT administrators, for example. I assume readers are familiar with the services available in a NT 4 environment and the networking essentials needed to grasp the TCP/IP concepts used to implement the Active Directory structure in Windows 2000.

I do try and keep things as clear and simple as possible. When introducing some of the new interfaces and features of the product, readers will have screen shots to guide them through the more obtuse interfaces. The product makes extensive use of Wizards, both for administrative tasks and user tasks. So, much of the learning can be done very quickly once an administrator starts working with Windows 2000. When the interfaces are intuitive but the concepts or services are new, I spend more time on theory and background than screen shots. I have taught many folks to use this product in its beta and release candidate versions and over time. I think I have developed a feel for where administrators will have problems.

I

Windows 2000 Fundamentals

1

Inside Windows 2000 Overview

THE ADVENT OF THE PC TO THE BUSINESS WORLD HAS changed the way we approach desktops from a tech support standpoint. In the good old days, if a terminal broke, you called the mainframe repairperson. They usually brought in a new terminal, hooked it up, and removed the old one. Although we are often sorely tempted to do the same thing with a troublesome PC, economics usually demand that we try and fix the machine instead of just trashing it and buying a new one. Because many companies only look at the up front costs of purchasing hardware and software in a new system, post-purchase PC tech support has become one of the hidden costs in today's business computing environments. Depending on which industry analyst's reports you read, estimated annual total cost of ownership (TCO) can range from just under $4,000 to just over $12,000 per PC. Multiply those costs by the number of PCs in your organization, and you can easily see why lowering TCO for PCs has become a prime objective in the industry. In fact, it might be one of the reasons that you bought this book. Microsoft has responded to these concerns by incorporating many sophisticated user and environment management tools in Windows 2000.

As we try to lower TCO, there are several things that we can do. One of the keys to success would be to decrease the number of tech support staff visits to users' desks. How do we achieve that lofty goal? Well, first we would try to identify and remove the variables that cause the most trouble. (No, you can't remove the user!)

Speaking of the user, wouldn't it be great to find a way to protect the user from themselves while still letting them have some control of their environment? What about providing automatic fault tolerance for their documents and files? How about being able to create transparent alternate network paths to critical resources? Wait, let's make those network resources look like they are all on the user's hard drive so they don't even need to know about networks! Wouldn't it also be nice to let someone else take care of the user administrivia? You know, those help desk calls asking you to change their mailing address or phone number in the user database. Windows 2000 will allow you to do all of this and more.

There is a power struggle going on in every organization I have ever worked with. The prize in this universal, and seemingly eternal, conflict is control of the desktop. The user faction is the first to remind administrators that the "P" in PC stands for "personal." Naturally, the administrative alliance has a rather different view of who should control the desktop. Not necessarily because we are a paranoid group of control freaks, regardless of what our user community thinks, but simply because a more standardized desktop has been repeatedly proven to be easier to support and most importantly, reconstruct in the event of a disaster, whatever the cause. Windows 2000 will not magically end this struggle in your organization, but it will go a long way to giving you the ability to delegate administration in a sane and controlled manner so that you can ease the tensions between the two factions.

Regardless of the level of control you need over the desktop, and whether you require a centralized or decentralized administrative model for your enterprise, Windows 2000 can be customized to fit your needs.

Users

I find it interesting that administrator or tech support people I have known have the same love/hate relationship with their users. Without their constant calls to the help desk, we would be unemployed, or at least bored. You have to admit, though, that they provide a perpetual challenge and constant stream of great war stories to tell at conferences and classes. Most of those challenges and stories arise from the incredibly inventive things they do to their machines and the amazing amnesia that befalls them when they call the help desk to report the incident. Windows 2000 won't fix all your user problems, but it goes a long way towards limiting a user's ability to be creative and restoring their environment to a pre-amnesia state.

What's New for User and Desktop Management in Windows 2000

How are we going to achieve these goals of lowering TCO, creating an appropriate administrative model, and delegating administrative tasks as needed? Well, there are three primary additions to Windows 2000 that I see as the core technologies for improving the way we manage the desktop and our users. We will discuss each of these in greater detail later in the book, but this section will give you a conceptual background for future discussions. The three new technologies are:

- Active Directory
- Group Policy Objects
- IntelliMirror Technologies

Although Active Directory is totally new to Windows 2000, group policy objects and IntelliMirror are actually evolutionary improvements to existing Microsoft capabilities. For example, group policy objects are an extension of NT 4's system policies—policies on steroids, if you prefer. IntelliMirror is an evolution of ZAK and ZAW technologies. In Windows 2000, both group policies and IntelliMirror gain their true effectiveness as tools through their understanding of the Active Directory structures and mechanisms. So, let's start our discussion there and make sure you also understand why Active Directory is such an important component of this new operating system.

Active Directory

One of the limitations of previous versions of Microsoft's network operating systems has been the lack of a directory service that allowed administrators to create a three dimensional, abstracted directory tree. This capability has existed in other network operating systems (NOSs) for some time. Just ask any Novell or Banyan Vines administrator. The Active Directory is Microsoft's answer to NDS, Banyan Vines, and X.500 directory services.

The Active Directory is probably the single new feature with the most impact in Windows 2000. It will change the way network administrators manage users and resources. This one feature provides the fuel for all the talk you've been hearing about Windows 2000 being a "revolution, not an evolution." The truth of that statement is suspect because if you dig a little deeper into the NT architecture, the registry, and trust mechanisms, for example, you will find very little difference between NT 4 and Windows 2000. Instead of claiming "revolution," perhaps we can claim more realistically that Microsoft has made an evolutionary leap with this product, something akin to the first creature leaving the primordial ooze to walk on land.

Although the benefits of a three dimensional directory service are undeniable, I have already found that traditional NT and LAN Manager administrators have to seriously readjust their thinking to adapt to the idea of the Active Directory. The switch from being tied to the physical world where shared resources are associated with a particular server to the virtual world of the three dimensional directory service can be a difficult change. I believe though that once you have made the switch, you'll look back on previous Microsoft systems as primitive and limiting. Trust me, the switch is a liberating experience! With that hopeful outlook in mind, let's take a closer look at this new directory service.

Why Three-Dimensional?

All network operating systems must employ some version of naming or directory services that allow a user to locate useful shared resources on the network. We talk about these services as being one-, two- or three-dimensional.

A one-dimensional name service requires that a user have an account on every server where there are shared resources that they need to access. An example of a one-dimensional name service would be an NT 4 workgroup. In this model, a user is authenticated only against each machine's SAM as they attempt to access that machine. So, they must have valid accounts in each SAM.

When using a two-dimensional model, a user is authenticated against a central authority and is only required to have one account for all resources that they wish to access. Sound like an NT 4 domain using pass through authentication to anybody else? You're right! NT 4's domain models are prime examples of two-dimensional name services. If you have done inter-domain administration, you have already encountered one of the drawbacks of two-dimensional services—the domain boundary. In theory, there need only be one user account for any user through which they can be authenticated in other domains, provided we set up the required trust relationships between the domains. In actuality though, it is often easier or advisable for security reasons to set up multiple accounts in different domains for the same user.

A true three-dimensional-directory service has several characteristics, the first of which is a single logon for **all** network resources throughout the enterprise. No matter where the resource is in the enterprise, a user should be able to use their currently logged on credentials for authorization provided that they have been granted permission to access the requested resource. Another characteristic of three-dimensional services is that information about the network's environment is kept in a distributed form. Replication of the directory among several servers increases the fault tolerance of the directory. This replication must occur in such a manner that the currency of the directory data is assured so that when a change is made to one directory server's database, all other servers will soon be updated to reflect the change. Further, a user should be able to search a directory by a specific resource's name or by the type of resource. As an example, I should be able to look through the directory for the "Accounting Dept. Color Laser Printer" or just search for "color printers."

Finally, these directory resources should exist independently of their physically installed location. This is the concept of object abstraction. This is the concept causing us old NT administrators some mental anguish. Instead of needing to know that the Accounting department's color laser is installed on PRINTSVR3, I can locate the printer where it makes logical sense in the directory, probably the same place I locate all those accountants.

Windows 2000 meets all of these criteria for a three-dimensional directory service with Active Directory services in Windows 2000. The Active Directory allows administrators to create and manage a tree or forest of domains. We'll discuss those concepts further in the next section, Active Directory Overview. Within that directory structure, resources can be grouped to reflect the organizational structure and ease administrative burdens through delegation. Users need only one user account to access all resources, and the data is kept on several servers distributed throughout the structure and replicated whenever changes occur to ensure data currency.

Directory Services and the X.500 Specification

As with Novell's NDS and Banyan Systems' Street Talk, Microsoft's Active Directory is based on the X.500 directory service model, but it is not X.500 compliant. Although the X.500 directory service specification sounded great on paper, as with many ISO initiatives, it was seen as too complex and unwieldy to fully implement in the real world. At the same time though, people realized that the underlying structure of the directory service described in the specification was sound and provided scalability, flexibility, and fault tolerance. As a result, software manufacturers have taken what they thought was best in the X.500 specification and implemented it in their own proprietary way. Once again, we are plagued by the non-standard implementation of an industry standard.

At the moment, there are a few interoperability initiatives that have been undertaken by Novell, Banyan, and IBM to port their directory services to other platforms. There was NDS for NT 4, for example, and Banyan has ENS directory services implemented in a limited way on several other platforms. These solutions sometimes pose problems of their own, though, such as needing a Novell server to run NDS on an NT network and only having limited directory services using Banyan VINES ENS for UNIX platforms.

Microsoft is hoping to achieve real interoperability between directory services currently on the market with its implementation of Active Directory and its supporting services and APIs. They are planning to achieve this interoperability by building Active Directory on existing industry standards that already define interoperable services, such as directories and security services. One reason that we say the Active Directory is not X.500 compliant, is that rather than using DAP as the directory protocol, Microsoft has chosen the Lightweight Directory Access Protocol (LDAP). Microsoft has invested heavily in this specification almost since its inception. In addition to using the LDAP standard to locate and affect resources in the virtual structure of Active Directory, the domain tree structure of the Active Directory uses DNS naming conventions. Finally, once a directory is fully converted to Windows 2000, the system can use the Kerberos security system for authentication services.

Using the LDAP naming conventions, Microsoft has designed a generic directory interface called ADSI that can be used in scripts and programs to create, modify, and delete directory objects in the Windows 2000 Active Directory. In the future, Microsoft hopes that ADSI will be the programming interface of choice to modify directories in all networking environments. Because it uses LDAP and has the added advantage of allowing application programmers to use only one API to access all resources in a heterogenous network environment, there's a better than average chance that they will succeed in that hope.

IntelliMirror

As I mentioned earlier, IntelliMirror is a natural evolution of Microsoft's Zero Admin initiatives (ZAK and ZAW). It is actually a collection of technologies that have been incorporated into Windows 2000. Some of these technologies already existed in whole or in part in other Microsoft software packages. Administrators of SMS systems will feel quite comfortable with the application deployment features of Windows 2000, for example, because they will already be familiar with them if they have used the Microsoft Installer service in SMS.

All the features of IntelliMirror are designed to make it easier to recover a user's workstation in the event of a fatal crash. The features of Windows 2000 that are collectively called IntelliMirror are:

- Client Side Caching
- Remote Boot
- Single Instance Storage
- Microsoft Installer for Automated Application Deployment
- Group Policies

Although I have dedicated Chapter 9, "IntelliMirror Features for Client Management," to a full discussion of IntelliMirror because being able to exploit its features is critical to your ability to manage the desktop effectively, let me briefly explain each functionality here.

Client Side Caching

Client side caching allows for the use of server based files when the network is unavailable. This is accomplished by setting up a cache on the client's hard drive. Files and their security permissions are cached automatically as the user accesses files on the server. Should the network become unavailable for whatever reason, the user accesses the files in exactly the same way as if the client were connected. Instead of following the designated network path, Windows 2000 redirects the request to the locally cached copy of the document. When the network becomes available again, the documents in the cache are automatically synchronized against the server's copy. If both copies have been changed, the user is asked how they want to resolve the problem.

Group Policy Objects

Group policy objects are sometimes listed as an IntelliMirror feature depending on which Microsoft paper you are reading. We will talk about those as a separate functionality within Windows 2000. They will be discussed in the following section and in great depth in Chapter 8, "Employing Group Policies".

Remote Boot

Remote Boot allows for the quick reinstallation of an operating system from a centralized location on the network. In the event that the operating system needs to be reloaded due to a hardware problem, the user receiving a new PC, or just one of those inexplicable software failures, an administrator designates that a particular user or machine is associated with a particular operating system. Using a bootstrap protocol floppy or a PC98 BIOS compliant system, the user boots the machine and the operating system is downloaded from the network. This can also be used for NetPCs should you have any on your network.

Single Instance Storage (SIS)

We often run into problems when users install software packages and make them network installs. This results in several copies of the offending package on the server taking up valuable hard drive space. SIS allows you to overcome this problem. When using SIS, the administrator designates a portion of the server's storage as SIS area. When a file is saved to that server, the server checks the file against the other files in the SIS area. If that new file is identical to an existing file, SIS doesn't save a second copy of the file. Instead, the server only creates a directory entry for the file.

Microsoft Installer (MSI)

The application deployment features of IntelliMirror are accomplished using a combination of the MSI tool to manage the mechanics of the installation and group policy objects to define recipients of particular applications. This tool can be used to deploy, update, repair, and remove applications from the user's machine. Applications can be set for mandatory deployment or they can be published for the user to install if the user wants to. Using just in time installation at the time of "installation" only the icon is actually put in place on the desktop. Only when the user launches the application for the first time does the installation of required files actually occur. This prevents the system from installing unnecessary application files for software that this particular user may never have need of.

Group Policy Objects

Group policies allow us to set user and machine settings, employ logon/logoff and startup/shutdown scripts, set security policies such as audit and password policies, use automated application deployment, and distribute required URLs and files to the user's desktop environment. These policy objects can de deployed selectively throughout the domain by user, machine, group, or organization.

As I mentioned earlier in the chapter, group policies are an expansion of the capabilities that were available to administrators of NT 4 systems. What we talked about as system policies in NT 4 are called software policies in Windows 2000, and they are just one component of group policies. The five categories of group policies in Windows 2000 are:

- Software Policies
- User Documents and Settings
- Scripts
- Security Settings (for users and machines)
- Application Deployment

Although we will discuss each of these in great detail in Chapter 8, I think a brief introduction is in order at this point.

Software Policies

As I mentioned, software policies govern the same registry settings that NT system policies affected. Policies affect the client by altering the registry settings of the target machine just as they did in NT 4. Among other things, software policies can be used to restrict the user's ability to alter the desktop, configure the desktop for all users of a particular machine, restore settings, and set default locations for user directories.

User Documents and Settings

You can use these settings to redirect folders to other locations. For example, you could redirect the user's My Documents folder to a network drive to achieve fault tolerance for their files. You could also distribute URLs to all users or a particular group or Organizational Unit (OU) with these policies. You might want all the Windows 2000 administrators to have a direct link to the Microsoft Knowledge Base or the Windows 2000 Server home page, for example.

Scripts

In addition to the logon scripting capability that was available in NT 4, with Windows 2000 you can now add logoff scripts for any user, group, or OU. You can also use start up and shut down scripts for machines, groups of machines, or machines in a particular OU. The Windows Scripting Host (WSH) is now fully supported in the deployment of these policies. WSH is a language independent scripting host for 32 bit Windows environments that includes both the VBScript and JScript engines. Microsoft anticipates that other software companies will provide engines that will allow the use of Perl, REXX, TCL, and Python. We will spend much more time with WSH in later chapters.

Security Settings

You can apply security settings in the domain through group policy objects. With the Group Policy Editor, you can set account policies, local policies (audit, user rights, and other local security options), event log settings, and define the membership of your restricted groups (such as administrators, power users, and server operators). You can also control system settings such as system service configurations, registry hive file security, and file system security.

Application Deployment

Inherited from SMS is the ability to automatically distribute software packages to the desktop. With these deployment policies, you can assign, publish, repair, update, or remove applications for an OU, particular users, or a group of machines. The MSI tool handles the mechanics of deployment, but the selectivity of deployment is achieved through group policies. We'll go over both these topics in detail in Chapter 8.

All of these types of group policy objects can be inherited or blocked at any level of the domain's logical structure. This means that an administrator has the ability to set a policy that will apply for the entire domain by creating it at the root of the domain and specifying that it be inherited down the tree. An administrator can also choose to exempt a portion of the tree from any policy by choosing to block inheritance of the policy. One may not want the default domain user policy to apply in the Administrators organization, for example.

Group policies will be one of the most powerful tools in your administrative arsenal to achieve that elusive goal of lowering TCO for the desktop. They will allow you to create managed desktop environments that can be tailored to the user's job responsibilities and level of their PC literacy. For that reason, I have devoted Chapter 8 to the subject.

Active Directory Overview

The information that makes up the Active Directory is kept in a collection of databases that are replicated to different parts of the enterprise tree or forest. Microsoft often refers to these databases in their documentation as naming contexts.

Each domain in the structure has a database for that domain. This is often referred to as the user naming context or a partition in the Active Directory. Information in this database is replicated to all the domain controllers in that domain. It is not replicated to the rest of the tree.

There are three other naming contexts that are kept by the Active Directory. They are the Global Catalog, configuration information, and the schema. The configuration information and schema are collectively referred to as the Active Directory metadata. All three of these naming contexts are shared by the entire directory structure so there is only one Global Catalog and a single schema and configuration definition for each directory tree or forest.

Because this information is shared by the whole structure, the metadata and global catalog are replicated to every domain controller in the enterprise. Any changes to these universal naming contexts will start a replication cycle throughout the enterprise. Besides the replication traffic, also keep in mind that a mistake at this level will be a mistake that is replicated throughout the enterprise. Think of it as messing up the registry, but on a global scale, where everybody knows about it! For these reasons, I recommend that changes to any of these contexts should be made with extreme care and some serious forethought.

Let's start looking at these components on a smaller scale than that though. Let's begin our look at the Active Directory components at the domain level and then move on to bigger things.

Domains

The domain concept from NT 4 still has a home in Windows 2000. The domain is the building block for the enterprise model of the tree or forest, which we will discuss in the next section. A domain in Windows 2000 still serves as a boundary in terms of administration, security, and policy distribution.

Everything that was true of NT 4 domains holds for domains in Windows 2000. On a standalone workstation, the domain boundary is the workstation and users authenticate against the workstation SAM. If a machine is a member of a domain where there are domain controllers at work, users are authenticated against the domain database. The only difference is that in 2000, we authenticate against the Active Directory instead of the domain's SAM.

Each domain in the Active Directory structure is referred to as a partition. Each partition has a database that holds information about all objects that exist in that partition. The information includes the object name, all filled in attributes, and the access control listing for that object instance and it's attributes. This database is replicated on all domain controllers in the domain. The concept of primary domain controller (PDC) and backup domain controllers (BDCs) has disappeared in Windows 2000. The domain controllers are peers that use multimaster replication mechanisms to achieve synchronicity in the domain. This means that you no longer have to panic if your PDC gets blown up or some fool spills coffee in it. As long as you have at least one other domain controller operating in the partition, you still have total administrative abilities for that domain. Gone are the user calls complaining that they can't change their password because the primary is offline for repairs!

One reason that the concept of domains still exists in Windows 2000 is to achieve backwards compatibility with existing NT 4 domain models. Realistically, Microsoft doesn't expect that the day you upgrade one domain controller to Windows 2000 Server, you will migrate everything else in the organization as well. In recognition of this piece of reality, Windows 2000 domain servers recognize two modes of domain operation: mixed and native.

A Windows 2000 domain operating in native mode assumes that all domain controllers have been upgraded to Windows 2000. In this mode, multimaster replication between domain controllers is switched on, Kerberos becomes the default authentication mechanism, and deep level nesting of groups is allowed as well as the recognition of the universal security group.

The default mode for a newly promoted domain controller is mixed mode. In mixed mode, the Windows 2000 domain controller operates exactly like an NT 4 primary or backup domain controller, using NTLM as the authentication system, applying all the group rules of NT 4, and using the master-slave replication method for NT 4 domain controllers. Whether the W2K DC impersonates a PDC or a BDC in mixed mode depends on its order of installation in the existing NT 4 domain. If it was the first W2K domain controller upgraded in the domain, it will take over and declare itself the new domain PDC. When additional domain controllers are upgraded, they will act as NT 4 BDCs until all DCs are upgraded and the administrator chooses to switch the domain to native mode operation.

Trees and Forests

Domains are grouped together to form a tree or forest. The differences between the two structures are clearly seen in Figures 1.1 and 1.2.

As you see in Figure 1.1, the tree is so named because it resembles an upside down tree with the root at the top and the branches extending downward. All the domains in the structure are linked together by trust relationships. All subdomains in the tree derive their names from the name of the root, creating a contiguous namespace.

Two or more trees can be linked together to form a forest. As you can see in Figure 1.2, the namespace is non-contiguous with each tree having it's own root domain name. This arrangement of domains is convenient for corporations that have pre-existing public DNS namespaces for their divisions or subsidiaries. It would also be convenient in the event of a merger between two companies.

Regardless of whether you have created a tree or a forest structure, notice that subdomains off the root use the DNS naming convention to derive their names. The namespace created by the tree can be a public namespace that is visible on the Internet, such as `microsoft.com` or a private namespace that can be seen only within your organization's intranet.

The trust relationships that connect domains no longer have to be manually created and managed individually as they were in NT 4. When a domain joins an existing tree or forest, two-way trusts are automatically created between the domain and its immediate parent. In addition, Windows 2000 trust relationships are transitive and implicit. We'll talk more about these in Chapter 2, "Domains."

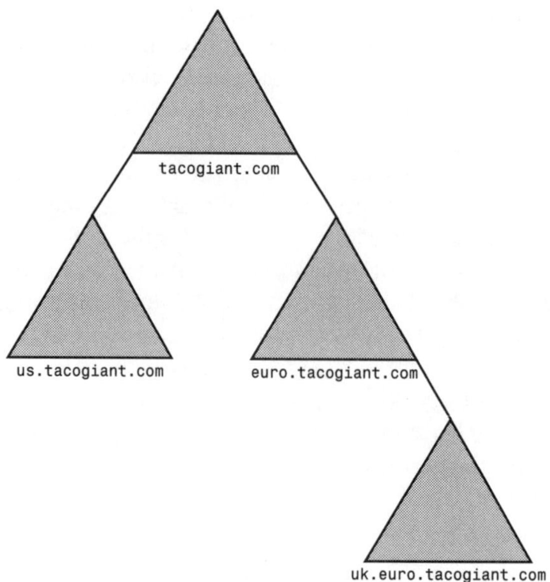

Figure 1.1 A directory tree created for Taco Giant, Inc., a wholly owned subsidiary of Fast Foods R Us, Inc.

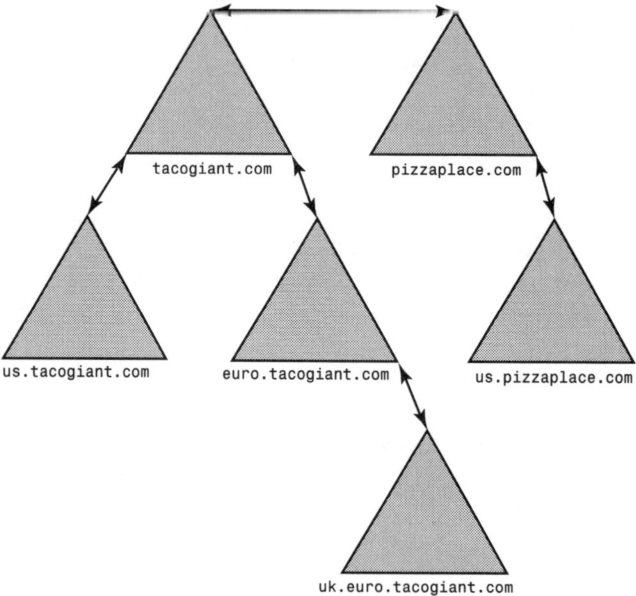

Figure 1.2 A forest structure created for the Fast Foods R Us Corporation made up of their Taco Giant, Inc. and Pizza Place, Inc. subsidiary's trees.

Earlier in the chapter, I mentioned that each partition maintains a database of objects that exist in that partition. These larger structures that constitute the Active Directory also have information that must be shared throughout the directory tree or forest. Remember that each tree or forest shares a common Global Catalog, configuration information, and schema. We'll talk more about these three naming contexts in upcoming sections.

Global Catalog

The Global Catalog's purpose is to make it easier and more efficient to search the entire directory for resources. Rather than having to know which domain a particular resource resides in, a user can search against the entire directory and find resources anywhere in the tree or forest. The Active Directory search engine supports both white page and yellow page type searches so that a user can search by the resource's name or just the type of resource.

The Global Catalog contains all the objects that exist in the individual domain partitions that have been selected by domain administrators for publication in the Global Catalog. In addition to the object, the Global Catalog maintains a subset of the attributes for that object. An administrator can also be selective about which object attributes they want to publish in the Global Catalog. This is accomplished through the Active Directory schema management snap-in.

Configuration Info

The configuration information naming context keeps track of information about sites, replication topologies, and trust relationships between domains.

Schema

Like any other database, the Active Directory database structure has a schema. The Active Directory's schema is actually a scaled down version of the X.500 schema. The schema defines the types of objects that can exist in the directory, the attributes those objects can have, the syntax for each attribute, a default permissions list for each one, and other information such as the legal parents and children that each object class may have.

The schema in Windows 2000 has the capacity to be extended. An organization can decide to add new types of objects or new attributes to existing objects. The only danger is that this extension is a one way process at this early stage of Windows 2000's lifetime. If a mistake is made, it is there forever (or until someone develops a toolset to reverse the process) and for everyone to see. Because there is only one schema for the enterprise, a mistake here will affect every entity that uses that definition anywhere in the enterprise.

Sites

If you are an administrator of Microsoft's BackOffice products, such as Exchange or SMS, you are already familiar with the concept of sites. The site concept has migrated to the Windows 2000 product although you may find the definition to be a little different than what you are used to in other BackOffice products. In their other products, sites are optimized for use in a particular application. The Windows 2000 definition of a site is related to the network topology instead. In Windows 2000, a site is a well connected network area. Microsoft's definition of well connected is surprisingly lenient. In their world, well connected means network connectivity in excess of 128 Kbps. In reality, you will probably be defining your sites as one or more TCP/IP subnets running at LAN speeds. I'm sure you can already guess the purpose of site definition, to allow you to differentiate your LAN connections from WAN connectivity, which is often achieved at much lower bandwidths.

Sites are used in W2K to define the physical world for the primary purposes of optimizing client logons and the replication topology for Active Directory components. In its default mode, Windows 2000 will self-manage the replication of the Active Directory based on site information. If desired, however, you can designate more than one connection for a remote site, and NT will then choose the lowest cost alternative that is available at the time. Site configuration will have a great impact on the efficiency of your Active Directory replication cycles. For this reason, it should be given careful consideration during the planning phase of your migration to Windows 2000.

Organizational Units (OUs)

OUs are the building blocks of the logical structure that we can create within each partition of the Active Directory. We create OUs for three purposes. The primary reason for creating an OU is to allow administrators to reflect the organizational structure of an enterprise and then use that structure to logically group resources together. Second, once resources have been grouped using OUs, group policies can be applied against those resources at the OU level. Finally, we can delegate the administration of the OU's resources to someone closer to the resource, a trusted user or local administrator, for example.

Using OUs would allow us to put all the company's accountants, their PCs, shared files, and printers in one OU. Once that is accomplished, we can then apply a group policy against that OU. The policy would ensure that the PCs always have the latest version of the primary accounting software package, and that the desktops have all necessary applications and network mappings, as well as URLs that the accountants have told us they need to access on the corporate intranet. Finally, we might designate one of the administrative assistants in the accounting group to manage all those changes to names and addresses for the accountants' user accounts and to be responsible for adding and deleting users from the groups in that organization. This use of group policies to automate software distribution and the ability to delegate administration to the OU level is one of the ways we will be lowering TCO with Windows 2000.

Objects

As it was in NT 4, every resource in Windows 2000 is treated as an object. File system resources, directory resources, shares, printers, and users; basically anything you can imagine in the system is an object. Objects can be described, manipulated, and audited. This whole idea of objects may be second nature to those object-oriented programming gurus in your organization, but for many of us in the network and systems administrators group, objects were just that—something that only programmers had to worry about. We administered our networks with NT and never really needed to understand object principles.

Although you could still administer a Windows 2000 system without knowing anything about object concepts, a little knowledge in this area can be very helpful in your administrative role. Like anything else in this industry, object orientation is surrounded by some pretty confusing technical jargon. Since you will probably be spending a lot of time working with directory objects, let's see if we can make things a little clearer in the next few paragraphs.

Object Definition and Encapsulation

Traditionally, a classical object is defined as data and the associated code that manipulates that data. An object definition consists of the object name, the attributes or properties of the object, and the methods that can be applied to that object. An object's name is also called the object class. Attributes define the information or data that we want to keep about an object class. Methods describe what functions you can perform on a particular object. When the object class is defined, it also specifies the syntax for any attribute. The definition of PASSWORD as 14 characters, alphanumeric, and case sensitive is an example of defining an attribute's syntax.

Imagine an object class called EMPLOYEE. In defining the attributes of an EMPLOYEE, we might like to keep information about their employee number, name, email address, hire date, SSN, and paygrade. When we define the methods for the EMPLOYEE object, we are basically asking, "What can we do to an EMPLOYEE?" Although some of you may think management has more inventive ideas, from a realistic standpoint there are only three things we can do to EMPLOYEE. Add an EMPLOYEE, delete an EMPLOYEE and modify an EMPLOYEE. This idea of defining both the attributes and the functions or methods of an object together is called encapsulation. Figure 1.3 demonstrates a typical definition format for objects using our EMPLOYEE object as an example.

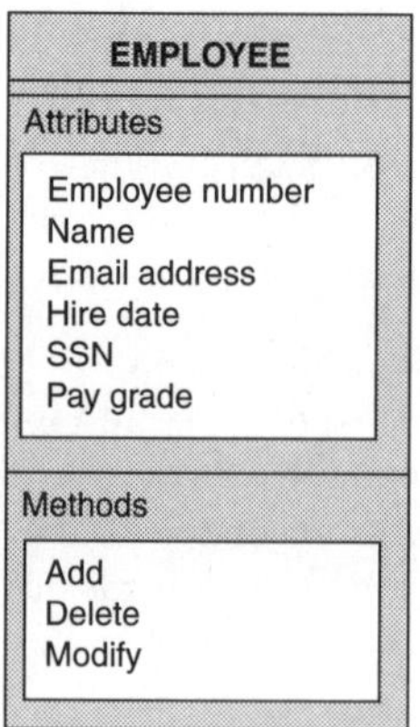

Figure 1.3 EMPLOYEE object with typical definition format.

Object Instantiation

Once we have completed the definition of the object, we probably want to start filling in real data. After all, just defining this object doesn't do much for us. It is just a definition of the structure. In order to be useful, the structure must have real world data in it. When we enter the information for Bob, one of our employees, we create an instance of the object EMPLOYEE. This process is called instantiation. If we fill in the structure with information about Mary, we have created a second instance in the database of the EMPLOYEE object. See, this is simpler than you thought!

Parent/Child Relationships

We could spend chapters on objects and their characteristics and rules, but let's keep this to the bare minimum that you need to understand to administer Windows 2000. You already know about encapsulation, but one of the other object concepts you will need to understand is the idea of inheritance. Part of the object class definition includes information about legal parents and legal children of that class. What types of objects can this object be placed in and what types of objects can be placed in this object, for example. A good example in our Windows 2000 administrative environment would be a group object. One of the legal parents for group objects is an OU. So if we had a group called Franchise Salespeople that lived in the SALES OU of the `uk.tacogiant.com` domain, and we looked at the legal parent list for that group, we would see the object class OU listed. If we were to look at the "legal children" list allowed for the SALES OU, we would see the object class GROUPS listed there. You would also see that OUs can be children of this OU, which means we can nest OUs within OUs.

Inheritance

Why am I annoying you with all these filial details? To explain how inheritance works for you. Inheritance is the concept that says child objects can inherit the attributes of their parents. In a strict object sense, this means I can partially define the attributes and methods of a child object, and it will obtain the rest of its definition from its parent. The attributes and methods are cumulative.

From a purely administrative standpoint, we can see an illustration of this concept when I create an access control list for our previously mentioned SALES OU that defines who can create new objects in that OU. I can then specify that the SALES OU ACL be inherited by objects that are legal children of the OU so that all OUs created in the SALES OU have the same ACL. That means I only have to define the ACL once and then propagate it down the OU tree. I also have the ability to block inheritance from parents, but more on that in Chapter 4, "Understanding Organizational Units: The Building Blocks of the Active Directory."

Planning the Active Directory

Just so we are all on the same page, I want to discuss how I am going to address the issues involved in planning the Active Directory in this text. Although we will discuss planning the structure of administrative components of the Active Directory in different chapters in this book, a complete discussion of planning and implementing the Active Directory is beyond the scope of this text. We will discuss creating a viable domain structure in Chapter 2, planning for the efficient use of OUs in Chapter 4, and group arrangements in Chapter 6, "Group Management." We will also be discussing using these Active Directory structures to implement centralized versus decentralized administration models. In essence, we will only discuss the planning issues that impact the administration of users and machines. I will not have time to tell you from beginning to end how to plan and implement an Active Directory structure.

I can, however, point you in the right direction for additional help in that area. For more complete planning guides, you can look on the Windows 2000 Server Web site at `www.microsoft.com`. You might also browse the whitepapers in the Knowledge Base while you're there. Another source of information can be found in the online books directory on your Windows 2000 Server CD (Beta 2 or higher versions). Finally, I can heartily recommend as required reading for migration team leaders a book called *Planning for Windows 2000* by Cone, Boggs and Perez, also published by New Riders. These guys taught me tricks I didn't know for migrating NT 4 systems. I feel it is an excellent reference for the design and implementation phases of your Windows 2000 migration.

2

Domains

As mentioned in Chapter 1, Inside Windows 2000 Overview the concept of domains has not disappeared with the advent of the Active Directory. Domains are very much alive and kicking in Windows 2000 and operating under the alias of "partitions" in the Active Directory's terminology. The question of why they still exist probably has many answers, but it seems the primary reason is to accommodate the requirement for backward compatibility. Maintaining the existing domain concepts allows you to integrate Windows 2000 into an existing NT 3.5x/4.0 environment and ease into the migration rather than using the big bang approach.

In this chapter, we will discuss the different domain models Microsoft has designed (actually, I think they just *evolved*, but that's a personal opinion!). We'll also investigate the differences between NT 4 domains and Windows 2000 domains and how those differences will affect you during your planning and migration phases. In order to have those discussions, though, we first need to understand some of the underlying mechanisms that make the whole NT world go 'round.

Domain Basics

The first question that needs to be addressed is why do we even need domains? Why not just use a whole bunch of workgroups to access all our resources? You probably already know the limitations of workgroups. The single biggest problem with NT workgroups is the security issue. Specifically, I'm talking about user authentication and implementing discretionary access control on resources. In workgroups, users are authenticated against the local workstation's or server's SAM database. This means that if you have 30 machines and Mary Jo needs to access shared resources on all machines, you either must have an account for Mary Jo on all 30 machines (imagine keeping all those passwords in synch!), or you must enable the guest account on all those machines. Thirty accounts also means 30 SIDs for Mary Jo in this workgroup because SIDs are created from a combination of machine name, timestamp, and username. Although Mary Jo could use the same username and password at each machine to log on (provided she never changed her password), each machine would have a different SID on its ACLs for Mary Jo.

In contrast, with a domain model, Mary Jo would only have to have one account and it would reside in a central location (the primary domain controller, specifically). When Mary Jo wants to access any domain resource, the local machine passes through the authentication request to the domain controller(s) for resolution. This means that administrators only have to worry about one instance of Mary Jo's account, and all discretionary access control is set by using the SID generated for that one account. This one feature of domains simplifies administration to the nth degree!

The next question that needs to be addressed is, exactly what is a domain? Is it a collection of geographically co-located users and resources? Could be. Is it a collection of shared resources and users within a particular organization? Might be. Actually, for years we have been saying that a domain is a logical administrative unit. Domains do not necessarily have anything to do with geography, network topology, or other physical environment factors. Remember from Chapter 1 that in Windows 2000, Microsoft uses the concepts of "sites" to represent the physical topology of a system. The real criteria in the pre-Windows 2000 world for defining the scope of a domain involved defining the access and administration requirements of the company's resources. The common wisdom was that network resources that were administered and shared by a common group of individuals should be grouped into a domain.

Is that the same criteria you would use to form Windows 2000 domains? Not exactly. The rules have changed, primarily because of the addition of the Active Directory's administrative structure and the increased size of the databases involved in maintaining objects for that structure. Some of the general advice you can follow for designing a Windows 2000 domain structure includes creating fewer and larger domains because the Active Directory will handle many more objects than an NT 4 SAM. Following that line of logic, you should reduce the number of grassroots domains in your organization. It is also recommended that you use a more stable criteria, such as geographic or geopolitical boundaries, to define the scope of your Windows 2000 domains. We'll discuss some more specific criteria for domain creation a little later in the chapter, under the section "Migrating Your Domain Model to Windows 2000."

Drawbacks of NT 3.x/4.0 Domains

Domains in previous NT versions had several limitations, but two stand out over all the others. The first has to do with administrative delegation of resources. In these prior versions of NT, the domain was the smallest administrative entity that could be defined. If you wanted to give someone the ability to create users, share resources, add machines to the domain and install drivers for a subset of the domain's servers, you had to give them domain administration rights for the whole domain and hope they didn't abuse the privilege.

Another drawback is Microsoft's top-end limitation on the size of the SAM database, the central repository for all user, group, and machine accounts in an NT 3.x/4.0 domain. We can all agree with Microsoft that a single domain's SAM should never grow to be more than 40MB. My clients are always asking me exactly how many users and groups could exist in a SAM that size. I'll give you the famous consultant's answer: it depends. No, no! Stop looking for the rotten tomatoes to throw. It really *does* depend. On what? Primarily, the way that you use local and global groups in your administrative environment. If you tend to use a large number of groups to set permissions, you may be able to squeeze in fewer users than an organization that only uses the predefined NT groups. You can use the guidelines in Table 2.1 to determine how many users can exist in *your* 40MB SAM.

Microsoft says that an NT 4 SAM can hold 40,000 users, but they immediately qualify that with caveats about the number of groups in the domain. In general, we say that an NT 4 domain SAM can support between 20,000 and 60,000 users, depending on the number of groups, trust relationships and machine accounts that also exist in the domain. Fair enough?

Table 2.1 **Account Size Requirements**

Type	Size
Each user account	1KB
Each machine account	0.5KB
Each local group	0.5KB, plus 36bytes per member
Each global group	0.5KB, plus 12 bytes per member

Okay, so your organization has 82,000 employees, they each have a PC, you have tons of servers, and want to use lots of groups. Does that mean you can't use NT? Of course not. Microsoft wasn't born yesterday. They want your business, too. For larger organizations, they created a model of domain integration that allows you to link multiple domains together to interoperate for user authentication. We'll talk about that model, as well as a couple of others, a little later in this chapter. In order for any of those models to work, though, there needs to be a mechanism for passing authentication requests between domains. In Microsoft-ese, that mechanism is called a trust relationship.

Trust Relationships

By default, NT domains, once created, are standalone entities. Just because you have created several domains in your organization and they are all running NT 4, does that mean that they have any relationship with each other for administration and resource sharing? The answer, as you probably already know, is a resounding no. Are they even aware that there are other NT 4 domains in existence? Except for perhaps being able to see the domains and display a list of them in Network Neighborhood, again the answer is no.

In order to be able to access a shared resource, you have to be able to check the ACLs of the resource against the SIDs in the domain where the user's account resides. In a single domain model, when a machine joins a domain, a secure authentication pathway is established by the NETLOGON service to accomplish this type of pass-through authentication. For example, if Mary Jo, one of our Pizza Place East Coast Operations domain (EASTOPS) users, tries to access one of the Office applications on the NT 4 member server, OFFAPPS1, as we see in Figure 2.1, the apps server will first try to resolve Mary Jo's identity in its own SAM. Remember that each machine, even though it is a member of a domain, still has its own local SAM database (except for domain controllers—they only maintain the domain SAM). When our apps server can't find Mary Jo's account in its SAM, it looks to a domain controller for the EASTOPS domain to solve the mystery of who Mary Jo is, whether or not she has any right to log on to the application server, and what her SIDs are. After it has those answers, the apps server can determine Mary Jo's permission levels.

When you have multiple domains and you want to have your users access shared resources in other domains, you have to create that same type of secure authentication channel between the domains. You activate this mechanism through the creation of a trust relationship between the two domains. In NT 3.x and NT 4.0, these trust relationships are one-way and have to be explicitly defined. If you'll look at the high level domains in Figure 2.2 that exist in our Pizza Place company, you'll see what I mean.

Figure 2.1 Pass-through authentication in a single domain from a local workstation to a member server and finally to the domain controller.

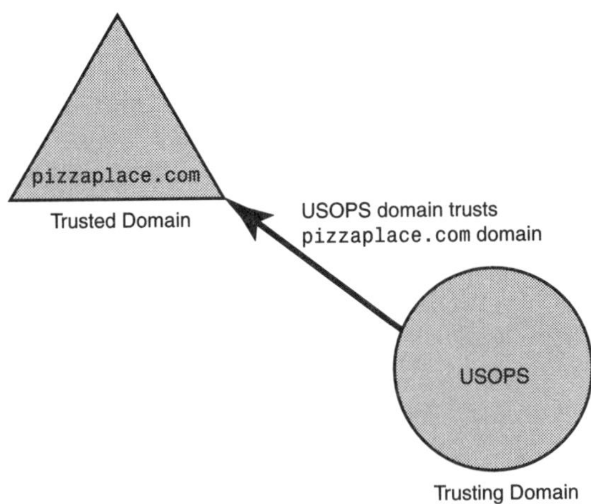

Figure 2.2 One-way trusts between `pizzaplace.com` and the USOPS domain.

Because we are just beginning our migration to Windows 2000 at Pizza Place, we still have many NT 4 domains in existence. Although the corporate headquarters domain, PIZZAPLACE (now called the `pizzaplace.com` domain in the Windows 2000 Active Directory structure) has already migrated to Windows 2000, all the US Operating Unit domains are still running NT 4. Because we have both versions of the domains, we will need to explicitly define the trust relationships between them as if they were all running NT 4. The domain structure shown in Figure 2.2 shows us some of the trust relationship mechanics (and terminology problems) that NT 4 administrators have to deal with. The headquarters division has a need to see resources from all the global operating units' domains to create financial reports and do quarterly tax reporting. In order to authenticate the headquarters' domain users against the ACLS in the US operating unit domain, it was necessary to create a one-way trust relationship between the two domains in which the USOPS domain *trusts* the `pizzaplace.com` domain. The `pizzaplace.com` domain becomes the *trusted domain* and the USOPS domain is referred to as the *trusting domain.*

From a functional standpoint, this relationship means that the users in the `pizzaplace.com` domain are able to view and use shared resources in the USOPS domain provided they have been given access permissions (via ACL entries). For the USOPS folks, the relationship means that when they set permissions on any resource, they can select users and groups from their own domain as well as users and groups from the `pizzaplace.com` domain. Figure 2.3 shows the pass-through authentication that happens when a user from `pizzaplace.com` attempts to access a resource on a USOPS server. An attempt is made to resolve the credentials locally, then at the domain controller, and, finally, at the `pizzaplace.com` domain controller.

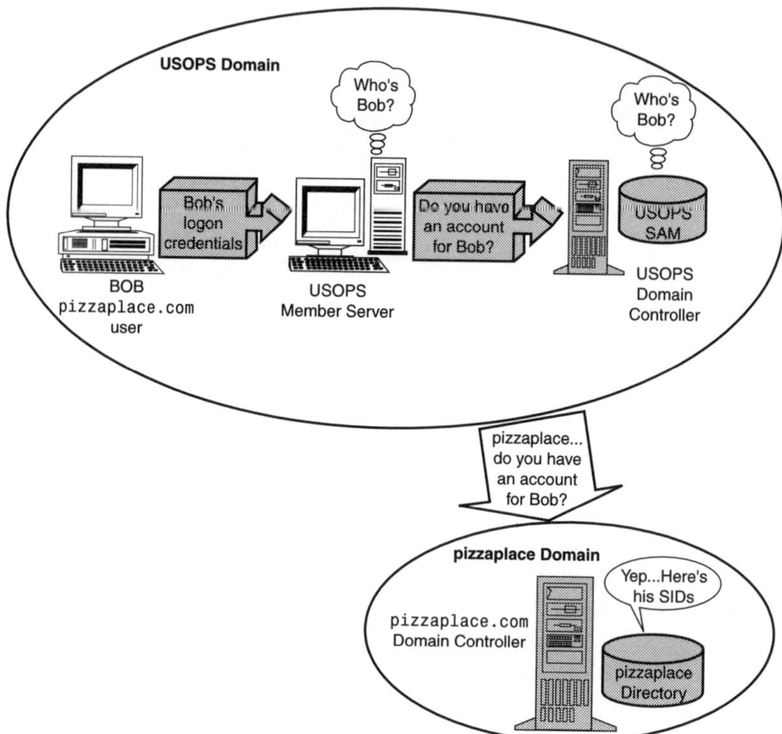

Figure 2.3 Pass-through authentication from member server in USOPS to `pizzaplace.com` domain through the trust relationship.

In a one-way trust relationship, such as the one in our example, the trusting domain's users (USOPS) have no means to look at resources in the trusted domain (`pizzaplace.com`). If you want that to happen, you would have to set up a second trust relationship between the domains where `pizzaplace.com` trusts the USOPS domain. After you established that second relationship, you would activate a mechanism for user authentication in the opposite direction. Now you would have a two-way trust between the domains, and users from both domains could access resources in the opposing domain that they had been given access permissions to. This also means that there would be an additional administrative burden on the domain administrators in each domain to set up and maintain those trusts. If you want to break a trust relationship, both domains' administrators should remove all references to the trust relationship from their domains' SAMs.

Because pizza is so popular in the US, the US operating unit has several regional offices. As you can see in Figure 2.4, each of these is also an NT 4 domain. The USOPS domain has a need to correlate data from the three US regional offices (East Coast, West Coast and Midwest), so the Pizza Place domain administrators have created a trust relationship between the USOPS domain and each of the regional domains. As you can see from the arrows in Figure 2.4, these are all one-way relationships with the regions trusting the USOPS domain. Given this structure, what is the relationship between the `pizzaplace.com` domain and the WESTOPS domain? Easy. In NT 4, there is none. Just because WESTOPS trusts USOPS and USOPS trusts `pizzaplace.com`, that doesn't imply any relationship between the lowest level and the highest. This is an illustration of the concept that all NT 4 trust relationships between domains must be explicitly defined.

Naming Windows 2000 Domains

When naming Windows 2000 domains, the domain name will be automatically appended by the parent DNS domain name. For example, the *USOPS* domain will have the Windows 2000 name of `usops.pizzaplace.com`. In addition to the Windows 2000 DNS style domain name, a downlevel logon name is maintained in the active directory for compatibility with NT 4 domains. In our example, the downlevel domain name will simply be *USOPS*.

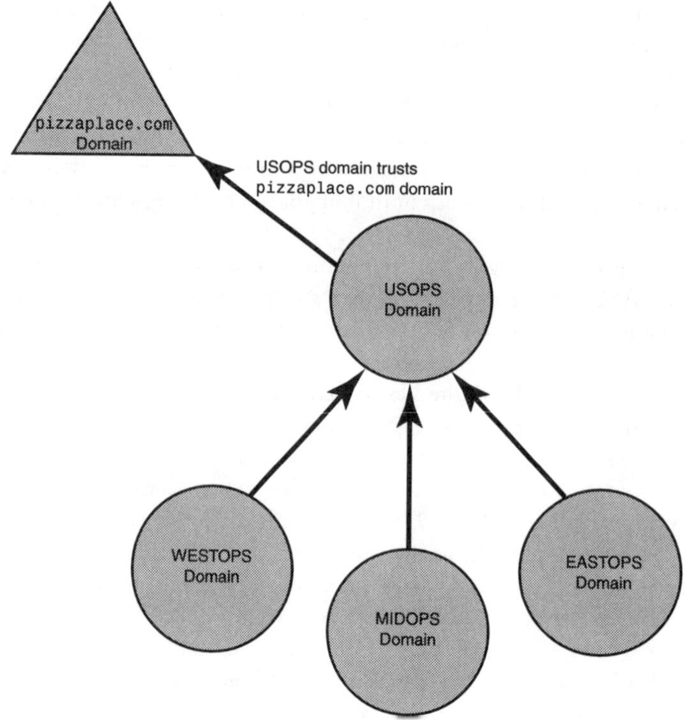

Figure 2.4 USOPS domain trusts `pizzaplace.com` domain

I have spent a lot of time and typing energy telling you about NT 4 trust relationships and how they operate. Why? This is, after all, a book about Windows 2000, right? There are actually two reasons I have subjected you to Trust Relationships 101. The first is so that you have a solid understanding of how NT 4 relationships work so that you can use them to connect your existing NT 4 domains to your new Windows 2000 domains. When configuring the two types of domains to interoperate, you will still have to establish these NT 4 type trusts between them. The second reason is so that you understand the limitations (and administrative headaches) of this structure and better appreciate the benefits of the Windows 2000 model.

Windows 2000 Trust Mechanisms

In comparison to NT 4 trust relationships, Windows 2000 trusts are largely self-managing. When a domain joins an existing tree structure, a new two-way trust relationship is established between the new domain and its parent domain. When joining two trees to form a forest, a two-way trust relationship is created between the top-level domains of each tree. In addition to these two-way trust relationships, the same type of two-way trust relationship is created between the new domain and all the other domains in the existing structure.

For example, let's take our previous example of the Pizza Place domain structure and convert it to a native mode Windows 2000 environment. Figure 2.5 shows the resulting web of trust relationships automatically created by Windows 2000 as we build the Active Directory tree. Solid lines show two-way trust relationships created when the tree is formed. Dotted lines illustrate the implicit relationships created throughout the structure.

Remember that in Windows 2000, the authenticating mechanism is not the individual domain SAM, it is the Active Directory database. In order to access all the partitions of the Active Directory for authentication and replication, these trusts must be in place. In order to reduce the administrative burden, thereby reducing total cost of ownership for the domain, Microsoft has made these trusts self-perpetuating and effectively self-managing.

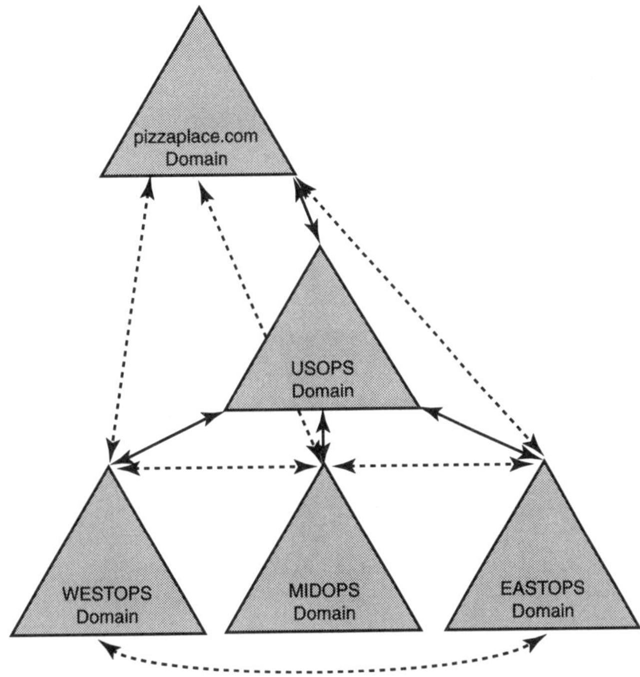

Figure 2.5 Windows 2000 model showing the trust web between our Pizza Place domains after they are all migrated.

Looking at our mythical company, let's say you have expanded and Pizza Place, Inc., has opened a new operating unit in Japan. If you were to create a new domain for that unit and add it to the existing Windows 2000 structure seen in Figure 2.5, implicit and transitive trust relationships would be automatically created between that domain and the rest of the Pizza Place tree. The dotted lines in Figure 2.6 show those transitive trust relationships. If there are security reasons that this trust model is unacceptable to your organization, you can always break the default model and set up explicit trusts with selected domains just like you would in NT 4. This is accomplished through the use of the Site and Trust management tool in Windows 2000 Server versions.

By the way, does this look a lot like the NT 4 complete trust model to anyone else? You know the one that even Microsoft recommended that you not use? Well, I can't fib to you. It is basically that model. However, if you remember *why* Microsoft recommended not using the model, you'll see that Windows 2000 overcomes those objections.

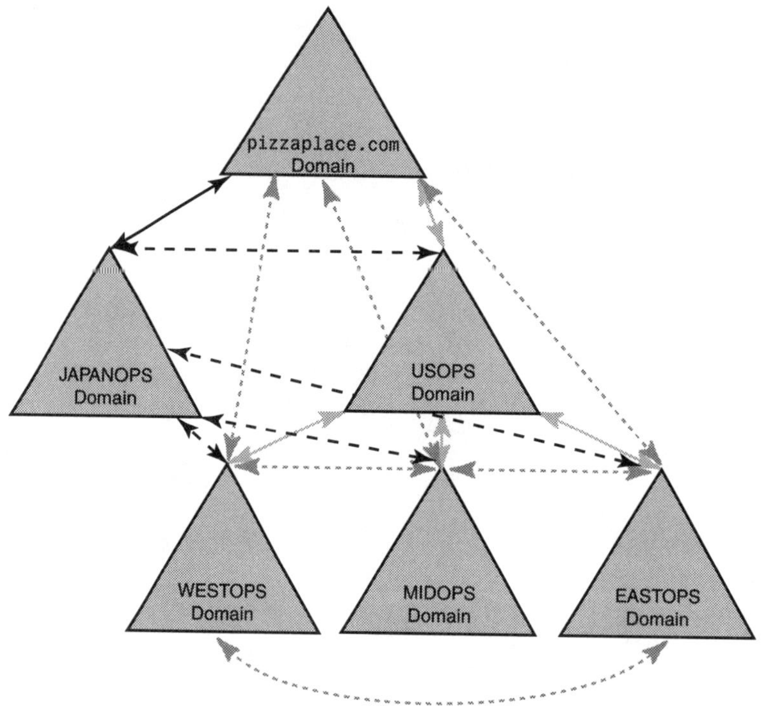

Figure 2.6 Adding a new domain to the Pizza Place tree creates the new implicit trust web shown in the bold dotted lines.

One of the main objections to the complete trust model was the high administrative overhead required to maintain the model. Remember that the number of trust relationships to administer was equal to the number of domains times the number of domains minus one (T = n[n-1] where T is the total number of trust relationships and n is the number of domains). So if we had 6 domains, we had to create and maintain 30 relationships manually.

Another question that needed to be asked when organizations implemented this model was "Why?" We said that one of the criteria for deciding the scope of a domain was to determine the shared resource needs of the users. If I implement a complete trust model, the assumption follows that users from all domains need to access resources in all the other domains. If this statement is true, why not create a single domain since everyone's sharing the resources. There were often sane reasons, such as too many users to fit in one domain, or perhaps the organization had adopted a decentralized IT administration model. Quite often, however, the reasons were not so logical. The implementation of a complete trust model was often done so that feuding political factions in an organization could get or maintain control of "their" resources, users, and groups. If this is the case, that organization can now combine those domains and use Organizational Units (OUs) to give administrative control to the factions.

In addition to these concerns, there were always administration and security concerns to overcome in the complete trust model. After all, just because you had secured your domain, did that mean the domain on the other side of that complete trust relationship had taken the same level of care that you did? Of course not, and after someone had violated their domain's security boundary, there was always a concern that they were now one step closer to yours.

Domain Models in NT 3.51 and NT 4

In previous versions of NT, the restrictions on the size of the SAM database made it necessary for larger companies to either choose another network operating system or split up their user and machine accounts into multiple domains. From Microsoft's standpoint, the first option was unacceptable, so they designed a few different domain models to meet the needs of larger organizations as well as organizations that have a requirement for decentralized administration of their NT network. Let's review those models, because I will bet that your organization is using one of them, even if it's not called by its Microsoft name. After we discuss the models, we'll discuss some of the ways you can consider migrating each structure to Windows 2000.

Single Domain Model

Obviously, this is the simplest model you can implement. There is only one domain. All user, group, and machine accounts are kept in a single SAM database on the PDC that is replicated out to the BDC(s). This model operates under three assumptions:

1. The SAM database will remain under 40 MB.
2. All users in the domain may have a need to access all the resources in the domain to some extent.
3. Management of the domain SAM will be centralized.

Master Domain Model (Single Master Domain Model)

One of the most popular multiple domain models is the single master domain model. This model uses two types of domains: a master account domain, where all the user accounts are created and administered, and one or more resource domains. There can be many resource domains, but in this model, there is only one master account domain. These domains are linked via a one-way trust relationship with the resource domains trusting the master account domain.

Because there is only one master account domain and the user accounts are kept in that domain, this model obviously does nothing to help you overcome the SAM size limitation. It wasn't intended to do that. It was intended to allow you to delegate administration of resources while at the same time maintaining centralized control of the user accounts and global groups. Here's how it works.

As you can see in Figure 2.7, the master account domain contains all the user and user-defined group accounts for the structure. New users and global groups are created in the master account domain as well and when users log on, they log on to the master domain even if they are logging on at a machine that is a member of the resource domain and they are planning to access resources in that resource domain.

Maybe the whole thing will be a little clearer if we look at an example. Let's use our favorite user Mary Jo, who works in the Pizza Place East Coast regional office. Mary Jo wants to access a share on the Human Resources server that is physically located in the office right next to hers in Atlanta. The machine account for the HR server is kept in the EASTOPS domain, a resource domain. Because they are using the single master domain model, Mary Jo's user account is in the USOPS domain. This means that she has to log on to the USOPS domain. There is no "Mary Jo" account in the EASTOPS domain, because it is a resource domain and only holds machine accounts. When she goes to access the share, the ACL has an entry on it for Mary Jo using the SID from her account in the USOPS domain. If Mary Jo needed to access a folder in the West Operations domain (WESTOPS), the same sequence would occur.

She would log on to the US Operations master account domain and the server in the West region would pass the authentication request back to her account domain before granting her access to any resource. Remember, this is why we create that one-way trust relationship—to create a secure authentication channel to pass authentication requests between these domains.

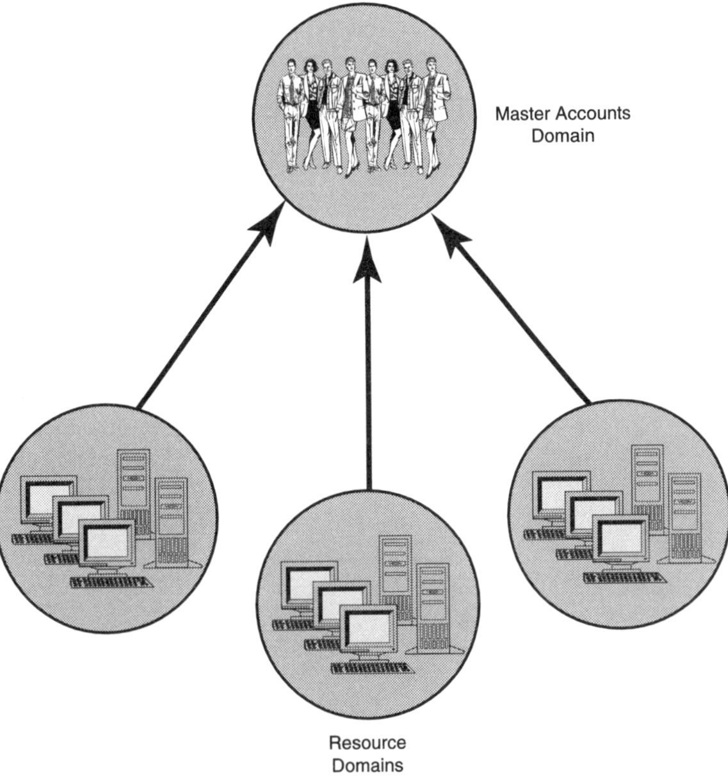

Figure 2.7 Generic single master model diagram. Notice the machine accounts reside in the resource domains and the user accounts reside in the master accounts domain.

Resource Domain Accounts

Although the single master domain model (and the multiple master account model as well) use concept of an "account domain" to hold user accounts, there are still going to be a few accounts and groups in the resource domains. The predefined accounts like Domain Administrator, Administrator, and Guest still exist in each and every resource domain. The predefined machine local groups and domain global groups also exist in the resource domains. The key to this whole structure is that the administrators of the resource domains are not allowed to create new user accounts in those domains. In other words, their user account from the master account domain is added to the local administrators group of the machines that they need to administer in the resource domains, but they are *not* added to any of the groups in that domain that have the power to create new users in the resource domain.

I said earlier that this model assisted in implementing a distributed administration model. Usually, the resource domains are administered by a different set of administrators than the group that administers the master account domain. This makes sense, especially because these administrators are usually physically located closer to the resources they are administering. Tasks such as formatting drives, creating shared resources, and adding machines to the domain can be handled at a local level. For example, if we look at the Pizza Place Operational units, the IT staff at headquarters will take care of all the users and groups, but the local staff in the Santa Fe office will take care of administering the servers in the Southwest regional domain.

Multiple Master Domain Model

The multiple master domain model (as shown in Figure 2.8) works on the same principles as the single master domain model with one important exception. In the multiple master domain, there are two or more master account domains. Notice another difference in the trust relationship web that links the model together. The one-way trust relationships between the resource domains and the account domain are still there, but a resource domain must create those one-way relationships with each master account domain. In addition, you will see two-way trust relationships that have been created between the master account domains.

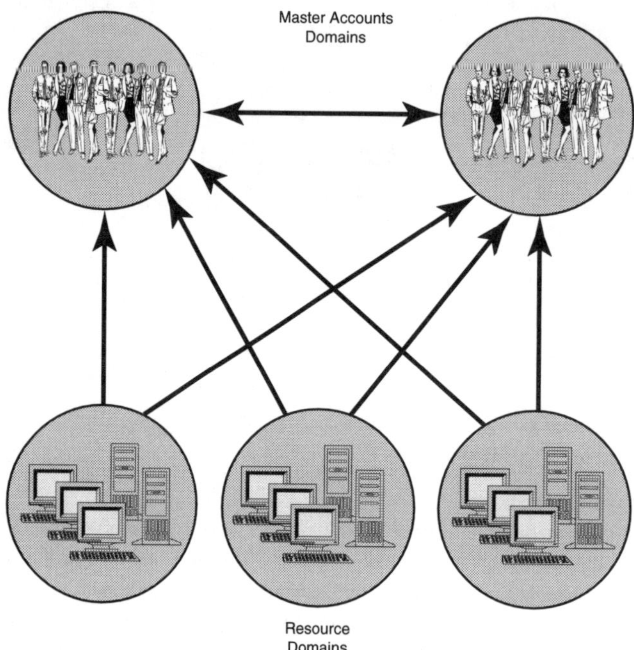

Figure 2.8 Generic multiple master model. Notice the similarity in functionality to the single master model. One difference: the two-way trust between the master account domains.

In addition to the overarching assumption that this model will be used to delegate administration of local resources, there are two additional reasons that a company may choose to implement this model. The first is that the company has too many users for a single SAM. In other words, they exceed Microsoft's 40 MB limit. Larger companies may be forced to implement this model. If this is the case, the way that accounts are divided between domains is really irrelevant. I've seen it done by functional units. I've even seen it done alphabetically. The second reason an organization might implement this model is that they have already divided up user management responsibilities among different support groups. Perhaps the MIS Support group is responsible for NT users in the HR, Accounting, and Payroll departments, and the PC Support group is responsible for all other NT users.

As with the single master domain model, the resource domains still have their own administrators, and those administrators are still concerned with machine administration, not user management. As with the single master, all users log on to one of the master domains regardless of where they are planning to access resources.

Complete Trust Model

The final Microsoft model I want to discuss is the complete trust model (shown in Figure 2.9). Each domain in the model is connected to every other domain with a two-way trust relationship. In this model, the assumption is that users in all domains need to access resources in all the other domains. If that's the case, the question needs to be asked, why didn't the company just set up a single domain in the first place? Well, I've heard three basic arguments from companies that have implemented this model. The first one is probably the only legitimate one:

1. The organization has made a deliberate, rational decision to go to a totally decentralized support model for their network. In this case, it makes perfect sense to locate the administrators, users, and machines in the same place and give the administrators responsibility for taking care of "their stuff." Unfortunately, this is not usually the scenario. More often, it is one of the next two.
2. In other organizations, the model just kind of evolves, as might be the case with an organization that doesn't migrate to NT 4 in an organized manner. As a result, they end up with several grassroots domains. Over time, they realize that there is a need to connect these domains and share resources, so they begin to create these trust relationships, and pretty soon you have the complete trust model.
3. The final reason the model comes into being might be due to political factors, such as territorialism within the company. You know, turf wars. Functional units all want to control their own users and resources, and there is no central administrative organization to take charge and change their minds. I have seen the worst administrative nightmares come from this kind of organizational thinking. One organization I know of had 1,000 machines, 1,100 users, and 22 domains in a complete trust relationship. Those administrators deserved a medal.

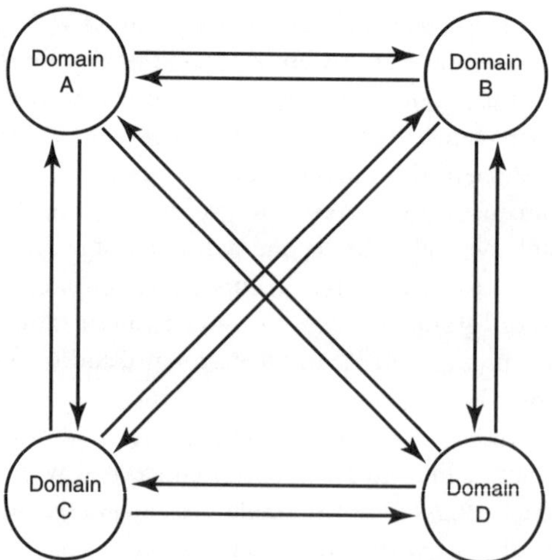

Figure 2.9 Generic complete trust model. Each trust is one-way and explicitly defined so it must be individually administered.

Although they recognize that this model exists, Microsoft does not recommend using this model with NT 4. The reason? It is incredibly hard to administer. As I mentioned in the earlier sidebar, the formula for figuring out how many trust relationships have to be created and manually administered is:

```
Number of trusts = n(n-1) where n = number of domains
```

So those poor administrators I mentioned with the 22 domains had 462 separate trust relationships to keep track of.

The "We Don't Really Have a Model" Model

Okay, so I'm being a little facetious here, but how many of you just experienced a physical pain of some kind because you know that, if you are really honest with yourself, this *is* your administrative model. Although it is not a recognized model, many of us have a multiple domain model that is organic in nature. It just grew and grew (kind of like crabgrass in an otherwise perfect lawn). People kept buying NT Server and creating their own grassroots domains. As they realized they needed to access other resources, they created trust relationships with other domains. The web of trust relationships hasn't evolved to a complete trust model yet. The end result is a model with lots of small domains, little individual kingdoms, with some access between them on an ad hoc basis. By the way, just to make things even more fun, these trust relationships usually aren't documented very well either.

If this is your model, you have a political struggle ahead of you in migrating to a good Windows 2000 administrative structure. There are organizational issues you need to address before you can even think about the technical issues of designing the structure. For example, how did those people get approval to purchase NT Server in the first place? Does your organization have any acquisition controls in place for server operating systems software purchases? If not, you may want to consider putting some in place—fast! Here's why.

With NT 4, you can create trust relationships between domains and access resources in those domains. A rebel organization that buys NT 4 Server and creates their own domain and trusts can still create a relationship with the existing approved NT 4 infrastructure. With Windows 2000, the picture changes slightly. Remember from Chapter 1 that when we create a tree or forest, the Global Catalog and schema are shared by the whole structure. If you have two existing Windows 2000 trees, one you created and one the rebels created, the trees have separate schemas. At the moment, there are no tools available to merge two existing Windows 2000 schemas. So the rebel tree cannot be merged into your authorized tree structure. This could result in some real headaches for you. I know that implementing configuration management and acquisition approvals is difficult, not to mention unpopular, but if you have rogue users, you should definitely try to do something to stop the creation of grassroots Windows 2000 domains.

Migrating Your Domain Model to Windows 2000

All of these models can be migrated to Windows 2000. If you wanted to, you could migrate them exactly as they are and never change a thing in your current model—other than the operating system, of course. You could keep the same number of domains, the same administrative model, and all the current trust relationships. If you did this, though, you would be doing a real disservice to yourself and your company.

With many of the limitations of NT 4 domains removed in Windows 2000, the logic used for creating NT 4 domains is very different than the criteria you should use to plan your Windows 2000 domains and tree/forest structure. As a result, with a little analysis and planning, you can create a more compact structure that better serves your administration needs while still providing your users with their accustomed autonomy. In order to achieve this design goal, the first thing you need to do is collect some information about the current environment so you can make educated design choices.

Analysis of the Current Environment

In order to really maximize the benefits of the Active Directory, before creating your new domain structure, you'll want to do an analysis of your current environment that includes the following areas of study:

- **Company's organizational and operational model.** This activity would document the company's actual business structure. Is the structure represented in terms of geographic distribution, like Pizza Place's Southwest and Northeast regions, or is it a functional business unit model, such as Marketing, Accounting, and Purchasing? This definition will begin to determine the possible domain boundaries as well as the needs that exist for OU divisions.
- **Administrative model of the organization.** You need to have an idea of the current administrative boundaries and entities that exist in your organization, including a clear picture of what the administrative needs are of each existing unit or domain and why the current model exists. One of the answers you may run into a lot during this phase is "We've done it this way since we migrated to NT several years ago." Understand that many of the people you will be interviewing will not have read this book and won't understand just how drastically the rules are changing between NT 4 and Windows 2000. You might find some resistance to challenging the existing administrative model, but keep your chin up and keep asking questions until you have a very clear picture of the environment.
- **Network/physical environment.** Analysis of the network and physical environment should include information about the geographic distribution of your offices and the number of employees at each location. An estimate of employee growth by location is also helpful to have on hand. Finally, the description of your physical network topology should include a full description of the existing links, their speed and utilization statistics. Although not technically required when deciding whether or not to create a domain, this information will assist you when you have to decide on your Windows 2000 site design to optimize domain replication traffic, and it provides helpful insights during the domain planning phase.

Creating Windows 2000 Domains

In NT 4, you might create domains to reflect your organization's business entities, because typically those functional units need to share resources. A good example at Pizza Place would be the Marketing and Logistics domains at corporate headquarters. They were created to service several thousand employees worldwide who need access to the same marketing and shipping information. This domain arrangement would coincidentally end up mirroring your functional business structure. Using domains to represent your organizational structure is specifically *not* recommended by Microsoft in Windows 2000. Instead, they recommend that you create fewer, larger domains using stable boundary criteria, like geography, as we have done with the Pizza Place operations domains. Then within those domains, you would create an OU structure to reflect the operational business environment in your company. If your company reorganizes, it's a lot easier to move OUs around than to merge several domains. We'll talk more about creating a viable OU structure in Chapter 4, "Understanding Organizational Units: The Building Blocks of the Active Directory."

So what advice can I give to help you decide when to create a Windows 2000 domain? The following list should help. You should create a new domain in Windows 2000 if

- You have a truly decentralized administrative model. If you had that complete trust model in your NT 4 environment, it may be very difficult for you to regain control of those domains and collapse them into an OU structure. Even though you can probably manage to give those groups the same level of control and administrative privileges with a delegated OU administrative model, you may find that they simply don't believe you (or Microsoft). In this case, your chances of success may depend on a management edict outlawing the rogue domains. There will be a lot of internal political pressure to re-create the decentralized model, even after you are finished with your Windows 2000 implementation and have created your new OU structure. People like to keep the control they are used to. If you are pressured to create these domains, I urge you to resist the temptation.
- You estimate that you will have more than 1 million objects in an Active Directory partition and have a need to balance the logon, search, and authentication load over multiple domains. Although the AD database's upper size limit has been stated to be 2 terabytes and Microsoft has tested the directory to 10 million objects, there is a serious degradation in performance when doing searches against the AD and during replication with directories more than 1 million objects.
- Your organization requires multiple, conflicting domain level policies. Some Windows 2000 policies are termed "domain policies" and are set at the domain level. These are different from group policy objects in that they cannot be applied by user, group, or OU. Many of the security policies fall into this category. One example of such a policy is the password strength policy. After you set passwords to expire every 90 days, or be at least 8 characters long, you have set that for all user accounts in the domain and cannot make it different for a particular group or OU within the domain. If you have an organization that requires a 30-day expiration, 10-character minimums, and password filtering as well, you will need to create another domain to accommodate their increased security needs.

- You have an organization that spans international borders and as a result needs to be able to reflect differences in language, time zones and currency. Our Pizza Place example has demonstrated this principle by creating a new domain for the new United Kingdom operating unit. Due to the differences in time zones, it also makes sense for Pizza Place UK to have their own administrators. How happy do you think the Memphis-based headquarters administrative staff is going to be when we tell them they need to be in the office at midnight British time so they can remotely install software and reboot that domain controller in London and stay until the upgrade is finished? That would pretty much soak up an evening.

Deciding on a Tree or Forest

Now that you have decided how many domains you will need, you need to make a decision about arranging them into a tree or a forest and whether or not to tie the new structure to an existing DNS public namespace. Although a full discussion of all the implications of this decision is beyond the scope of this book, I can give you a few things to consider when trying to decide which structure is best for you. For more information, you can refer to "Planning for Windows 2000" and the Windows 2000 Active Directory Planning White Papers at `http://www.microsoft.com`.

When deciding whether you need a tree or a forest, you should consider your company's overall business architecture. I'm referring to the really high level stuff—for example, are you organized as a joint venture, partnership, subsidiary to a larger firm, or some other organization? This is important because you want to make the overall domain structure mirror the information needs of your employees. If your company operates as a single entity, a single tree structure would probably be best for you. The tree structure forms a contiguous namespace and simplifies searches through the Active Directory. An example of how a tree might look for my consulting firm is shown in Figure 2.10. This structure is also easier for users and administrators to navigate and administer. In addition, LDAP referrals can be used to resolve searches within the tree.

The choice to use a forest is made when an organization has a structure that is actually comprised of several distinct business entities. This might be the case with a joint venture, holding company, or conglomerate, such as our fictional parent company Fast Foods R Us. Because each of Fast Foods' child entities operate as independent business units; they have formed their own administrative models and staffs as well as domain policies. In order to leverage the power of marketing research, however, they have a need to share resources related to marketing, sales, and some management information reporting between the three corporate entities. For these reasons, a forest like the one illustrated in Figure 2.11 would be a good choice for their domain structure.

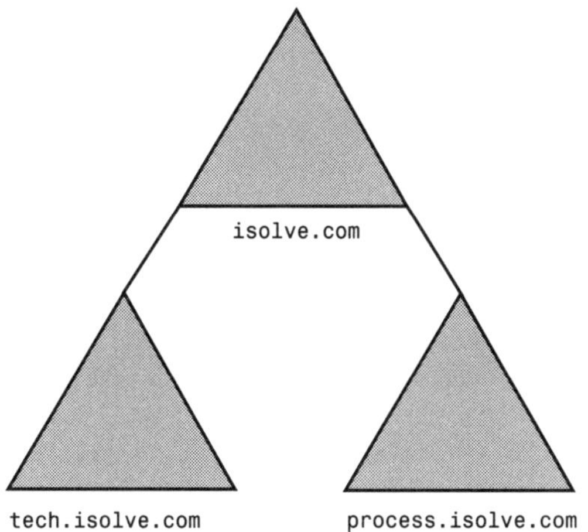

Figure 2.10 isolve.com single tree diagram.

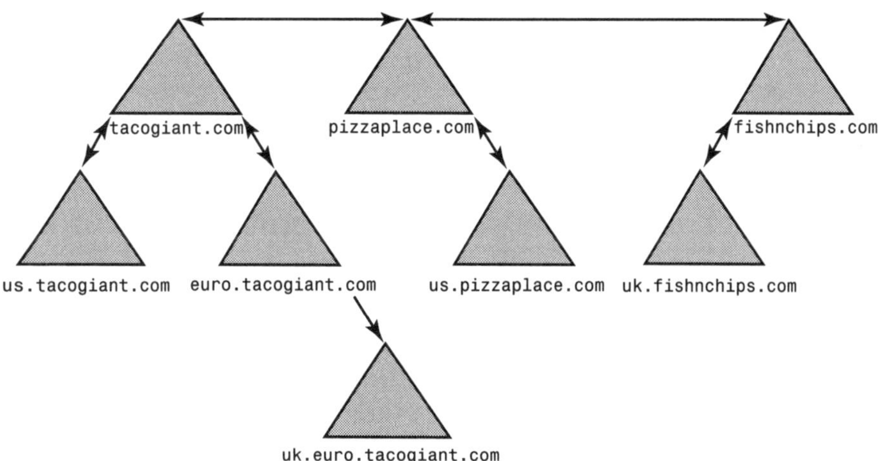

Figure 2.11 Fast Foods R Us forest structure with Pizza Place, Taco Giant, and Fish 'n' Chips domain structures illustrated.

With a forest, the domains would form a non-contiguous, disjointed namespace still connected through Kerberos transitive trust relationships. Although this structure allows each business unit to keep its administrative independence and still share resources, there are two distinct disadvantages to the forest structure that has been chosen. The first is the complexity of the structure itself. Even though the DNS naming convention is used to form the trees of the forest, this structure is more difficult for users and administrators to navigate. In addition to that drawback, LDAP referrals cannot be used to resolve searches between the trees in the forest, so searches of the forest are restricted by the attributes published in the shared global catalog that surrounds the tree. If the attribute is not published in the catalog, the search will not be successfully resolved.

Naming Your Top-Level Domains

After the tree versus forest decision is made, it will be time to start naming those domains. One of the most important choices you will make is the name of your top-level domain or domains. Because that name will be the root of all your other DNS names in the structure, you should carefully consider its selection. After the name is selected and you have configured Windows 2000 to use Dynamic DNS as defined by the Internet Engineering Task Force to register new machines and domains, changing the top-level domain name will be exceedingly difficult, if not impossible.

The first question that needs to be answered is whether or not you have a publicly registered DNS namespace on the Internet, and if so, whether you want the internal domain structure to be derived from that namespace. For example, if Pizza Place had a registered Internet DNS server with `pizzaplace.com` as the root domain, you need to decide if you want the Pizza Place employees to be working off that same namespace for their servers. For a discussion of the advantages and disadvantages of using the same public namespace, see the sidebar entitled "Comparing Public and Versus Private Namespaces."

Other than the choice of public versus private DNS namespace, there are a few other guidelines for naming your top-level domains. First and foremost, choose a stable name. As I mentioned earlier, all your subdomain names will be derived from this one, so choosing a name that might change is not something you want to do. Also, the KISS principle should definitely apply (Keep It Simple, Stupid). Because all the other names are derived from this top level, they can get very long. Making the name short and representative of the company will help the logic of the DNS structure be easily seen by employees and administrators. It goes without saying that you should obey the DNS naming rules in terms of the allowed character set (A-Z, a-z, 0-9, and the hyphen, although the hyphen has been known to cause some problems in SQL Server environments, so beware).

Finally, even if you have decided to use different internal and external namespaces, register your internal DNS name with InterNIC, just as you did your external name. This prevents someone else from capturing the domain name and having your internal users being redirected to another company's servers when they are trying to access their local resources. It's a situation that is frustrating for users and quite embarrassing for the responsible administrator.

Comparing Public and Private Namespaces

If you have an existing public namespace on the Internet or if you are planning on a future Internet presence, you need to decide whether to tie your new Windows 2000 DDNS structure into that existing or planned space, or to keep a independent namespace for your internal structure. There are advantages and disadvantages to both scenarios, so let's briefly examine those.

Option 1—Dueling Namespaces

First, let's assume you decide to keep two separate namespaces, internal and external, with different DNS root domains. This would be similar to what we have done with the Pizza Place example in this text. Pizza Place has an external, public DNS namespace with the root domain of `thepizzaplace.com`. Their Web server is `www.thepizzaplace.com`. They have also started an internal DNS namespace design beginning with a root domain of `pizzaplace.com`. It is common to have an internal root domain name that is very similar to the external root domain as is seen in our example.

This organization of namespaces provides some benefits. First, it hides the internal IP addressing scheme from the external DNS servers because there should be no need to cross-reference the internal and external environments. This means that the external server's lookup tables will not be required to have entries for hosts inside the firewall. Each namespace is a independent DNS zone, maintained by its own DDNS server. Second, configuration of this environment is simpler because there is no need to mirror servers to maintain a logical separation between the zones or to configure proxies to understand the difference between two identically named servers where one is inside the firewall and the other is outside.

Finally, if the existing public namespace is already set up and running in a DNS environment that does not support SRV resource records (for example, UNIX with BIND 4.x, NT 4 with SP3 or below, or other third-party DNS software without SRV RR support), you can still implement the internal namespace without the worries of converting the external environment to some DNS platform that meets the Active Directory's requirement for BIND 8.1.2 or above. These SRV records are required for Windows 2000 domain controllers to locate other domain controllers (which are also the DDNS database repositories) and accomplish zone transfers.

The only disadvantage of this arrangement would be the need to register two namespaces with InterNIC. Other than that, implementation and maintenance are easier than with your other option, a single namespace.

Option 2—The Unispace Solution

The single namespace is not seen as often in companies that have an Internet presence. Some of the reasons for this are security concerns as well as implementation and configuration difficulties.

The security issue stems from using a single set of host records to resolve resource names for both internal and external users. Doing so would compromise all your IP addresses should the list fall into the wrong hands. So the goal is to hide the internal IP addressing scheme from external users while still providing internal users with a way to resolve host names for both internal and external resources.

One way to do this is to mirror your external servers to internal servers behind a firewall and configure the DDNS servers on either side of the firewall so they can resolve only those hosts on their side of the firewall. In addition, no replication occurs between the internal and external DDNS servers. Although they do share the same domain name, because each is configured differently and there is no replication, they are essentially two separate zones.

For example, if my company decided to use its InterNIC domain name `isolve.com` as both an internal and external namespace and we had an intranet as well as an Internet presence, both my employees and my customers would need to access a web server called `www.isolve.com`. Should these physically be the same machine? Naturally, no. What I could set up instead is a mirrored web server inside the firewall. Next, I would configure the internal DDNS server to forward my internal web requests to the internal mirrored web server. Similarly, external Web requests would be routed to the external Web server by the DDNS server that was maintaining the external namespace. Because they are physically detached databases, using this system I have met the design goal of protecting my host tables from prying hacker eyes and still have a mechanism for employees to access resources that are the same as those outside the firewall.

Naturally, what you choose to do will depend on your situation, but I can testify to you that generally, if you have an Internet presence, the dual namespace concept is the easiest to implement.

Naming Your Subdomains

As with your top-level domain, there are some general guidelines you should follow when naming lower-level domains. First, remember the general domain creation criteria we discussed earlier in this chapter. Because you used those criteria to create the domains, the names will probably reflect the divisions you chose earlier, such as geographic boundaries. Also, remember that these names must be unique in the structure, so a lower-level domain should never be named the same as a higher-level domain. Although DNS could decide where it belonged by using the fully qualified domain name for resolution (for example, `sales.usops.pizzaplace.com` and `sales.europs.pizzaplace.com` are different DNS names), remember the issue of the downlevel domain names. Windows 2000 would make both of those downlevel names simply SALES. This could get confusing for logons.

Domains should never reflect organizational boundaries (that's what OUs are for), so naturally, their names shouldn't either. For example, that `sales.usops.pizzaplace` domain I just mentioned is a bad domain name.

Finally, keep your names as user friendly as possible. I work with one organization that has more than 60 domains in their organization and uses such cryptic domain names that users have no idea what they are looking at in the logon screen. They are trained to look for xyz123 domain and always log on there. Not a problem so far, but what happens when a user needs to set ACLs on one of his resources or access a resource in another domain? That's when it gets a little strange. He may know that the person he's looking for is in a particular department, such as Accounting, but the domain name GDWQ887 has no logical correlation to the accounting department, and yet, in fact, GDWQ887 is the domain name for Accounting. The powers that be thought they would increase security by using these nonsense names. I suppose they have achieved that goal, but in the process, they have made it much more difficult for their user community to get any work done.

A Few Final Thoughts

Now you know all about Windows 2000 domain concepts, naming rules and operational guidelines. Over the next few chapters, we'll expand on the administrative framework we have started for Pizza Place. Domains are just a part of this new, wonderful world of the Active Directory.

Just remember, you're not in Kansas anymore, Toto. The rules that you are used to have changed. Overall, I think it's a change for the better, but it is still hard to put aside all the guidelines you've used for years and adopt new ones. Especially when you are essentially dealing with the same product line. Well, this field is always a challenge and always changing, but that's why they pay you the big bucks! Okay, maybe they don't—but at least you're not going to be bored for the next few months. I think you can see that there will be some serious planning going on to revamp your domain structure as well as some education and possibly even some political battles until everyone jumps on the Windows 2000 bandwagon. When you're done, though, you can start planning the rest of the directory structure and begin simplifying your life as an administrator. There, now you have something to smile about!

3

Authentication and Resource Protection in Windows 2000

BECAUSE THIS IS A USER ADMINISTRATION BOOK, not a security book, I'm not going to go into a huge amount of detail about all the new security features in Windows 2000. There are security improvements in many parts of the product: Kerberos for authentication, an encrypting file system, support for certificates, and in networking, IPSEC. Although this is a chapter on security, we aren't going to discuss all of Windows 2000's new security features. I am going to try and keep the discussion to the security features that impact your user or desktop administration duties. In this chapter, we'll discuss how Windows 2000 handles authentication, authorization, access control and auditing. There are other security functions we will discuss in later chapters. For instance, we won't discuss how to control visibility and permissions on directory objects until Chapter 4, "Understanding Organizational Units: The Building Blocks of the Active Directory." Some of the security features in Windows 2000 are implemented as policies—IPSEC is an example. We will discuss those security functions in Chapter 9, "IntelliMirror Features for Client Management," when we are talking about creating and deploying policies.

In the real world, you really should at least have a passing familiarity with what Windows 2000 security can do for you as an administrator, so in this chapter, we will have a high-level discussion of some of the new security features, talk about some basic security concepts, and finally discuss how to secure your file system resources and implement auditing on those resources. As I mentioned in Chapter 1, "Inside Windows 2000 Overview," the permission and inheritance model has changed quite a bit in Windows 2000, so we will spend a considerable amount of time on that at the end of the chapter to make sure you fully understand the security implications in administering the system. Let's start with some general security terms and concepts, and see how Windows 2000 implements these functions.

Security Perimeters

When I was first learning about computer security, I was always told that there are four major security perimeters in any computer system:

- Physical security
- System security
- Application security
- Data Security

I was also told that these four layers could be thought of as being arranged in a bull's-eye pattern. As you move toward the center of the eye, each ring you pass through provides a higher level of security for the resources contained in that ring.

In Figure 3.1, you can see that the outer ring is the physical security ring. The fence around the installation, locked doors, and bulletproof glass would be considered physical security measures. Moving toward the center of the bull's-eye, the next ring is the system security perimeter. The idea of a network logon to an NT domain is an example of system security. After the system ring, there is the application ring and finally the data ring. Often we use the system logon to determine access to the innermost rings by using pass-through authentication to determine access levels for a particular user.

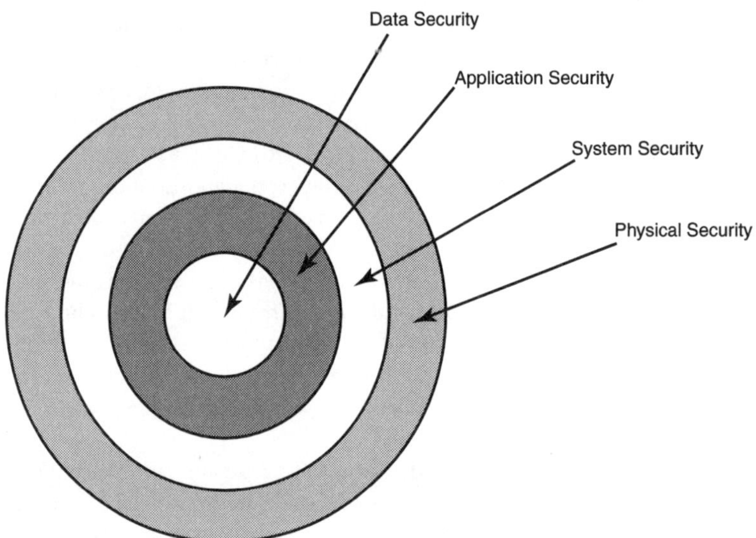

Figure 3.1 Security bull's-eye.

Security Activities

Any decent security system has to allow for the implementation of certain basic security functions. Naturally, every system implements these differently. Five of the basic security activities are identification, authentication, authorization, access control, and auditing. How strong a security system is depends on how strong and trustworthy each of these implementations is.

Identification

Identification is the concept of identifying yourself to the system. Depending on the perimeter, the method of identification differs. In physical security systems, this may be a badge. In system, application, and data security, you are typically identified by your username: your logon ID.

Windows 2000 can use two methods of identification for local and network logons. One is the traditional username and another is the Smart Card.

Authentication

When you authenticate to a system, you are proving that you are who you say you are. That picture on your badge is an example of authentication in the physical layer. In the system security ring, your password is a typical authentication mechanism. The certificates on a Smart Card logon are also examples of authentication.

In order to achieve authentication, a network must know how to authenticate. What methods are followed? What input is acceptable as an authenticator? How do we securely pass those authenticators to a machine that can validate them? How do we let a client know they have been authenticated? All these questions are answered by the choice of an authentication protocol. Windows 2000 supports three authentication protocols: NTLM, Kerberos, and SSL/TLS. We will discuss these protocols in detail a little later in the chapter.

Smart Cards

There is a lot of talk in the Windows 2000 documentation about Smart Cards as an identification and authentication mechanism. Exactly what is a Smart Card? A smart card is a credit-card-sized device that is inserted into a smart card reader, which is either installed internally in your computer or connected externally to your computer. The combination of the card (something you have) and a PIN that you enter (something you know) becomes the identification and authentication mechanism. To provide further security in a public key infrastructure environment, certificate information can also be placed on the card. As you probably already know, a certificate is an encrypted set of authentication credentials. These credentials are then passed to the system to be used as you access different servers. In order to use certificates in Windows 2000, you must use activate Certificate Services.

Authorization

When the system allows you to cross any given security perimeter, we refer to that as the process of authorization. You are being given the "authority" to cross the perimeter. When the door opens after you swipe that badge, the system has authorized you to enter a secure perimeter. When NT logs you on after you enter your username and password correctly, you have been authenticated at the system security perimeter.

Access Control

After you have been allowed to cross a given perimeter, there are usually further controls on your activities within that perimeter. After all, just because you have gotten in the gate doesn't mean the house is unlocked too. From a physical security standpoint, that is why you see multiple security levels within a facility, with more locked doors protecting each area. In general, how access control is handled on a system level depends on whether the particular system invokes share-level or user-level security (see sidebar).

Share-Level or User-Level Security?

Share-level security is the type usually offered by less secure peer-to-peer networking systems, such as Windows for Workgroups. Windows 9x can implement either share- or user-level security. With a share-level system, access restriction options are rather limited. Typically, they are Read Only, Full Control, or, at most, the access level can be set depending on the password supplied. There would be one password for Read Only and another password for Full Control. All the Read Only users share the same password to access the share. I call this "secret knock" security. If you know the secret knock, you get in. People being what they are, when a password is out for a share, it typically ends up being given to unauthorized users for one reason or another. Another aspect of this type of security is that there is only one checkpoint—the share. After you get into the sharepoint, all files and folders that exist in the share are visible to you and, if you have full control, alterable by you.

User-level security, on the other hand, requires that each user of a system be uniquely identified. This concept of a unique identifier for users and groups is then used to implement discretionary access control on resources in the system—discretionary because your access depends on your identity and the permissions set on the resource using that identifier. Typically, discretionary access controls are applied at each level of a system's resources. For example, there would be a list governing access to the sharepoint, then to the folder, then to subfolders, and finally to individual files. This allows an administrator to be very specific with permissions on resource levels. If a user wants to use a resource, he must have correct permission entries on all the lists leading to the resource he wants to access, based on either his personal identity or a group he is a member of. In Windows 2000, these permissions lists are called Discretionary Access Control Lists (DACLs).

Like its NT predecessors, Windows 2000 implements access controls through the use of identifiers that uniquely identify users and groups. It then sets permissions using those identifiers to restrict or allow access using access control lists attached to the resources. As always, the system operates on the model that if there is not an explicit entry on the list for a user, that user gets no access. There is no such thing as an implied permission in the NT world. In addition, permissions setting is still the responsibility of a resource's owner or an administrator who has taken ownership of a resource on a user's behalf. There are a few differences in both the permissions available and the inheritance model that Microsoft has implemented in Windows 2000. We will discuss those differences in detail a little later in the chapter in the section on "Setting Object Permissions and the New Inheritance Model."

Auditing

One requirement of a good security system is the capability to track what has happened on your system. Auditing is the security function that watches and then records security events of interest to the system administrator. Like all the other security activities, this may happen at any and all perimeters as needed. I remember one of our door entry systems was protected by a keypad system where we had to swipe our badges and then enter a PIN for entry. Each and every entry was then logged to a system in the security manager's office for auditing purposes.

Windows 2000 implements auditing of many system and access-related events through the use of an overall security policy that defines what type of security events to audit. In addition, each Active Directory and file system object can be protected by a Security Access Control List (SACL).

Secure Authentication Services in Windows 2000

An authentication protocol determines the method a system uses to verify a user's identity and access levels. In Windows 2000, more authentication methods are available for use than in previous NT systems. Microsoft has accomplished this by including additional authentication protocol support to the security architecture.

For backward compatibility with previous Microsoft systems and standalone logons, Windows 2000 still supports the traditional NTLM authentication protocol. As you have no doubt already heard, Microsoft has also opted to use the Kerberos security system as the default protocol for network authentication. The final authentication protocol that is supported is Secure Sockets Layer/Transport Layer Security (SSL/TLS). Using this protocol and X.509 certificates, Windows 2000 can authenticate Smart Card users and provide protection for unsecured networks, such as the Internet.

NTLM Authentication

NTLM is Microsoft's legacy authentication protocol from NT 4. Prior to Windows NT 4.0 Service Pack 4 (SP4), Windows NT supported two kinds of challenge/response authentication: LAN Manager (LM) challenge/response and Windows NT challenge/response (also known as NTLM challenge/response). In addition, Microsoft has developed a new version of NTLM known as NTLMv2.

A brief explanation of all three is in order so you can make informed decisions about allowing support for these protocols in your Windows 2000 environment.

LM authentication is the weakest of the three protocols because, although the passwords in LM can be longer than 7 characters, the algorithm allows longer passwords to be attacked in 7-character chunks. Password characters can be drawn from the set of uppercase alphabetic, numeric, and punctuation characters, plus 32 special ALT characters.

In contrast, NTLM uses all 14 characters in the password as a single contiguous unit and allows lowercase letters. Basically, increasing the length and character complexity in this manner means that although an eavesdropping hacker can attack in the same way as with the LM authentication protocol, it will take far longer for him to be successful. Naturally, if your users are choosing shorter passwords, whole words, or blank passwords, NTLM won't help!

NTLM on steroids is called NTLMv2 by Microsoft. NTLMv2 improves both the authentication and session security mechanisms of NTLM. In addition, the NTLM Security Service Provider (SSP) now allows clients to control which version of NTLM to use and allows servers to decide which alternatives to accept. Finally, NTLMv2 allows clients and servers to require the negotiation of message confidentiality (encryption), message integrity, 128-bit encryption, and NTLMv2 session security. NTLMv2 is available on NT 4 systems with Service Pack 4 or higher.

In Windows 2000, you have the capability to turn off NTLM support and go with a purely Kerberos model that provides a higher level of security for your network. However, you may find that you need to continue NTLM support on your Windows 2000 system for several reasons.

The first reason to continue NTML support is if you have downlevel clients and servers that use one of the LM/NTLM authentication protocols listed above. Computers with Windows 3.11, Windows 95, Windows 98, or Windows NT 4.0 use the NTLM protocol for network authentication in Windows 2000 domains. Second, your Windows 2000 machines use NTLM when authenticating to servers with Windows NT 4.0 and when accessing resources in Windows NT 4.0 domains. These first two reasons apply if you have a mixed Microsoft network environment.

Other reasons to keep NTLM support have to do with, believe it or not, UNIX compatibility. Even though we think of Kerberos as a UNIX standard, you may also have to consider keeping NTLM support if you have UNIX clients connecting to your Windows 2000 domains. If they are using an SMB client to connect, whether the UNIX clients are configured for Kerberos or not, they need to use NTLM to connect because of the requirements set forth by the SMB client. If the UNIX clients are using standard TCP/IP application protocols, such as Telnet and FTP, exclusively, you can then eliminate NTLM support. Finally, if your Windows 2000 clients are connecting to a UNIX server using an SMB daemon and you want to keep that model, you will still need NTLM. Another option in this situation would be to turn off the SMB daemon and use an NFS client for the Windows 2000 boxes. Microsoft provides that client as part of their UNIX interoperability package, Services for UNIX.

Kerberos Authentication

In Windows 2000, Microsoft is implementing Kerberos version 5 with extensions to support public key authentication as the preferred network authentication protocol between Windows 2000 machines. In this section, we will discuss the advantages of this decision as well as how Microsoft's implementation of Kerberos works in the simplest possible terms. As I mentioned before, an in-depth discussion of Kerberos v5 is way beyond the scope of this book. But if you are a nuts and bolts kind of person and want all the gory details of Kerberos, there is good news. Because Kerberos has been around for more than a decade and is an established industry standard security protocol, there is lots of information out there on the system. To look at Kerberos strictly from a Windows 2000 viewpoint, Microsoft has a white paper titled "Windows 2000 Kerberos Authentication." *Windows NT* magazine has also published a couple of good, understandable articles on Kerberos. You can get those archived articles from their Web site at `http://www.winntmag.com/` if you are a subscriber.

Advantages of Using Kerberos

Kerberos has a few advantages over NTLM as an authentication protocol. The number one advantage may very well be that it is an industry standard protocol. Kerberos v5 is outlined in RFC 1510 from the IETF and is on standards track. In their whitepaper on Kerberos Authentication in Windows 2000, Microsoft says that their implementation of Kerberos "closely follows the specification defined in Internet RFC 1510." That's Microsoftese for "we did it our way." To be fair to Microsoft, though, that's true of all standards implementations. From what we have seen of the product so far, it is generally agreed that cross-system authentication between Windows 2000 and existing Kerberos-based authentication systems should be possible. Let's look at some of the other advantages of Kerberos in the following section.

Quicker Server Connection Time

As we discussed in Chapter 2, with NTLM, an application server connects to a domain controller to authenticate clients. This happens each time a client establishes a session with the application server. If a client connects to OFFAPPS1, disconnects and reconnects a few minutes later, the machines go through the whole authentication process again. With Kerberos, after the client and the applications server are both authenticated, and the client is approved for access, a set of credentials is issued for a session between the two machines. The client can then reuse those credentials for subsequent conversations with that server. Because no further authentication is necessary, the use of Kerberos speeds up server connection time by eliminating the need to authenticate each time a connection to the same server is made. This can provide a noticeable improvement for users who are coming in over slower WAN connections.

For improved security, these credentials have an expiration time associated with them. You can set that expiration time to match the security levels required in your organization. By default, the time to live on a session ticket in Windows 2000 is eight hours.

Mutual Authentication

NTLM is a one-way authentication protocol that allows clients to authenticate to a server. How does the client know it is really connecting to the server that it is supposed to be connected to and not some hacker's proxy? With NTLM, you don't know and can't be sure. NTLM was designed in an era where servers were assumed to be genuine. This is an invalid assumption in today's open Internet environments.

Kerberos, in contrast, is based on mutual distrust. The Kerberos server makes all machines in the domain prove their identity before they are allowed to participate in the domain, even the servers. Through the use of shared private keys, Kerberos can guarantee that all the parties involved in the conversation are who they say they are.

Delegated Authentication

Windows services often have a need to impersonate clients when accessing resources. For example, this must be done when accessing a remote server. NTLM had no capacity to impersonate a client and access a remote service. Kerberos has a proxy function that allows a service to impersonate its client when connecting to other services on remote servers. For example, if a user is accessing an application on the Personnel server and that application requires a resource from the Payroll server, the Personnel server pretends to be the user and passes the user's credentials when requesting authentication on the Payroll server.

Simplified Trust Management

Because Kerberos employs mutual authentication, it can implement a trust model that allows for trust relationships that are two-way and transitive. Mutual authentication guarantees that any machine in a domain truly is a member. Kerberos forces servers to authenticate as well, so that all the domain controllers are also legitimate. In view of that assumption, the domain controllers become trusted security principals in a multidomain network and can be organized in a tree of transitive, mutual trust. Kerberos credentials issued in one domain can then be used and accepted anywhere in the tree or forest.

Interoperability

As mentioned earlier, Microsoft's implementation of the Kerberos protocol is based on IETF standards-track specifications (RFCs 1510 and 1964) from the Internet Engineering Task Force (IETF). Therefore, the implementation of Kerberos in Windows 2000 gives you a basis for interoperability with other networks where Kerberos version 5 is used for authentication.

In Windows 2000, Microsoft has implemented extensions to the Kerberos protocol that permit initial authentication using public key certificates rather than the conventional Kerberos shared secret keys. This enhancement allows the protocol to support interactive logon with a Smart Card.

How Kerberos Works

How does this paranoid security system work? Get yourself a cup of coffee and open your mind—this can be a little hard to follow if you've never seen it before.

Keep in mind two things as we go along. First, remember that Kerberos operates on the concept of symmetric (or shared private key) encryption, meaning you must use the same key to decrypt a message as you used to encrypt the message in the first place. I call this the secret decoder ring method of encryption. If we both have the same secret decoder rings, with identical keys, we can encrypt and decrypt messages we send to each other. However, if you have the Batman decoder ring, and I have the Superman ring, we can't send secret messages to each other. Kerberos works on this same concept by issuing symmetric keys for authentication and work sessions.

Another thing to remember is something I mentioned briefly earlier. Kerberos works on the assumption of mutual distrust. It doesn't believe that anyone is who he say he is until his identity is proven by his ability to decrypt messages encrypted in the private key he shares with the Kerberos server.

Finally, in this shared private key system, there must be a place that keeps track of and distributes these algorithms. In Kerberos, this function is called the key distribution center (KDC). In the Windows 2000 implementation of Kerberos, the KDC is hosted in the Active Directory and is, therefore, resident on each and every domain controller. This gives the KDC all the advantages of the multimaster domain controller replication and fault tolerance. So in this discussion, whenever KDC is mentioned, think "domain controller."

In theory, the functioning of Kerberos is rather simple. A centralized security server (or replicated servers) issues each security principal in their domain a secure key to talk to the Kerberos server. This is often referred to as the long-term key. Long-term keys are typically derived from the user's password and other information through a one-way hashing algorithm and stored in the local credentials cache. The credentials cache is an area of protected volatile memory that is destroyed when the user session is ended. Each security principal has a different key than its neighbor, and the security server is the only other party that knows what each key is. This key is used to get another set of credentials, called a ticket-granting ticket (TGT), that allows a user to request access to other servers.

If one security principal wants to talk to another security principal—Mary Jo wants to access that OFFAPPS1 server, for example—Kerberos has to issue a session key (sometimes called the short-term key) to Mary Jo and the applications server so that those two can send secure messages to each other. Each session key is unique and has an expiration time on it to further enhance its security. Session tickets can be renewed if the administrator chooses to set this up as part of the domain's Kerberos policy. See, simple…in theory! Let's look at the implementation of the details.

Logging On

We'll start with Mary Jo's logon. When Mary Jo logs on to her local machine, the Kerberos client software running on her workstation converts her password to an encryption key and saves the resulting key in its credential cache. Then the client sends an authentication request to the Kerberos server. The first part of the authentication request identifies Mary Jo and the name of the service for which she is requesting credentials. Because this is her logon, she is requesting credentials for the ticket-granting service. As I mentioned, most people don't log on to the domain to talk to the security system, they want to access applications and other resources. When she has logged on successfully to the domain, the KDC will issue her a TGT that she will use when talking to the Kerberos server (during this session) to request access to other servers. The second part of this authentication request message contains pre-authentication data that proves Mary Jo knows the password. This is usually a timestamp encrypted with Mary Jo's long-term key. Other forms of pre-authentication data can be accepted by the protocol.

When the KDC receives this package, it checks its database for Mary Jo's long-term key, decrypts the pre-authentication info, makes sure the timestamp is within allowed parameters, and then issues Mary Jo a TGT that she will use to obtain future session tickets. To accomplish this transaction, the KDC invents a session key for itself and Mary Jo to use for their conversations. Then, it encrypts this logon session key with Mary Jo's long-term key. Next, it embeds another copy of the logon session key and other authorization info about Mary Jo. It encrypts these two things in its own long-term key. This portion that is encrypted in the KDC's long-term key is the actual TGT.

When Mary Jo's station receives this reply, it decrypts the session ticket using Mary Jo's long-term key and stores the session ticket in its credentials cache. It also extracts the TGT, still encrypted in the KDC's long-term key, and stores it in the credentials cache.

Accessing Other Servers

Now that Mary Jo has been authenticated onto the domain and has a TGT to request access to other resources, she can ask for permission to talk to the OFFAPPS1 server. From the user standpoint, all this is invisible. Mary Jo probably goes to My Network Places, searches the Active Directory, or clicks the Microsoft Word icon on her desktop. When she does, the Kerberos client on her machine sends a Ticket Granting Service Request message to the KDC that includes Mary Jo's name, an authenticator (again, usually a timestamp) encrypted in the logon session key, the TGT (still encrypted in the KDC's long-term key), and the name of the service for which Mary Jo is requesting a session key (OFFAPPS1, for example).

When the domain controller receives this message, it decrypts the TGT with its long-term key and extracts the logon session key it embedded there. It uses that key to decrypt the authenticator portion of the request. If the authenticator is within bounds, the KDC creates a session key for Mary Jo to use when talking to the applications server. Now, at this point, the KDC could send the session key to Mary Jo and a second message to the applications server with that same session key in it. This method of key distribution would be inefficient because it requires the KDC to send two messages. Problems would also be caused if there was a network disturbance and Mary Jo tried to use her session key before the applications server had received its copy of the key. In order to overcome these potential problems, the KDC's response to Mary Jo's request for access to the applications server looks like this: the response contains two parts. The first part is the session key for the Mary Jo-OFFAPPS1 session, encrypted in the Mary Jo-KDC logon session key. In the second part of the response, the KDC embeds a second copy of the Mary Jo-OFFAPPS1 session key and Mary Jo's authorization data and encrypts this second portion in the OFFAPPS1 server's long-term key.

When Mary Jo's machine receives this response, it decrypts the first part of the message and stores the OFFAPPS1 session key in its credentials cache. It then extracts the second part of the message, the part encrypted in the OFFAPPS1 long-term key, and stores that in its cache as well.

When Mary Jo goes to access the applications server, a message is sent from the Kerberos client on her machine to the Kerberos client on the applications server. This message is called a Kerberos Application Request and contains an authenticator encrypted in the Mary Jo-OFFAPPS1 session key and the ticket that was sent back to Mary Jo's machine encrypted in the applications server's long-term key.

Upon receipt of the Application Request, the applications server decrypts the session key and Mary Jo's authorization data using its own long-term key and then uses the session key to test the authenticator that is encrypted in the session key. If the authenticator checks out, it sends a response to Mary Jo's machine, and the conversation between Mary Jo and the applications server can proceed.

I warned you! Is that coffee cold yet? And that was the executive overview version of logging on within a single domain! When you are working within an Active Directory structure that has more than one domain, Kerberos accepts authentication credentials from other domains in the tree or forest. The way that those are forwarded from one domain to another is a little more complicated than what we have discussed here. Again, if you want the fine details, go to the Microsoft white paper on Kerberos authentication. I think this discussion was enough for you get the idea, though. I'm sure you can see why Kerberos is considered a good authentication protocol.

Remember, Kerberos is just that, an *authentication* protocol. It does very little to help with implementing access controls after the initial logon to a machine or service. All right, in our example, Mary Jo has been allowed to log on to the applications server, but can she run MS Excel? Kerberos plays a small role in determining the answer, but those kinds of permissions questions come under the mantle of discretionary access control.

Secure Sockets Layer/Transport Layer Security

The final authentication protocol supported in Windows 2000 is SSL/TLS. This protocol is already supported in other Microsoft products, such as Exchange and IIS. It is used primarily to authenticate Smart Card users using a combination of this protocol and X.509 certificates, and to protect connections on unsecured networks. It can be used to secure your email and I'net (Internet and intranet) applications.

Security Access Tokens

As mentioned earlier, in order to implement discretionary access control, each security principal must be uniquely identified to the system and there must be a mechanism to compare that identifier to a list of approved users for each resource in the system.

In Windows 2000, as it was in NT 4, security principals are uniquely identified by a SID (Security Identifier), a unique alphanumeric value consisting of two parts. The first part identifies the domain in which the SID was issued, and the second part uniquely identifies the account within that domain. Keep in mind that in Microsoftese, a domain can be the individual machine if it is a standalone box or a member of a workgroup. Regardless of the scope of the "domain," Microsoft guarantees that a SID will always be unique and never reused. SIDs are used to identify individual users as well as groups within the domain. These SIDs are used by the Local Security Authority (LSA) on each local machine to build a Security Access Token (SAT) that follows a user's processes throughout the system. The SAT contains the user's individual account SID as well as all the SIDs for any groups he is a member of. Based on those SIDs, a list of system rights is appended to the access token as well—the right to log on interactively to a domain controller, for example, or permitted logon hours.

In standalone machines, workgroups, and domains not using Kerberos for whatever reason, NTLM is used to build SATs just as they were built in previous versions of NT. In a native mode domain where Kerberos authentication is enabled, the KDC prepares authorization data in two steps to assist in the access control process.

Step one takes place when the KDC prepares a TGT for a user. When the TGT is requested, the KDC queries the Active Directory for the user's account. In the attributes of the account there is a field for the user's SID and another attribute field for the SIDs of the security groups the user belongs to. Both of these attributes are returned and embedded into the authorization data field of the TGT. In a multidomain environment, the KDC also queries the Global Catalog for universal groups that include the user's SID or the SIDs of any of the domain security groups of which the user is a member. If those are found, the SIDs for the universal groups are also included in the authorization data field.

Step two happens when the KDC prepares a session ticket for conversations between two parties. When a user requests a session ticket for a particular server, the domain controller (KDC) in the server's domain copies the authorization field data from the TGT and embeds it in the session ticket's authorization field. If the server is in a different domain than the one where the user account was created, the KDC in the server's domain will check its Active Directory for any domain local groups that contain either the user SID or group SIDs that are already in the authorization field. If it finds any, it adds these to the session ticket's authorization field before it is passed on to the target server. This authorization data is signed by the KDC.

Wait a minute, what happened to the LSA and the access tokens? They are still in existence. When this session ticket is received by the target server, the LSA process takes the information in the authorization field and creates an access token for that user on the local machine. At that point, the functioning of the system is essentially the same as an NT 4 box.

Discretionary Access Control Lists (DACLs)

Now that the user is authenticated onto the server, the user's SAT can be checked against the permissions list for the objects she wants to use on that server. The header of every object in the system contains a security descriptor with a list of permissions embedded in it. This list is called the Discretionary Access Control List (DACL) and contains SIDs and permissions levels for each SID listed. If there isn't an explicit entry on the list for a user or one of her groups, it is assumed by Windows 2000 that no access should be allowed. The permissions list is maintained by the owner of the object. Only the owner is allowed to grant and revoke permissions to the resource.

Administrative Ownership of Resources

In the event of an emergency, an administrator can take ownership of a resource and even reset permissions because he is the new owner. This ability is usually exercised when unexpected events happen (like poor old Bob gets hit by a bus at lunch) and it is necessary to transfer ownership to another user. To take ownership, the administrator would go to the Properties screen of the resource and select the Security tab. On the Security screen, select the Advanced button and, finally, the Ownership tab shown in Figure 3.2, and select the new administrative owner. An administrator can elect to set himself as the owner, in which case the resource's size would be counted against his personal disk quota space if disk quotas are being used. He can also elect to set the ownership to the Administrators group. The Administrators group is exempt from disk quotas.

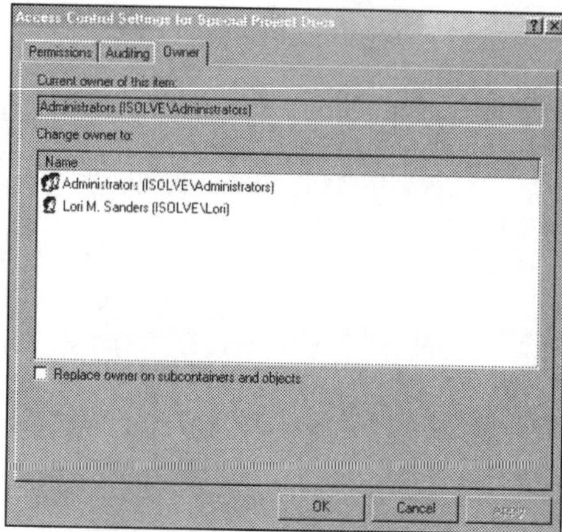

Figure 3.2 Changing ownership of a resource.

To pass ownership to another user, the administrator can go directly to the Access Control Settings screen by using the Advanced button on the Security tab of the Properties screen. From there, click on the Add button, and select the desired user. Then, the Permission Entry screen will pop up. Now, scroll down to the Take Ownership permission on the Permission Entry screen and put a check in the Allow box to enable the chosen user to take ownership of the resource.

Now, when that user logs on and accesses the Security Properties for that object, he will have the ability to go to the ownership tab and select himself as the new owner of the object. One interesting thing about the ownership interface: In the list of users and groups that are displayed to select from, only users and groups that have the permission to take ownership will ever show up. As a further security precaution, only the currently logged-on user and his authorized groups will show up in the list. For example, if I were logged on and had been given the permission to take ownership of a resource, the list would show my "Lori" account as well as the "Administrators" group for my machine. Because ownership can only be taken and never given, this makes sense. Otherwise, an unscrupulous administrator would have the ability to take ownership and then give it back without the resource's true owner ever knowing about it. Not a good thing, especially if it's the payroll file or strategic, sensitive corporate information.

Setting Object Permissions and the New Inheritance Model

One of the key things to remember about Windows 2000 and permissions is that there are different types of objects you can set permissions for. It can be a little confusing at first, but if you are used to Novell or Banyan, or are familiar with the idea of shares in the Microsoft world, I think you'll have no problems here.

When we discuss permissions in Windows 2000, we talk about setting permissions on file system objects or directory objects. In this section, we'll discuss setting permissions on file system objects. Those would be limited to files, folders, and shared folders. We'll talk about directory object permissions in the next chapter. The interface for setting permissions on both types of objects, file system and directory, is almost the same. Also, the inheritance model is very similar, so when you get it for file systems, the directory should be a breeze.

Setting File System Permissions

When setting permissions for file system objects, we are actually going to limit access to the object. As with NT 4, the default permissions mask on the Windows 2000 file system is basically everyone has complete access. If you are coming from the Novell or UNIX world, you are probably breathless with shock right now. Instead of opening access up to an NT/Windows 2000 system like you would in other environments, you must do the opposite. You must shut it down. If you don't believe me, just go have a look at your system volume. By default, it will say Everyone, Full. There are exceptions to this mask in Windows 2000. The `%systemroot%` directory where Windows 2000 is installed, as well as the Program Files and Documents and Settings directories, has a different default mask that allows average users less access and administrators full access. But, trust me, almost everything else is wide open. And remember, because the guest account is part of the Everyone group, that means whatever Everyone has, Guest has if the account is enabled. If it is enabled, anyone *without* a valid account will be logged on as a guest. It's kind of like putting out a big welcome sign for Hackers, Inc. That's why we're going to spend a little time on setting permissions.

Because Windows 2000 uses discretionary access control, you can think of access to a resource as being similar to passing through several locked doors in a building to get to your office. In order to access a file, the user must have all the right "keys" to get through the file system path that leads to the file, as well as the correct key to open the file. Having the right keys means having the necessary permission entries on the DACLs of the volume, folders, subfolders, and finally the file. If the right permission level is missing at any of these preliminary DACLs, access to the resource may be denied. If it is a shared resource, and users are coming in over the network to access it, they must also have correct permissions on the sharepoint to proceed with their entry into the file system.

Standard Permissions Sets

As with NT 4, there is a set of standard permissions for files and folders that you can use to make your life as an administrator easier. You also have the ability to set very specific "special" permissions on a file system resource if necessary. We saw an example of this in the sidebar on taking ownership.

Setting standard permissions can be accomplished using the first screen of the Security Properties dialog box as shown in Figure 3.3. To get to this dialog box, right-click on the desired object, select Properties from the menu, and then select the Security tab.

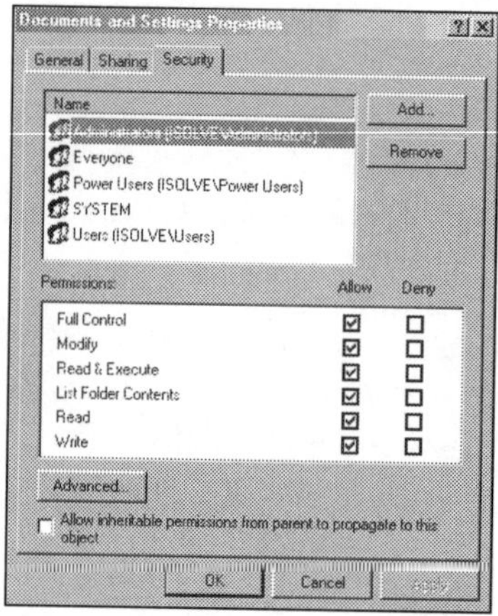

Figure 3.3 Security Properties dialog box used for setting standard sets of permissions.

This dialog box is just the first of three that you can use to set permissions on resources. The permissions set shown applies to the highlighted user or group. In this case, our screen shot shows the permissions for the Administrators group. To see the other permissions levels, you would need to move the highlight bar to the appropriate group or user. Adding and removing users from the list is very easy. Simply choose Add or Remove. This part really is intuitive!

Table 3.1 shows the standard permissions sets for files and folders and exactly what those sets mean in Windows 2000.

Table 3.1 **Standard Permissions**

Standard Permission	Specific Permissions Granted as a Result
Read	List Folder/Read Data Read Attributes Read Extended Attributes Read Permissions Synchronize

Standard Permission	Specific Permissions Granted as a Result
Read and Execute	List Folder/Read Data Read Attributes Read Extended Attributes Read Permissions Synchronize Traverse Folder/Execute File
Modify	Create Files/Write Data Create Folders/Append Data Delete List Folder/Read Data Read Attributes Read Extended Attributes Read Permissions Synchronize Write Attributes Write Extended Attributes
Write	Create Files/Write Data Create Folders/Append Data Read Permissions Synchronize Write Attributes Write Extended Attributes
List Folder Contents	List Folder/Read Data Read Attributes Read Extended Attributes Read Permissions Synchronize Traverse Folder/Execute File
Full Control	Change Permissions Create Files/Write Data Create Folders/Append Data Delete Delete Subfolders and Files List Folder/Read Data Read Attributes Read Extended Attributes Read Permissions Synchronize Take Ownership Write Attributes Write Extended Attributes

You might have noticed the new column for "Deny" in Figure 3.3. In NT 4, you had the option to set a "No Access" flag, but you couldn't get specific about what permissions you wanted to deny someone. For example, if you wanted to deny someone the Write permission in NT 4, you had to set all the other permissions to allow access and leave the Write permission check box blank. As you can see from the interface, you can now explicitly deny someone the right to write! Denying Full Control has the same effect as the NT 4 "No Access" flag. All the Deny permission entries in a DACL will be at the top of the list. This improves the efficiency of the permissions checks. If a person or group is denied any one of the requested set of permissions, they are thrown out at the top of the list rather than having to read the whole DACL to determine that they don't have that Write permission.

When an access request comes into the system, the permissions that are requested are considered a set. This means that whether a person is allowed access is an "all or nothing" proposition. Let's say, for example, that I tried to open a document. This would spawn several requests. One request would be to Read and Execute the program's .exe file and its associated DLLs, plus there would probably be a second request for Modify access to the document file. You can see from the standard permissions list in Table 3.1 what Modify means. If I am denied any of those permissions on the document, I will receive an "Access Denied" message. I will not get a message that says, "You can Read and Add Data to this document, but you can't Delete the document." That's what I mean by "all or nothing."

Permissions are cumulative in Windows 2000, as in NT 4. If a user is granted Read permission, but a group he belongs to is granted Write and Delete, the user's access is Read, Write, and Delete. When trying to determine a user's access level to a resource, there are three ways a permissions check can be terminated. The DACL entries will be checked until one of the following three conditions is met:

- The full set of requested permissions has been satisfied by SID entries for the user or the groups of which the user is a member
- One or more of the requested permissions has been denied for the user or one of the groups of which the user is a member
- The entire DACL has been checked and there was no entry for one or more of the requested permissions; therefore, access is assumed to be denied

If you are troubleshooting a permissions problem and need to know the actual ordering of the DACL, you can view the DACL by using the Advanced button on the Permissions tab. This will bring up the screen in Figure 3.4, which shows the ordering of the entries. From an administrative standpoint, you might find this screen easier to use because it gives you the whole list and the permissions levels without having to move the highlight bar. If you want to know specifically which special permissions have been set, simply highlight the entry in question and click on the View/Edit button. This will take you to the Special Permissions dialog box.

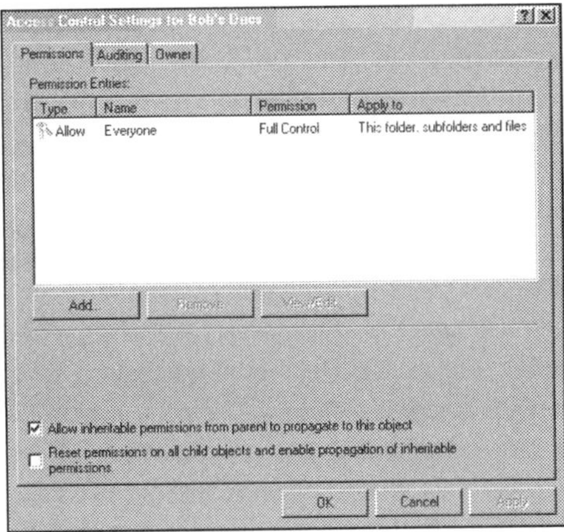

Figure 3.4 Access Control Settings screen used to view the ordering of the DACL on objects.

Setting Special Permissions

As was mentioned earlier, an administrator or owner of a resource can be very granular about what permissions they want individuals to have. Besides being able to explicitly Allow or Deny a permission, the screen shot in Figure 3.5 shows the special permissions that can be set on folders or files. The interface is a little more self-explanatory than it was in NT 4.

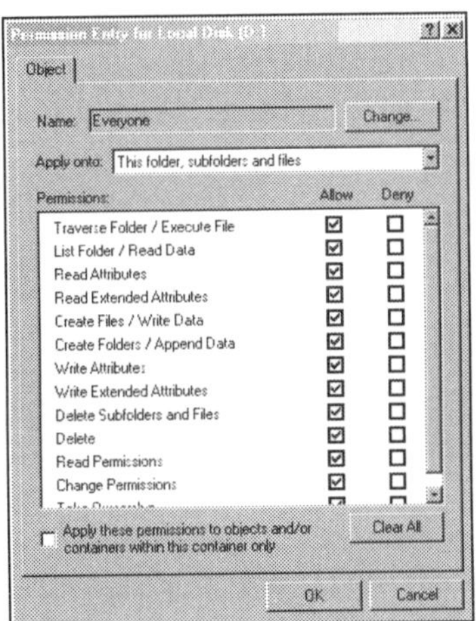

Figure 3.5 Permission Entry screen used to view the details of a particular DACL entry.

Naturally, whenever possible, you should use the standard permissions and set permissions using groups instead of individuals. Doing these two things and using the capabilities of the new inheritance model should make this part of your job as an administrator much easier. Permission inheritance will be discussed in the next section.

Shared Folder Permissions

There are a few things to remember about shared file system resources and permissions. First, a share is nothing more than a folder that has been designated for network access. If you have a folder called DOCS that you share out, a user who logs on locally to your machine will be governed by the DACL on the local file system folder. When you share the folder out, you have the option to set an additional DACL for the share that would govern users coming into the resource over the network. Oh, and by the way, guess what the default permissions mask is on all shares...that's right: Everyone, Full. If there is a conflict between the share DACL and the folder DACL, the most restrictive permissions set is used. For example, if you have an entry for Bob on the share DACL with Full Access set, and the folder DACL also has an entry for Bob, but with only Read access, Bob will only get Read privileges.

There are fewer choices for standard permissions settings on a share. Basically, you have Read, Change, and Full Control. The capability to set special permissions is not available at all on the share level. You can still set those special permissions at the folder level if you need them, and they will apply for your network users as well. The standard permissions that can be set on a share are shown in Table 3.2.

Table 3.2 **Standard Share Permissions**

Standard Permission	Specific Permissions Granted as a Result
Read	Traversing subfolders Viewing data in files and running programs Viewing filenames and subfolder names
Change	Adding files and folders to the shared folder Changing data in files Deleting subfolders and files Traversing subfolders Viewing data in files and running programs Viewing filenames and subfolder names
Full Control	Adding files and folders to the shared folder Changing data in files Changing permissions (NTFS only) Deleting subfolders and files Taking ownership (NTFS only) Traversing subfolders Viewing data in files and running programs Viewing filenames and subfolder names

Permission Propagation and Inheritance

In NT 4, you could set permissions at the top levels of a file structure and then push that permissions mask down through the structure to subfolders and files, as long as you were the owner of the resources. You had some control over how far you wanted to push the mask, but there weren't a lot of options in the interface. After you set a new mask and chose to push it down, NT 4 had the rather annoying habit of replacing *all* permissions. So, if you had set special permissions somewhere down in the bowels of the file structure, these were erased and replaced with the new mask. There was no way to preserve those explicitly set permissions. Pretty aggravating after you had gone to all the trouble to set them in the first place!

Windows 2000 has improved on that model by recognizing two sets of DACLs on a resource: the inherited DACL and the explicit DACL. Now, it is possible to set a default mask at the top level, push it down, and still keep those special permissions you had to set for Bob last week.

Naturally, there are some new rules to know with this new capability. I mentioned previously that Deny permissions would be listed at the front of the DACL to improve access request response times. It's simply more efficient that way. Well, let's complicate that picture just a little. If you have both types of permissions set on a resource, explicit and inherited, the explicit permissions are always checked first. So, the real search order on that resource would be Explicit Denies, Explicit Allows, Inherited Denies, and finally Inherited Allows. Figure 3.6 shows the Access Control Settings screen. I told you earlier that this screen was the easiest one to use to troubleshoot permissions, and you can see why if you look at it closely. I have created a DACL with both inherited and explicit permissions, as well as an Allow and a Deny for each type. They are listed on the interface in exactly the same order they are searched by Windows 2000. If you look closely at the first two entries, you will see that the icons to the left of the entries are nice and clear. These are explicit entries. The icons for the next two entries look a little fuzzy and faded. It's not your eyes; relax. These are the inherited entries. The icons are designed that way to give you a graphical clue to let you know which ones are explicit and which are inherited.

As you can see in that same figure, the explicit deny is listed first, followed by the explicit allow, then the inherited deny, and finally the inherited allow. The DACL will be searched in that order, and the three conditions listed earlier in the chapter will be used to terminate the request. That means *explicit permissions will override inherited permissions*. In our list, Lori will be denied Read access even though she inherits a Full Control permission from the parent folder. This happens because when the request comes in for access, the system will see the explicit deny listed first, terminate the request with an Access Denied message, and never search the list any farther, so it would never even see that Full Control entry. The logic here is that if the owner of the resource went to all the trouble to explicitly set a permission for Lori that is different from the inherited mask, there must be a reason and therefore the explicit must be the more important permission.

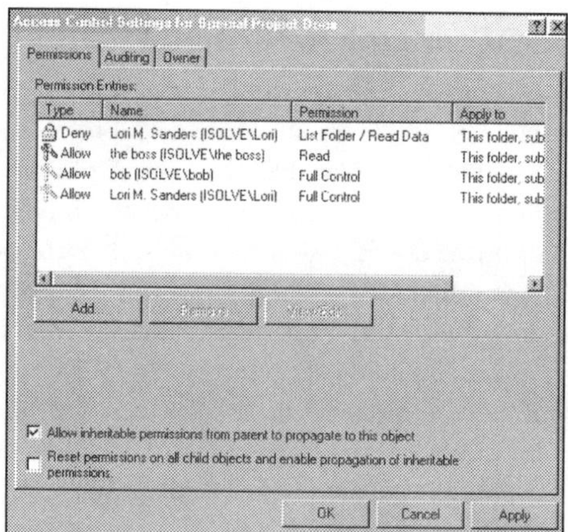

Figure 3.6 Using the Access Control Settings screen to view and troubleshoot file access problems.

If you don't need that much detail, you can get some of the same information on the first Security tab of the resource. Notice that inherited standard permissions are indicated by gray backgrounds in the check boxes, like those in Figure 3.7, while explicitly set permissions have clear backgrounds, as you can see in Figure 3.8. As always, you will have to move the highlight bar around to determine who has what.

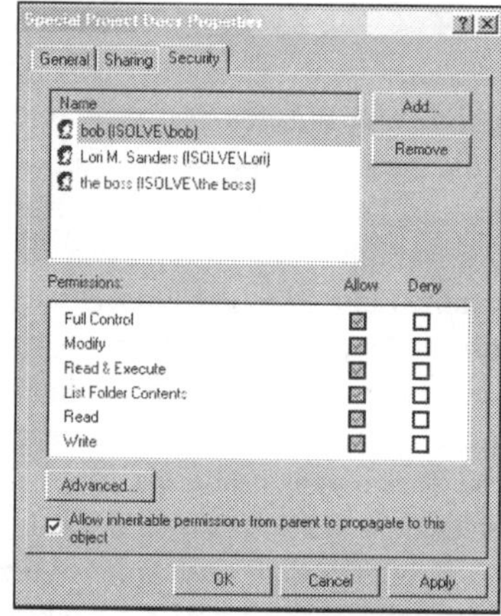

Figure 3.7 Using the Security Properties screen to view the inherited permissions set.

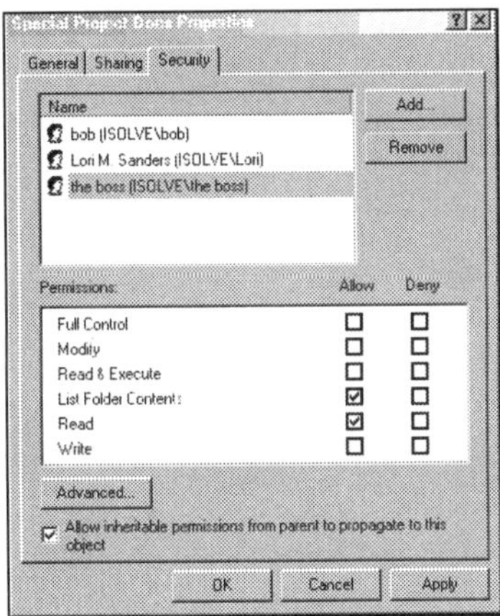

Figure 3.8 Viewing explicit permissions using the Security Properties tab.

There is one small glitch in this first interface that I want to make sure you are aware of. Look at Figures 3.7 and 3.8 again. Notice that there is only one entry for "Lori" on the first properties page, even though you can clearly see both entries listed on the Access Control Settings screen back in Figure 3.6. Be aware that multiple entries for the same account might not show up. Even worse, the general page shows only that Lori has inherited Full Control permissions. It says nothing about that Explicit Deny for Read access. This could be very deceiving (and aggravating) if you are trying to troubleshoot a problem. This is another argument for just going to the Access Control Settings screen in the first place.

So, if these explicit entries are going to be preserved, what do you do if you mess up the mask and need to reset the permissions to the inherited default? It takes a little work and forethought, but you can still recover from this type of mistake. One option is to simply go in and remove the offending explicit entries and then propagate that mask down to the files and subfolders (I'll tell you how to do that in the next section). If the mask is so messed up that you can't determine for sure which entries are good and which are bad, but you know they are correct above that point in the tree, you can simply move up in the file tree to the level where they are correct and choose to propagate the correct mask from there. If you are at the top level and moving up is not an option, you can do it the old-fashioned way. If there is a correct mask anywhere on the partition, copy the tree structure so that it becomes a child of the resource with the correct mask. Then, check that the permissions are correct and move the structure back to its original spot. Remember the mantra: move retains, copy inherits. It works for permissions and compression states. This method only works within a single partition, however, because moves across partitions behave like copies, and in that case, all permissions will be inherited from the target parent folder.

You can think of propagation of permissions as pushing permissions down the file system tree. Inheritance, on the other hand, has to do with receiving a permissions mask that has been propagated. On the interfaces I have shown you, there are actually a couple of entries that deal with permission propagation and inheritance. Let's look at those two functions and their associated interface entries separately so you get a better understanding of each.

Propagation Controls

There are basically three screens we have discussed that are part of the permissions module in Windows 2000:

- The Security Properties screen, where you see the standard permissions
- The Access Control Settings screen, reached by using the Advanced button on the Security Properties screen
- The Permission Entry screen, which gives the details for each entry on the DACL

The last two screens have entries that control propagation. Earlier we discussed the problem of needing to replace an incorrect permissions mask that contained explicit entries. I mentioned that this is a problem because those explicit settings are preserved by default and checked before the inherited entries in the DACL. If that's the case and you want to replace the whole set of permissions on all subfolders and files, simply go to the Access Control Settings screen and check the box shown with the arrow in Figure 3.9.

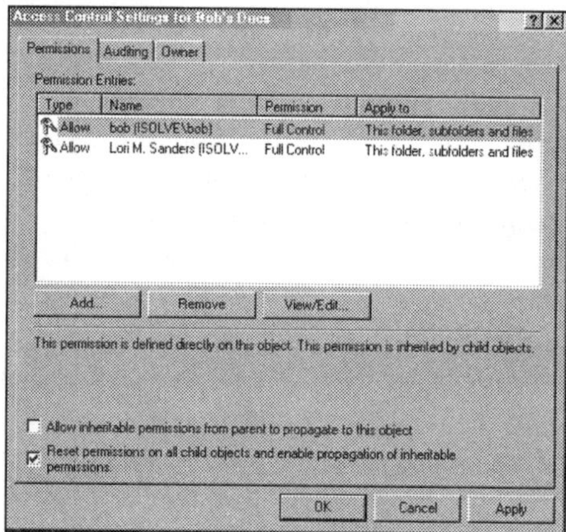

Figure 3.9 Using the Access Control Settings screen to replace explicit permissions and propagate the desired mask down through the file tree.

Because this is such a drastic action, you get a warning message telling you that this will remove all explicitly set permissions and turn for inheritance for all subfolders and files. If you are familiar with NT 4, you should know that turning on this check box makes the system act like the NT 4 file system did when you elected to replace permissions on subfolders and files. As you might imagine, the system default is for this check box to be blank.

If, on the other hand, you only want to propagate selected DACL entries or have a need to finely control how far a particular entry should go, use the Permission Entry dialog box. As you can see in Figure 3.10, by using this interface, you can be very selective about just where you want this particular entry to be applied. I think this is pretty intuitive. Just be aware of the granularity you have in this interface. By the way, the default is for the entry to be applied to "This folder, subfolders and files."

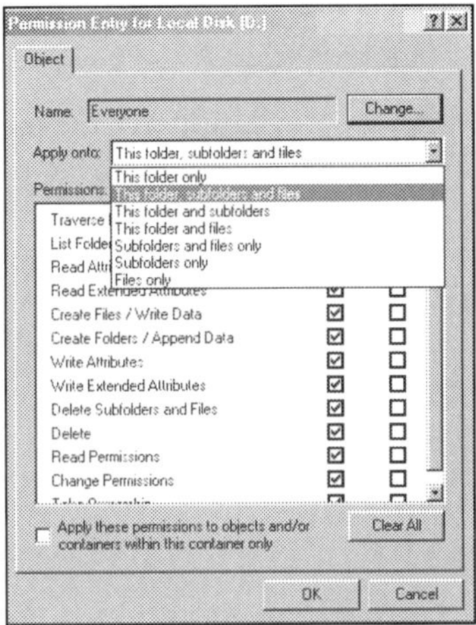

Figure 3.10 Using the Permission Entry dialog box to precisely control the application of permissions and limit propagation to the desired level.

At the bottom of that dialog box you will notice another check box. This one says "Apply these permissions to objects and/or containers within this container only." If you turn this feature on, propagation will be limited to the folder and its immediate children. Its children are defined as the subfolders and files that exist within that folder. The grandchildren objects—the files that exist in a subfolder, for example—will not have the mask applied to them.

These two boxes work together. If you do not limit the propagation by checking the box at the bottom of the screen and select to have these permissions applied to "Subfolders only," all the subfolders at all levels below this one will have the permissions reset. So, if you have five levels of subfolders, all will be affected. On the other hand, if you choose to limit the propagation, only this folder and one level of subfolders will be set.

Controlling Inheritance

Inheritance can be controlled from either the Security tab or the Access Control Settings screen by simply checking the box that says "Allow inheritable permissions from parent to propagate to this object." This box is available on either screen. As with many things in Windows 2000 interfaces, enabling and disabling inheritance in this way is incredibly easy. To block inheritance of upper-level permission masks, simply clear the check box.

What's a little more difficult is understanding what happens to permissions when you change this setting. If that little check box is turned on and you choose to disable the setting, Windows 2000 will ask you what you want to do with the current settings. Your choices are:

- Copy the current set to the resource and make them explicit permissions
- Remove all the permissions and start with a clean slate
- Oops...I don't really want to do this! Also known as the Cancel button

No matter what you choose to do, you always have the option to re-enable inheritance in the future and reapply the inherited DACL. Should you decide to do that, just remember that you will now have two DACLs, an explicit and an inherited, and that the explicit settings will take priority over your inheriteds.

The default setting is that inheritance is enabled on all file system objects, so beware. When you make changes to masks at the top levels, they can propagate to lower levels as long as inheritance is turned on at those lower-level resources. To be honest, I've messed up a whole file system this way. "Gee, all I did was click OK instead of Cancel." Wow, that one hurt! I'm trying to save you from suffering that pain.

Auditing Security Access Control Lists

Now that you've got your permissions set up the way you want them, you might want to keep track of who is trying to get into those resources. This is accomplished through the application of file system auditing.

Turning on the capability to audit a resource is a two-step process in Windows 2000. In the first step, you have to enable Audit Object Access, using the Group Policy snap-in for MMC. If you forget this step, don't worry, Windows 2000 will remind you with an error message when you try to set up auditing on a particular file or folder. It will accept the entry, but until you do turn it on, no auditing will take place. This can be accomplished either through the domain group policies or the Local Computer Policy Editor, if there is no domain group policy being used.

Another thing to remember: In order to enable this setting or audit, you must be logged on with an account that is a member of the local machine's Administrators group, or have been given the right to "Manage Auditing and Security Log."

The second step in setting up auditing is pretty easy. Go to the resource, right-click, and head for that Access Control Settings screen. You'll see that the middle tab is the Auditing tab. There, the interface looks a lot like the interface to add a user to the DACL. Select Add, choose the user or group you want to audit, then choose the event you want to audit and whether you want to audit successes or failures of that event. As you add entries, a list is built. This list is called the Security Access Control List (SACL). This list is kept in addition to the DACL. If you look closely at the interface, you'll notice that the text for the inheritable permissions check boxes has changed. They now mention inheriting and replacing inheritable *auditing* entries, as indicated by the arrows in Figure 3.11. You can also go one step further and use the Permission Entry screen to precisely set an audit setting or limit its propagation in exactly the same way you set and propagated the DACL, except that this time you use the Audit tab instead of the Permissions tab.

Editing Local Group Policy Objects

You won't find the Local Group Policy Editor installed on the menu bars of a Windows 2000 system. In order to run this, you'll need to start an MMC console using Start+Run and typing in mmc. When the console starts, select Console and select Add or Remove Snap In from the drop-down menu. Choose Add and select Group Policy from the list. You will get a dialog box that tells you the Group Policy object selected is the Local Computer. Click Finish, and you'll return to the console, which will now have an entry for Local Computer Policy.

To turn on auditing for objects on the local machine, select Computer Configuration and drill down through Windows Settings, Security Settings, Local Policies, and finally Audit Policy. Expand this and double click on Audit Object Access. When the dialog box appears, turn on the check boxes to enable auditing on successful events and/or failed events. Select OK and you will be returned to the main console screen. The Local Setting column entry should have changed from the default of No Auditing to an entry that says Success, Failure. The Effective Setting column might still say No Auditing. Don't worry, this will change when you exit the console and re-enter. You do not have to save your settings as you exit the console to have these changes take effect. When the system asks you if you want to save the console settings, it is referring to the way the console appears; what trees you have open for example, not the changes that you made. Those were applied when you hit the OK button in the dialog box. Now, you have the capability to go to a resource and set auditing for either successful access events or failed events.

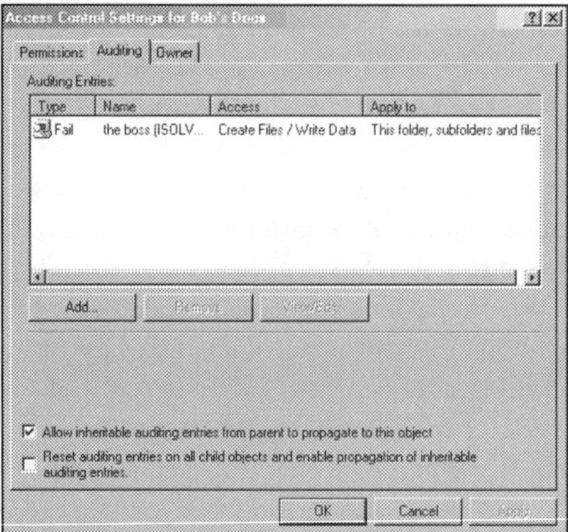

Figure 3.11 Viewing the SACL and determining SACL propagation limits.

Auditing activities are recorded in the system's security log. You can view the results of your auditing efforts through the Event Viewer. You can get to the Event Viewer several ways, but the easiest is going to the Administrative Tools menu and selecting it from there. Event Viewer hasn't changed much since NT 4. After you're in the security log, you'll see that successful access events are still represented by keys and failures by padlocks. To see the details on an event, double-click on the event. Pretty simple.

One last thing. I always get a kick out of the calls I get from paranoid security folks who have just discovered this auditing function. Typically, they aren't very selective about what they audit. Many just turn on all the settings and audit everything! Not long after they do this, I get a call. Their complaint is usually that their machine has turned into a slug. Yeah, right after they turned on auditing! Please remember that the very act of auditing and producing these log entries carries an overhead in terms of performance. My advice is to be selective about what you choose to audit. Give it some thought and remember that opening one icon can spawn several programs. Teach your users that too, especially those security officers!

A Few Last Words

In this chapter, we have covered how Windows 2000 handles authentication and how to protect your file system resources. As I mentioned at the start of the chapter, there is a whole lot more to know about Windows 2000 security mechanisms. When Microsoft started delivering the betas for this product, people began predicting that no one would be able to know it all because the product was so huge. They predicted that specialties would develop within the administrative ranks—that there would be desktop/user administrators, network experts, security experts, Active Directory administrators. My focus here has been to help you become more of an expert in desktop/user security issues. As I said, we'll touch on other security issues throughout the rest of the book as they come up in our conversation. If you get done and still want to know more, check out `http://www.microsoft.com/` and browse the Windows 2000 security white papers to get the details. If I were you, though, I'd be sure and get some caffeine first! The papers are well written, but those details are…how should I say this? Well, let's just say they can cure insomnia!

4

Understanding Organizational Units: The Building Blocks of the Active Directory

WE MENTIONED OUs EARLIER IN THIS TEXT, but now it's time to really delve in and see what they are all about and how to plan for an efficient OU structure that meets your design goals. Over the last few months, I've spent some time reading a few things from Microsoft and other sources about strategies for deploying Windows 2000. I find it very interesting that all these sources spend a lot of time talking about how to plan a serviceable domain scheme or how to design your sites for the most efficient replication topology, but relatively little time telling you about the OU structure.

I have a secret theory that the reason not much time is spent on OUs is that this area isn't very well understood yet because OUs are one of the newest parts of the Microsoft universe. As a matter of fact, when you read these different sources, you will get conflicting advice about how to make the best use of OUs. Some say to structure OUs by location, and others say to go by business unit. Even others say to structure them strictly for your administrative needs. Who's right? It depends. I know, the consultant's answer again, but in this case, it is very true. OU structures should be as individual to companies as fingerprints are to people because so many factors involving the company's organization and culture should be considered when creating this grouping.

Certain things about OUs are unarguable. OUs are container objects in the directory that can contain any other directory object, including other OUs. OUs are directory objects. So, like all other directory objects, they have a DACL and a SACL associated with them that governs who has access to the OU and what security events affecting the OU will be audited and entered in the security log. As with file system objects, directory objects such as OUs are subject to permission inheritance rules.

Then there are other questions surrounding OUs that don't have such hard and fast answers. I've already mentioned one of them. How should you set up your OU structure? When do you create an OU? What is the most important criteria for the design? What rules should you follow when designing your OU hierarchy? Those are the questions I'll try and help you with a little later in the chapter. First, examine some general guidelines to follow in your design process.

Creating an OU Hierarchy that Works for You

This design process seems more like art than science sometimes, but there a few general guidelines you can follow that will give you a better end product.

The first principle to remember is that the users might not navigate the directory to find resources, but the system does. Those LDAP distinguished names we talked about a couple of chapters ago have to be resolved by the operating system. As a result, very deep OU structures can cause performance to suffer. From the operating system's standpoint, you could nest 40 levels if you wanted to. Windows 2000 would certainly let you, you'd just end up waiting a long time for your searches to come back! Microsoft's official advice is that such structures should be no more than 10 levels deep. In preliminary customer testing, however, performance has been known to suffer in as few as five levels. So, the guideline is to limit OU levels for more efficient LDAP searches.

Another thing you want to try and do regardless of what OU model you choose is to organize around relatively static business entities. Although we all seem to suffer frequent company reorganization nowadays, there are usually company boundaries that remain relatively static. Large divisions such as Sales, Finance, Personnel, and IT will probably stay around for awhile. Geopolitical boundaries are also less likely to change, which is not a guarantee either nowadays but less subject to reorganizing than your operating unit—I'll bet!

Because it is so easy to create, delete, and move OUs around within the directory, it's tempting to create OUs for projects. This is not a good idea because when the project ends, all those resources have to be moved to new OUs. That isn't hard to do—so what's the big deal? Well, for one thing, to move something, you have to have Delete permissions where it is and Write permissions where it is going. That usually means a pretty high-level administrator has to do it. I personally don't want to have to worry about moving 100 users to 10 other OUs when the project ends. Once they've been moved, you also have to rethink what policies will now apply to those users in their new OU. If you are trying to lower TCO, temporary OUs are not going to help you.

We'll talk more about this in the next section, but one thing you should definitely keep in mind as you create this model is your administrative requirements. Are you a centralized administrative staff? Decentralized? How much administration are you planning to delegate to user groups? How will you use group policies? How big is your staff? How big is your backlog? How can creating this OU structure help you fix that problem? If you do it right, it can help. So, now that we have some general guides, let's start looking at specific design orientations.

Reasons to Create OUs

When Windows 2000 was in its earliest releases, OUs were advertised as the directory components that could be used to reflect the organizational structure of your company. Many people took this to mean the organizational chart and started creating OU structures that reflected that. In labs, we quickly found that this was not the most brilliant way to organize this structure. It is certainly one of the ways you *can* construct your OU model, but only if your administrative needs closely follow those little lines on your organizational chart.

Another way people first tried creating their OU model was to optimize it for the organization of users and resources within OUs, putting all the accounting users, printers, and servers in the Accounting OU, for example. Microsoft makes the assumption that users are not going to be traversing the OU tree when searching for resources. Instead, they are expected to use the Directory Search functionality, and so you shouldn't have to create OUs to help users locate directory objects. If you have valid administrative reasons to group users and resources into an OU, it's a good strategy, but otherwise, it actually ends up creating extra work for the administrative staff. How? Well, if you have only one policy that governs all users and another policy for all printers, what is gained by separating users or printers into separate OUs? The administrator might end up creating identical policies at different branches in the OU structure. Additionally, if resources or users transfer between OUs, it becomes necessary for an administrator to move them, creating additional administrative overhead.

So what's the magic formula? When *do* you know you have a valid reason to create an OU? There are basically four reasons to create an OU:

- Delegation of administration
- Group policy application
- Simplified resource administration
- Controlling the visibility scope of resources

When you design your OU hierarchy, you should take all four of these into consideration. To be most efficient, focus on one area at a time, but work through the logic in all four before you create the first one in the Active Directory. This should really be a paper exercise (or whiteboard if you're like my company). Create a design as you focus on one area, and put it aside. Then move to the next area, and repeat the process, optimizing for that view of the model. When you have finished all four areas, you will have a clear picture of what the real needs of your organization are. Once you have defined those, you can start deciding which is the most important to you and where the duplication of OUs occurs. When you do this, it might be the first time that all those factors have been considered together, and I can almost guarantee that you will end up with a more efficient system after you spend this time.

Let's look at each of these reasons to create an OU.

Delegation of Administration

Microsoft actually recommends that you let your OU structure mimic your administrative model rather than your business model. Certainly, many people consider this the most important consideration in creating the structure. The delegation model is going to be near the top of the list if you are planning on decentralizing administrative tasks. Even organizations using centralized administrative models can take advantage of the capability to delegate the administration of certain properties of an object. As you will see a little later in this section, we can now get very specific about just what we want to let users do for themselves and on what types of objects.

The first thing to determine when trying to design a structure based on administrative delegation is what you want to delegate and to whom you want to delegate it. This is absolutely the hardest part of this exercise. It involves looking at your administrative model and seeing if it still makes sense. Why are you having your users call the Help desk to change their addresses or phone numbers in the directory, for example? Why not let them take care of that task themselves? Would they do it? Would they know how to do it? Do they have the tools to do it? Should you designate someone in their workgroup, such as their administrative assistant, to be responsible for this task instead? Those are the types of questions that need to be asked when delegating.

This idea of administrative delegation will be a hard concept for most administrators to grasp, because they've never done it this way before. The systems that were available in the past simply didn't have this capability. In addition, there is an element of trust involved in giving up functions that have always been under your direct control. Will users do it right? Will they be as careful as you were? What happens when they mess it up? Don't worry, I've already been suffering through this process, and you can survive. It's kind of like letting your newly licensed teenager take your car out for the evening for the first time. Letting go is always hard!

Consider the following issues when looking at delegating administrative tasks:

- Are there security issues that prevent you from delegating administrative tasks to lower levels? Is there some overarching security policy that dictated the centralized administrative system you have now?

- What are your most common administrivia Help desk calls? Usually, a large proportion of calls are simple things that could be delegated to user groups, such as clearing print queues, resetting user passwords, and changing user properties pages. As always, realistically consider the consequences of the task not being done properly. What percentage of the whole may be improperly performed? What will the financial impact of fixing those errors be?
- How do you want to divide your administrative delegation?
  - **By physical location.** For example, objects in Pizza Place's West Coast Operations unit can only be managed by a particular set of administrators.
  - **By business unit.** For example, objects belonging to the Accounting organization can only be managed by a certain group of administrators.
  - **By role or task.** This division is according to the type of object being managed. For example, a set of administrators might be responsible only for printer objects.

Once you have considered all these questions, you are ready to start designing the structure. When creating a structure based solely on delegating administration, make sure that you delegate Full Control at the higher levels of the structure and then delegate by object class at the lower levels. Look at Figure 4.1, for example. We have an OU called Finance in this diagram. On that OU, we have a group of administrators that have Full Control permissions. We have four child OUs off Finance: Workstations, Servers, Users, and Printers. What's in those OUs is pretty self-evident from the names. In this design, each OU has a different set of people who are allowed to administer the objects contained in that OU. Looking at the DACL on the Printers' OU for example, we see that one tech support group has full control for printers. If we were to look at the Users OU DACL, we would see that there is another group with Full Control permissions for User objects in that OU.

Once you set the DACL on the OU, all the objects created or placed within that OU inherit that permission set. In our example, that means that all printers moved to, or created in, the Printers OU would inherit the Printer Support group's Full Control entry. If we directly examined the DACL on a particular printer instance, we would see that entry as well as the inherited entry from the Finance OU, giving Administrators full control of everything.

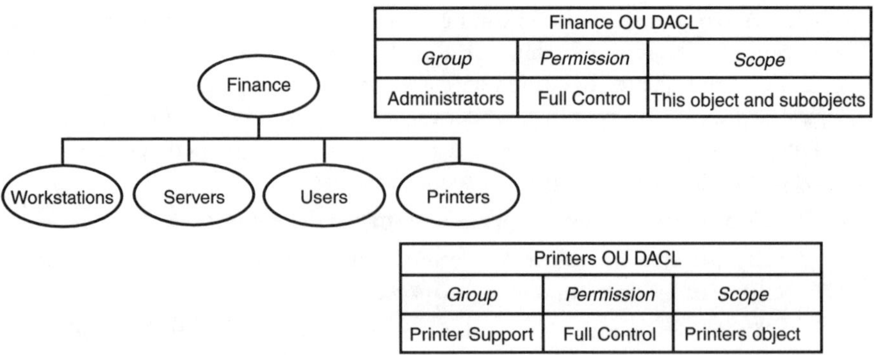

Figure 4.1 Division of administrative responsibilities using the OU structure as a framework.

Group Policy Application

Another way to look at the OU model is to focus on your group policy needs. If you have one domain-wide policy for all users right now, you probably don't need to go through this part of the OU design exercise. On the other hand, if you have looked at the new features available to you with Windows 2000 group policy objects and want to use them, you need to start by grouping your users and resources based on their policy needs. Objects that can have identical policies applied may be grouped together in a single OU to simplify the group policy structure.

Remember as you design this structure that policies are cumulative and apply from the container that is most distant from the affected directory object. So, if you have a default domain policy and your user is buried three OUs down in the structure, the domain policy applies first, then the highest OU, the middle OU, and finally the OU the user lives in. This can be very useful in that you don't have to recreate policies set at a higher level in the structure, but on the downside, you have to make sure you are not overwriting important settings as policies are applied on top of one another.

As far as who you will group together, it will depend on their desktop environments, software distribution requirements, and other settings that can be affected by policies. You may find that these requirements closely follow your organizational chart boundaries, and that's okay. It's only a bad idea to organize around the organizational chart if there is no valid administrative reason for doing so. If your use of policies is organizationally centered, you have a valid administrative reason to recreate the organizational chart.

Simplified Resource Administration

Another criteria to use when creating an OU model is simplified resource management. When you create the DACL and SACL for an OU, you can also create DACLs and SACLs for different object classes that will reside in the OU. For example, you can create a DACL/SACL combination to cover all instances of Printer objects in a certain OU and then create a different DACL/SACL for SharedVolume objects in that same OU. Whenever a new printer is created in that OU, it will inherit the DACL/SACL you set at the OU level. In a like manner, new shared volumes will inherit those permissions from the OU template.

DACLs on directory objects serve two purposes. They govern both who can see and use a resource using the Directory icon in My Network Places or when searching the directory, *and* who can administer the resource. In the case of printers and shared volumes, that makes it very easy to set a single mask at the OU level that says Mary can read a share, Bob has Modify privileges, whereas Alan is the only one who can create new shares and delete shares in that OU. Altering a single DACL on the OU does all that. In addition, if new OUs are created within that OU, it can inherit these settings if you want. Of course, you'd never use Bob, Mary, and Alan—you'd put them in groups and then use groups, right?

Controlling the Visibility Scope of Resources

Tied closely to our last discussion is the idea of putting resources into an OU and then setting the DACL on the OU so that the resources contained within it have limited visibility, if any at all, in the directory. The best example I can think of is all those hidden shares you have running around your organization. For whatever reason, the owner of the resource doesn't want them to be visible when browsing the network, and so you create the shares and plop a "$" behind its name. Now it's hidden from the browser, but somebody is always forgetting to put the "$" on the end, and then complaining they can't get to the share. By using the DACL on the OU, you could set the DACL for SharedVolume objects so that no one except a specific group can see those shares. Then, when you create the directory objects, they all inherit that access permission list. You can also hide those really big, expensive color printers this way!

Just remember from our earlier discussions, the DACL we set through the Active Directory Users and Computers console only covers the directory object, which is a logical entity only visible when using the Directory icon or search engine. If someone is looking at the share through My Network Neighborhood, he will still be able to see it unless you have taken away his privileges at the sharepoint ACL or protected it from the browser with a "$" at the end of the sharename.

DACLs and SACLs on OUs

Like file system objects, OUs have DACLs and SACLs associated with them. DACLs on OUs actually serve two purposes. First, they control who can "see" the resources contained in the OU. Second, they determine who can administer the OU and its resources. We'll cover how both of those functions work in a few minutes. For now though, let's get familiar with the interface and the similarities and the differences you'll see when setting permissions on directory objects as opposed to file system objects.

Examining OU Permissions

To look at the permissions set on an OU, or any other directory object, you will use the Active Directory Users and Computers snap-in. By default, no matter who you log in as, you will not be able to see the security settings for your directory objects. To see those, you have to enable the advanced features of the interface. To do this, go to the console menu bar, select View, and then click Advanced Features. If you don't do this, the only tabs you will see when looking at the properties of OUs you have created are General, Managed By, and Group Policy. For system-created OUs, you would only see the General tab. When you activate the Advanced Features, two additional tabs are displayed: Object and Security. When you select the Security tab, you'll see the interface shown in Figure 4.2.

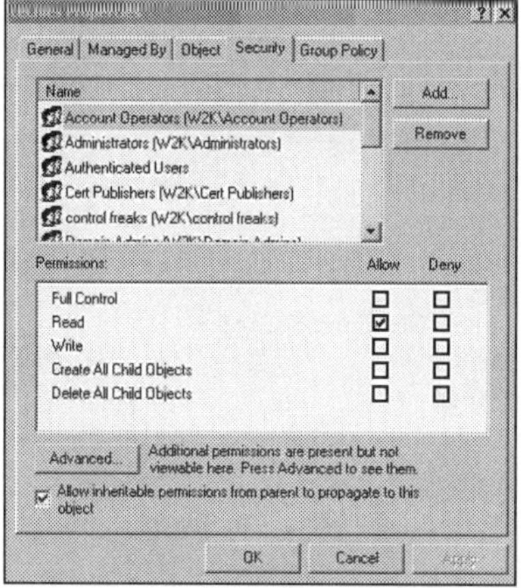

Figure 4.2 Basic security interface for Techies OU.

This should look familiar to you from our last chapter, where we discussed setting DACLs and SACLs for the file system. You'll see the Allow and Deny columns and the inheritance check box at the bottom of the page. In fact, the actual interface is exactly the same except for the standard permissions shown in the lower text box. You'll notice that these permission entries are more directory oriented. When we talk about directory objects, we can set permissions on the object as well as each property of the object. That's how we achieve a high degree of granularity when delegating administrative tasks in Windows 2000, but it also makes the DACL for an object and its associated properties rather complex. In addition, the list of properties displayed changes based on what type of object you have chosen to look at in the directory. So, the properties that show up for a group object aren't the same as those for an OU object. Table 4.1 shows you what each of those standard permissions means in terms of the advanced permissions for both the OU object and properties.

Table 4.1 **Standard Permission Sets for OUs**

Standard Permission	Associated Advanced Permissions on Objects	Associated Advanced Permissions on Properties
Full Control	Full Control	Read All Properties
	List Contents	Write All Properties
	Read All Properties	Read adminDescription
	Write All Properties	Write adminDescription
	Delete	Read adminDisplayName
	Delete Subtree	Write adminDisplayName
	Read Permissions	Read countryCode
	Modify Permissions	Write countryCode
	Modify Owner	Read gPLink
	All Validated Writes	Write gPLink
	All Extended Rights	Read gPOptions
	Create All Child Objects	Write gPOptions
	Delete All Child Objects	Read Managed By
	Create Computer Objects	Write Managed By
	Delete Computer Objects	Read postalAddress
	Create Contact Objects	Write postalAddress
	Delete Contact Objects	Read postalCode
	Create groupPolicyContainer Objects	Write postalCode
	Delete groupPolicyContainer Objects	Read postOfficeBox
	Create IntelliMirror Group Objects	Write postOfficeBox
	Delete IntelliMirror Group Objects	Read st
	Create IntelliMirror Service Objects	Write st
	Delete IntelliMirror Service Objects	Read street
	Create Organizational Unit Objects	Write street
	Delete Organizational Unit Objects	Read uPNSuffixes
	Create Printer Objects	Write uPNSuffixes

continues

Table 4.1 **Continued**

Standard Permission	Associated Advanced Permissions on Objects	Associated Advanced Permissions on Properties
	Delete Printer Objects Create Shared Folder Objects Delete Shared Folder Objects Create User Objects Delete User Objects	
Read	List Contents Read All properties Read Permissions	Read All Properties Read adminDescription Read adminDisplayName Read countryCode Read gPLink Read gPOptions Read Managed By Read postalAddress Read postalCode Read postOfficeBox Read st Read street Read uPNSuffixes
Write	Write All Properties All Validated Writes	Write All Properties Write adminDescription Write adminDisplayName Write countryCode Write gPLink Write gPOptions Write Managed By Write postalAddress Write postalCode Write postOfficeBox Write st Write street Write uPNSuffixes
Create All Child Objects	Create All Child Objects Create Computer Objects Create Contact Objects Create groupPolicyContainer Objects	No permissions defined on object properties

Standard Permission	Associated Advanced Permissions on Objects	Associated Advanced Permissions on Properties
	Create IntelliMirror Group Objects	
	Create IntelliMirror Service Objects	
	Create Organizational Unit Objects	
	Create Printer Objects	
	Create Shared Folder Objects	
	Create User Objects	
Delete All Child Objects	Delete All Child Objects	No permissions defined on object properties.
	Delete Computer Objects	
	Delete Contact Objects	
	Delete groupPolicyContainer Objects	
	Delete IntelliMirror Group Objects	
	Delete IntelliMirror Service Objects	
	Delete Organizational Unit Objects	
	Delete Printer Objects	
	Delete Shared Folder Objects	
	Delete User Objects	

As with the file system, there are two additional security pages that can be called up. The first is accessed by using the Advanced button. Just as in the file system interface, this shows you the actual DACL for the object under scrutiny. This is the best page to use for troubleshooting access problems because it will display the DACL in the proper search order: explicit Denies, explicit Allows, inherited Denies, and inherited Allows.

The final security properties page is invoked through the use of the View/Edit tab on the Access Control Settings page and shows you the specific Permission Entries for both the object and all its associated properties. This gives you the details of each ACE set on the previous screen.

I need to point out a couple of things to you about the advanced pages. On the second properties page where you can see the actual DACL (the Access Control Settings page), you should note that there is no check box to "Reset permissions on all child objects and enable propagation of inheritable permissions" as there was in the file system interface. That means that if the DACLs on an OU are messed up, there is no quick, check-the-box way to fix it. To fix a problem like that, you need to be able to *copy* the OU to another OU with an acceptable DACL so that it would inherit the desirable DACL—and guess what? You can't do that. Directory objects can't be copied between OUs, only moved. Remember the inheritance rule: move retains, copy inherits.

Another thing to take note of is on the Permissions Entries page. When you select the Properties tab, you will see the properties for the object class that you have highlighted in the directory. I just want to warn you that at first you might not recognize these properties as valid properties for the object. When you talk about writing the postalCode property for an OU, for example, it sounds a little strange until you become really familiar with the system. Just think about all the fields that show up on all the tabs when you are viewing an object's properties. Those are the things that will show up here. For example, postalCode for the OU is really the postalCode of the person who is listed on the Managed By tab for the OU.

Default Permissions for OUs from Schema

Like all other objects in the directory, there is a default schema DACL for OUs. Table 4.2 shows those permissions. As with all other default DACLs, this one can be changed to suit your needs. You can specify a new default in the schema, if you want, through the Schema Management tool or choose to specify a new DACL at the highest OU level and let it inherit down through the OU levels.

Managed By

Let's talk about that Managed By tab for a minute. If you are going to dole out administrative duties to the field and have users managing their own objects, groups, OUs, and so on, *please* make your life easier by requiring that this tab be filled in for objects with delegated administration. Go to the Schema Manager tool, and make these properties mandatory! Trust me, you will be happy you did when you have to track down the offending local administrator of a particular group or OU that is having problems.

Table 4.2 **Default Permissions on OU Objects**

Group	Permission	Scope
EXPLICIT PERMISSIONS		
SYSTEM	Full Control	This object only
Domain Admins	Full Control	This object only
Account Operators	Create/Delete Computer Objects	This object only
	Create/Delete User Objects	
	Create/Delete Group Objects	
Print Operators	Create/Delete Printer Objects	This object only
Authenticated Users	List Contents	
	Read All Properties	
	Read Permissions	
INHERITED PERMISSIONS		
Administrators	List Contents	This object and all child objects
	Read All Properties	
	Write All Properties	
	Delete	
	Read Permissions	
	Modify Permissions	
	Modify Owner	
	All Validated Writes	
	All Extended Rights	
	Create All Child Objects	
	Create Computer Objects	
	Create Contact Objects	
	Create groupPolicy Container Objects	
	Create IntelliMirror Group Objects	
	Create IntelliMirror Service Objects	
	Create Organizational Unit Objects	
	Create Printer Objects	
	Create Shared Folder Objects	
	Create User Objects	
Enterprise Admins	Full Control	This object and all child objects

continues

Table 4.2 **Continued**

Group	Permission	Scope
INHERITED PERMISSIONS		
Domain Admins	Full Control	User Objects
SYSTEM	Full Control	User Objects
Account Operators	Full Control	User Objects
SELF	List Contents	User Objects
	Read All Properties	
	Read Permissions	
	Change Password	
	Send As	
	Receive As	
	Read/Write Personal Information	
	Read/Write Phone and Mail Options	
	Read/Write Web Information	
RAS and IAS Servers	Read Remote Access Information	User Objects
	Read Account Restrictions	
	Read Group Membership	
	Read Logon Information	
Authenticated Users	Read Permissions	User Objects
	Read General Information	
	Read Personal Information	
	Read Web Information	
	Read Public Information	
Everyone	Change Password	User Objects
	Read Property	
Cert Publishers	Read/Write Property	User Objects

Controlling Access and Auditing with OUs

As I mentioned a little earlier, you can use the OU to specify access permissions for certain types of resources that are created in OUs. The two object classes where this can be very effective are SharedVolume objects and Printer objects. If you know that you are going to be creating several shared volumes in your Techies OU and that all those shared volumes will have the same basic DACL and SACL entries, you can save time and work by setting the permissions at the OU level by object class. As you can see in Figure 4.3, we are adding the Geeks & Nerds group to the OU DACL and giving them Read and Write permissions only on Shared Folder objects.

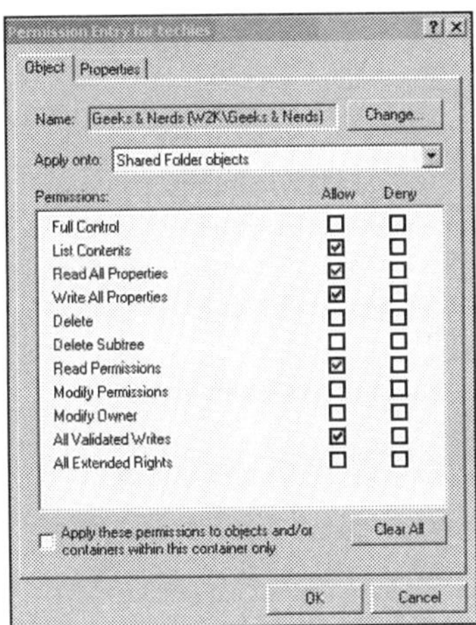

Figure 4.3 Adding a new ACE for Shared Folders in the Techies OU.

When we go in and create a new shared folder called Clipart in the Techies OU, you can see in Figure 4.4 that there is now an inherited entry for Geeks & Nerds with Read and Write permissions. All other shared folders created in this OU will have the same entry. In situations where the same group of folks will need the same permissions on all their shared resources, this strategy will be a real work-saver!

With this capability, you can control the visibility of objects you place in a particular OU. If you grant Everyone and Authenticated Users Read access to an OU and all its object classes, everyone will be able to see every object in the OU. If, on the other hand, you remove the Read privilege for Everyone and Authenticated Users, that OU becomes a black hole to most of the enterprise. You can then open up the OU and assign Read permissions to only those users and groups that need to see a particular kind of object in the OU. In our example, we might allow only the Geeks & Nerds group to see the shared volume objects. If we set that at the OU level, it will apply to all shared folder objects created in that OU. What if we just want to set those permissions for the Clipart shared folder? Simple. Right-click on the Clipart shared folder object, and use the Properties tabs to make explicit entries that reflect the permission level you want to set on that object.

In addition to using access permissions, you can also save time by setting your SACL at the OU level if all instances of the object class in the OU have similar auditing requirements. To do this, use the Advanced button off the initial security properties page, and select the Auditing tab. Then use the interface just as you would if you were setting file auditing. You will notice in Figure 4.5, which shows the auditing screens, the events have changed to reflect a directory orientation.

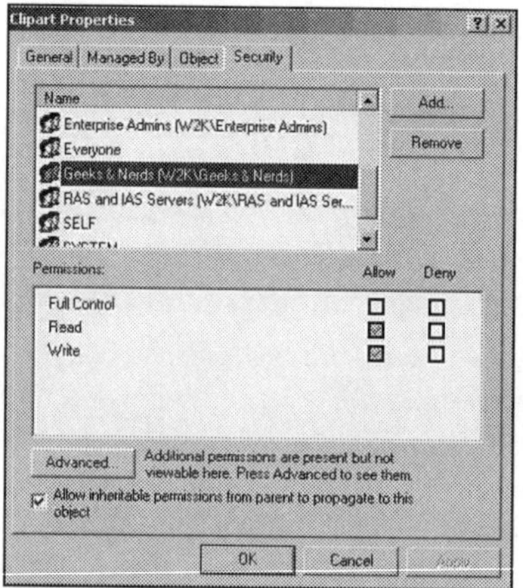

Figure 4.4 Inherited permissions on the new shared folder object Clipart.

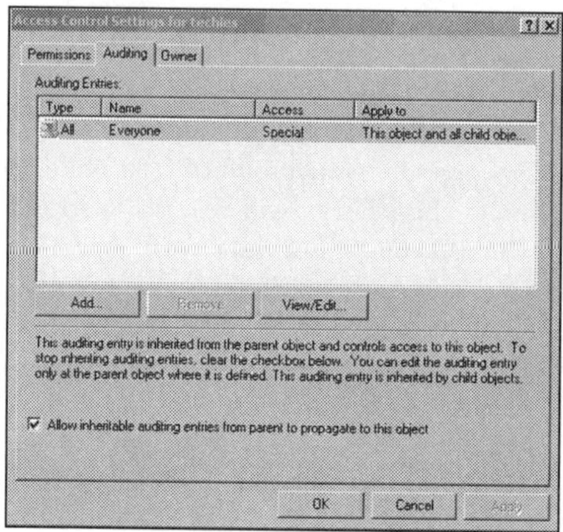

Figure 4.5 Setting up auditing on an OU.

Directory Object Inheritance Model

As I mentioned earlier, the inheritance model for directory objects operates exactly like the inheritance model for file system objects. Explicit permissions still take precedence over inherited permissions. Denies take precedence over Allows within the explicit and inherited sets of permissions. The directory object DACL is checked in the same order as a file system DACL; explicit Denies, explicit Allows, inherited Denies, and finally inherited Allows. About the only difference you will have to think about when applying inheritance is that, with the directory, you have so many more object classes that can have DACLs applied to them. You can have a DACL on the OU for the OU object class that will govern that OU and any OUs created within that OU. You can then have another DACL at the same OU level that applies to only shared folder objects created in that OU.

Delegating Administration Tasks with OUs

We use OU DACLs to scope the visibility of objects that we place in an OU and also to determine who can modify the OU and its child objects. We have covered the visibility part, so let's look at delegating administration.

There are two ways to change the DACL on a directory object: by manually editing the DACL or by using the Delegation of Control Wizard. We have already seen how to explicitly set a DACL; so we won't go through all that again, but I want to mention a couple of things about setting administrative DACLs before we move on to the Wizard.

Manually Changing the DACL

First, there will be times when you might need to manually change the DACL because the administrative task you are delegating is so specialized. If you do choose to change the DACL this way, keep in mind what you are trying to accomplish and what actions a user must be able to perform. For example, if you want your Geeks & Nerds group to have the responsibility of creating users in their OU, you must actually set two permissions. The first is on the OU. You must first give them the right to create a user object in that OU. Then you must also give them permissions to write the attributes on a User object. If you don't give them the second permission, they can't create a user—to create a user, they have to give them attributes, such as a name and password. It can really give you a headache when you start obsessing about it. If you want Martha to be able to reset a user's password, you have to make sure she can see the user (List Contents), read the attributes (Read All Properties), and write the password attribute (Change Password).

Delegation of Control Wizard

That headache you feel coming on is why Microsoft has spent some programming effort creating the Delegation of Control Wizard. With the Wizard, you can delegate common tasks very quickly, such as giving Geeks & Nerds permission to create users or even one of the more customized tasks such as having Martha change passwords but none of the other user properties.

To access the Wizard, simply right-click on the OU or object that you want to delegate control of, and select Delegate Control from the context menu. (Intuitive so far.) Then you select the group that you want to delegate control to. In our case, let's select those Geeks & Nerds. Then you can select a common task to delegate from the list shown or choose to create a custom administrative task. In our example of giving the Geeks & Nerds permission to create users in our Techies OU, we would have to select a custom task because we just want them to create, not delete or manage the accounts they create. When you create a custom task, the next several screens allow you to specify the scope of the authority, the type of object you want them to have permissions on, and finally the actual permissions you want to allow. You'll probably want to spend some time playing with this tool until you know it like the back of your hand. If you are planning to use decentralized administration, you'll need it.

There is one drawback to the Delegation of Control Wizard that you should be aware of. You can only add permissions with this tool. To remove existing permissions, even permissions that you have set using the Wizard, you will have to manually edit the DACL as mentioned in the previous section.

Pizza Place Case Study

One of the advantages of the Active Directory is that you can enlarge your domains, because the directory will handle more objects than the NT 4 style SAM would. If you do this, you'll probably be using OUs to represent your old domain structure.

In Chapter 2, "Domains" I described Pizza Place's existing domain trust model. Because you've probably slept since then, Figure 4.6 is what it looked like.

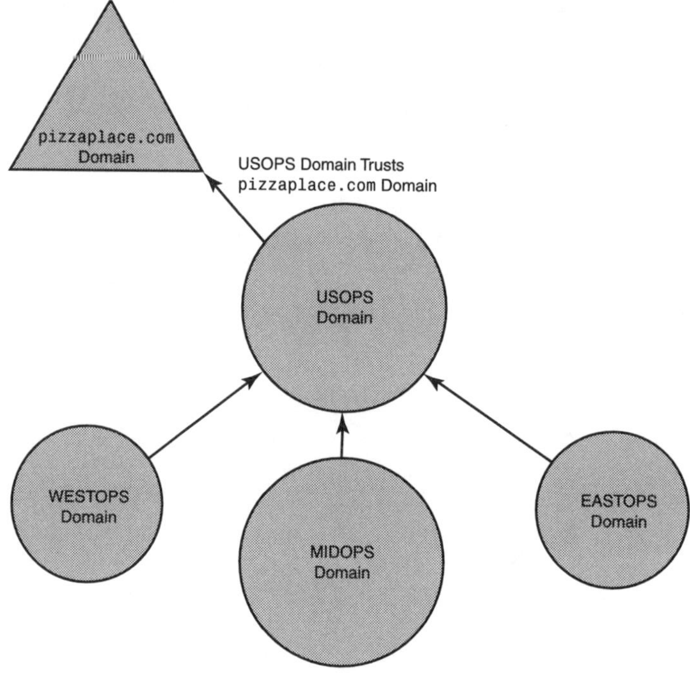

Figure 4.6 Pizza Place's original domain structure.

Now we can take that structure and turn it into an OU structure like the one shown in Figure 4.7. As you can see, we have taken the old operations domains and created a hierarchy of operational units. You'll notice that the OU model is loosely structured to reflect both static organizational entities and geographic boundaries.

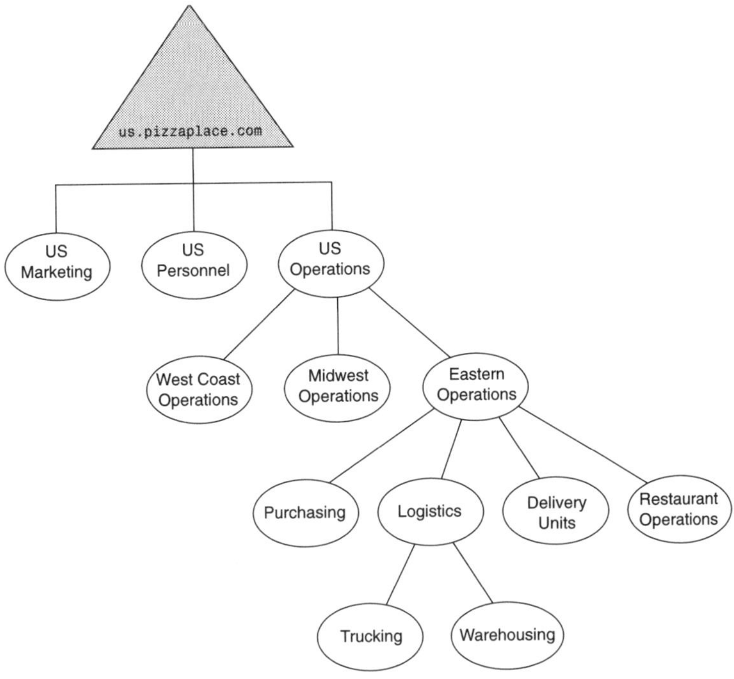

Figure 4.7 The new domain with its internal OU structure that replaces the domain web shown in Figure 4.6.

Our assumption here is that the Operations units probably have similar policies that will apply. So, we can set a policy at the U.S. Operations level and have it inherit down to the three regional OUs. We've also chosen a decentralized administration model so that each regional operations office has its own support staff. Unfortunately, after that, the similarities in structure between the three regions ends. The Eastern unit's sub-OU model is entirely different than what they are doing out on the West Coast, and so these administrators are free to create that model any way they choose. This is just a quick example to demonstrate that an OU structure can be set up for resource sharing, delegation of administration, and efficient application of group policies, yet still give enough flexibility to remote administrators to create a substructure that works for them.

I hope this chapter has been a help to you. As I said earlier, this is the creative part of your Active Directory design. As a result, I couldn't really give you many hard and fast rules, but if you follow the general guidelines put forth here, you should be just fine. We've now finished our discussion about creating the structure your users will be living in. The Active Directory design should be done at this point. All that is left to do now is fill the structure with users and groups and start managing them. Our next section of the text covers just that topic, so let's push on to Chapter 5, "Managing User Accounts."

Managing Users and Groups

5 Managing User Accounts

IT'S TIME TO START FILLING THAT EMPTY OU structure with users and groups. In this chapter, we'll talk about creating and managing your user accounts, including the built-in accounts provided by Microsoft.

It doesn't matter what size your organization is, user management is always a challenge. For one thing, users don't like to be managed. Another problem is that there are probably other administrators out there who are helping manage your users. Sometimes communication between these groups can be a problem. In Windows 2000, you can delegate some or all of the administrative tasks associated with users. Although this will probably relieve a lot of your daily workload, it may give you an ulcer until you get used to the idea. One thing you can do to make your ulcer less active and also help the users to whom you're giving these responsibilities is *train them*! You'll feel better and so will they once they know what they are supposed to do, how to accomplish it, and how to be sure they aren't going to mess something else up by accident. If done correctly, you should be able to prevent most disasters through your OU DACLs.

Predefined User Accounts

As with previous versions of NT, there are a few predefined user accounts shipped with all versions of the Windows 2000 product. You have seen some of them before, and others might be new to you.

On workstations and member servers, there are only two predefined accounts: Administrator and Guest. On a domain controller, you will see those two accounts, and you will also encounter `TsInternetUser` and `krbtgt`.

Administrator

This account can be renamed, but not deleted. By default, it is also exempt from being locked out after a certain number of bad logon attempts. As in previous versions of NT, this account is the most powerful account on the machine. It is the only account that is automatically given all rights and privileges in the system. That means it has control of the local machine. If the local machine just happens to be a domain controller, this account has control of the domain. This account is automatically added to the Administrators group of the local machine, as well as the Domain Admins group on a domain controller. If the machine is a domain controller of a root partition, the account is also automatically added to the Enterprise Admins group. The Domain Admins group is then added to the Administrators group on every machine that participates in the domain, and the Enterprise Admins are added to the Domain Admins group in domains lower on the tree.

Naturally, you can see that a hacker who is able to log on to your system using this account has full access to the machine and can, therefore, do much more damage than if he logged on as an average user. Virus attacks launched with this level of privileges can be devastating. To protect your system, this account should be renamed to look like any other user account so that it is indistinguishable from Joe User's account, in case a hacker is browsing the system. In addition, the password should be set to the maximum length and be fairly complex. These settings should be written down and then locked away. The account should never be used except to initially set up a machine and in case of an emergency at a future date.

The first thing you should do after a machine is fully installed is create at least one other administrative account, and start using that account. One important reason to do this is for auditing. If a machine has three administrators and they are all using the Administrator account to log on, you will never know who did what to the system. For example, if you have a Take Ownership event, even if the new owner is chosen to be the Administrators group, the audit log would show the logon name of the administrator who actually spawned the event. One school of thought says that if you have to worry about administrators, they shouldn't be administrators. True, because it is almost impossible to guard against a malicious administrator. On the other hand, I think it would be incredibly negligent to make *no* attempt to audit the important administrative events on your system. Naturally, how carefully you handle this account depends on the scope of the machine it resides on as well as your security policy.

Guest

The Guest account is designed to be used by people who have an occasional need to access the system. It can be helpful in situations where there is a low level of security required and you have chosen to use an automatic logon so that logon is transparent to the user. An information kiosk in a mall and a library catalog terminal are good examples of times when the Guest account might be employed. The Guest account is a security hazard for two reasons. First, if a user doesn't have an account, and the Guest account is enabled, the user will be allowed to log on to the system. Although the only right that a Guest has by default is the right to log on over the network, the system puts this account in the Everyone group. So, any rights and permissions given to the Everyone group are also given to the Guest by the account's membership in that group.

The second problem can be overcome by employing the Authenticated Users group to set all rights and permissions. Doing this excludes Guest and Anonymous logons. The Guest account can also be renamed, but not deleted. The Guest account is disabled by default on all machines.

TsInternetUser and *krbtgt*

`TsInternetUser` is only found by default on domain controllers. This account is used by Terminal Services and is enabled by default. `krbtgt` is also an account that only appears on DCs. This account is used by Kerberos. It is the Key Distribution Center Services account and shows up disabled by default.

Creating Users

Naturally, you aren't going to run your system with just those predefined users, so you will need to create some user accounts. There are several different methods that can be used to accomplish this task. You can create the accounts one at a time, you can copy existing accounts, you can use ADSI scripts to create users in specific containers, and you can do bulk uploads and migrations from other systems. What method you choose will depend on your situation.

Local Users

On member servers and workstations, you can only create local users. The term "local" refers to the scope of the user. A workstation and a member server both have local databases to keep their users in, just as we had in the NT 4 SAMs. Local user accounts are only valid on the machine they are created on, and an individual SID tracks each account. If you have a user named Jim who logs on to several workstations in a workgroup, he must have a Jim account on each machine, as we discussed in Chapter 3, "Authentication and Resource Protection in Windows 2000." Each Jim account will have a different SID, and the Jim account on the first machine has no scope on any other machine in the workgroup. Those machines might have an account that has the same account name, Jim, but it is not the same account because the SIDs are different.

Local accounts are created on workstations and member servers by using the Computer Management console Local Users and Groups node. This Local Users and Groups node is only available on machines that are not domain controllers. On domain controllers, when you initiate a computer management session, hovering over the Local Users node you will see a big red circle with an "X" in it, indicating that the function is disabled. This has changed, by the way, from NT 4—where you could create a local user on a domain controller.

To create a user with the Local Users and Groups tool, simply open a Computer Management session, and select Local Users and Groups. You can right-click on the Users folder in the right pane, and the interface shown in Figure 5.1 comes up. If you have worked with NT 4 workstations, you may notice that this looks a lot like the User Manager interface that came with NT 4 Workstation. The attributes available for a local user are very limited. You would have to be using the Active Directory database in order to create a user with the 50 or so available attributes we have talked about.

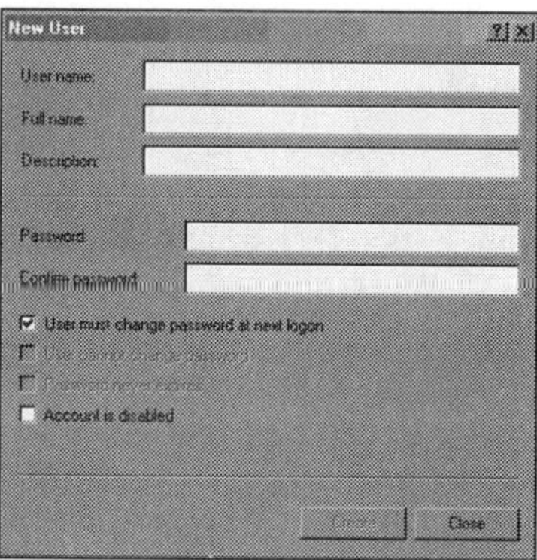

Figure 5.1 Creating a Local User.

Using Active Directory Users and Computers

Using the Active Directory to create a user is very easy as well. Naturally, in order to create a new user in a location, you must first have Write permission to that OU and permission to Write the attributes of user objects. Given that you have those permissions, use the Active Directory Users and Computers management tool. Expand the domain, and then simply right-click on the OU that you want to put the user in. Select New...User from the context menu. Then fill in the blanks. There are a couple of things about the interface that I should warn you about, though. Remember that I told you there are 50 attributes that can be filled in for a user? Well, you won't do that here. In this interface, all you can do is set the user's name, logon name, logon domain, password, and password options. Setting the other attributes will require that you go in and enter them after the user account is created. I'll show you those options in a few minutes when we discuss maintaining accounts. You can see the two user creation screens in Figures 5.2 and 5.3.

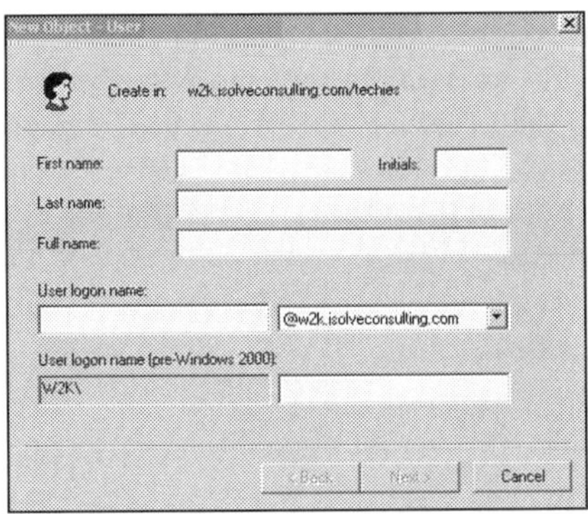

Figure 5.2 Creating a user, step 1, the basic account information.

In Figure 5.2, notice that the user's full name and his logon name are very different things. I told you that with LDAP, you could have two Bob Smiths in a domain as long as their logon names were different. The rule is that full names are allowed to duplicate in a domain, but logon names must be unique. So in our `us.pizzaplace.com` domain, you can have Bob Smith from the Accounting OU and Bob Smith from the US Operations OU as long as you have one logging on as `bobs@us.pizzaplace.com` and the other one logging on as `bsmith@us.pizzaplace.com`. Logon names are limited to 20 characters and are not case sensitive. Also in Figure 5.2, when looking at the logon domain—that's the "`@`" part of the user logon name—note that the system fills this in automatically for you. One small catch: currently, it tends to fill in the name of the top-level partition in the tree. If this user resides in a lower domain, you must select that domain from the drop-down list. Notice that a downlevel logon name is automatically created using the domain in a NT 4 recognizable format and the first part of the user logon name.

The password options are as they have always been. Passwords can be up to 14 characters long and are case sensitive. You can see the password options in Figure 5.3. For security's sake, you want to give the user a first logon password and require that he changes it at the next logon. This way, no one but the user knows his password. Alternatively, you can specify that the user can't change the password. This can be very useful for the Guest account and other shared-access accounts. You can set accounts with passwords that never expire, a useful option for service accounts. Finally—an option that has nothing to do with passwords—you can disable the account at creation. Remember the rule: Always disable before deleting an account! If someone leaves the company and you destroy his account, that SID is lost forever. If you hire someone to replace that individual, you must create a new account, which creates a new SID, and then reset permissions using the new SID. If you had disabled the old employee's account, you could have simply renamed it and all the permissions would still have been valid for your new user. Disabling an account is a method that is also employed when creating template accounts, also known as cookie cutter accounts in some circles. For more information on how and why you would want to use cookie cutter accounts, look to the following sidebar entitled "Template Accounts."

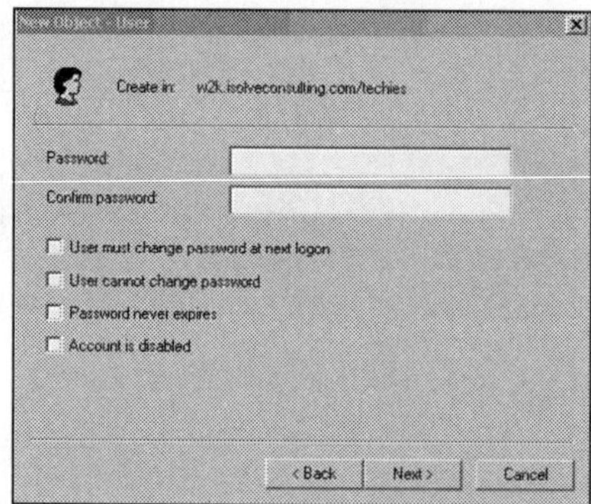

Figure 5.3 Creating a user, step 2, the password information.

Template Accounts

Let's talk about template accounts for a moment, just in case you've never used them. A template account is one you set up with all the right options for a particular class of user—engineers, for example. You set the user's profile path, home folder, perhaps even log on with the account and set up the desktop environment in a certain way. You then disable the account for security purposes. Now, when the company hires a new engineer, you can take this account and copy it to save yourself some time in setting up the new employee's account. As long as you use variables such as `%user%` and `%homedrive%`, there is no problem using a template account like this. This approach saves tons of work in an environment where you have well-defined user classes, but I've also seen it used where just one template account was set up called DomainUser. Whenever *anybody* was hired, they copied that account template to the new employee's account.

Using ADSI, LDAP, and Windows Script Host (WSH)

As we discussed earlier, ADSI scripts can be used for many types of tasks in the Active Directory. One of the most common will be the creation and management of users. In Appendix B "Custom .ADM Template File Example," I have provided some examples of common tasks that can be performed this way. In these examples, I have used VBScript, but any scripting language that is supported by ADSI can be used. Currently, WSH supports the use of VBScript and JScript. It is the general expectation in the industry that in the near future there will be third-party extensions to the host that will allow the use of other scripting languages to be used, such as PERL and REXX. Several vendors have already stated that they have these interfaces in development. In order to use this method to add or maintain users, you need to know three things: your scripting language of choice, LDAP naming conventions, and the WSH. As you will see when you browse the appendix, the scripts have to be built from the top down, so to speak, by navigating the LDAP structure from the highest level and providing a path to the place where you want to get the work done.

Scripts written in the WSH are not confined to the world of Windows 2000. They can also be run on legacy NT systems and Windows 95 and 98 environments. WSH is included in the Windows 2000 and Windows 98 products. Scripts can be run with WSH using two programs: `cscript.exe` and `wscript.exe`. `cscript` runs at the command line, and `wscript` runs in the background. `cscript` supports error levels; `wscript` doesn't. This means that `cscript` can be more useful when a script is part of a larger batch file that is running. Other than that difference, both programs run scripts equally well.

You can get much more information about WSH and ADSI from the Microsoft Web site. There is a whitepaper entitled "MS Active Directory Service Interfaces (ADSI)" and another that specifically covers WSH in detail, titled "Windows Script Host: A Universal Scripting Host for Scripting Languages." Both of these subjects are also covered extensively in the Software Development Kit (SDK), if you have access to that. Let me warn you that this is not a topic for lightweights. In NT 4, it was relatively easy to create a little batch file to perform simple administrative tasks within the SAM. Using WSH requires more programming knowledge than many of us have. If you aren't interested in learning scripting, it's time to start taking those programmers down the hall to lunch every now and then,because you're going to need them someday soon!

Bulk Creation Tools

There are third-party NT 4 tools that allow you to do bulk creation of users. You may also have used a resource kit tool or created scripts of your own to add users to the SAM in a NT 4 domain. These are called *bulk creation tools* because they are designed to take a large group of users and add them to the database all at once. Depending on the tool, there is a possibility that it might still work in a Windows 2000 environment, as long as you are running in mixed mode. Many of the NT 4 tools and template files work for Windows 2000 as well because Microsoft has designed Windows 2000 for backward compatibility with NT 4. Remember that a mixed-mode Windows 2000 domain controller will operate exactly as a NT 4 PDC or BDC would. Maintaining that backward compatibility means maintaining the same registry keys and many other features.

Upgrading from an Earlier Version of NT

What happens to all your users and groups when you upgrade from earlier versions of NT to the Active Directory model? Do you have to create those users and groups again in the correct containers of the Active Directory? Quite simply, no. It would be pretty dumb on Microsoft's part to let that happen! When you upgrade from earlier versions of NT, Windows 2000 will take your existing users and place them into certain Active Directory containers. The two that will be used are Users and Builtin.

- **Users container.** Most of your users and groups will be migrated to this container at upgrade. This container holds all user accounts and all user-created groups. In addition, this is where the system-defined, domain-level groups are kept, such as Domain Admins and Domain Guests.
- **Builtin container.** The Builtin container holds all the system-defined local groups that are used to assign rights on the local machine. Groups such as Administrators, Server Operators, and Power Users are kept in this Active Directory container. These groups are exactly the same as their NT 4 equivalents, and in an upgrade the membership lists of each corresponding NT 4 group are migrated to these groups.

Windows 2000 Working and Playing Well with Others...Specifically Novell

Now that Microsoft has a more sophisticated, industry-standard directory environment, it is possible to achieve better synchronization between the different networking systems operating in your environment. Because it is most likely that if you have another NOS operating in your environment it's some version of Novell, Microsoft has spent their development time making Windows 2000 and Novell work and play well together.

There are several tools available on Windows 2000 that allow interaction between the Windows 2000 and Novell environments. Some of these tools are focused to achieve cross-network access and authentication, such as the Client Service for NetWare that is available with Windows 2000 Professional or the Gateway for NetWare that is available in the Windows 2000 Server product line. We are not really interested in these tools in this text. There are two tools, though, that directly impact the way you administer users. They are the Microsoft Directory Synchronization Services and the Directory Service Migration Tool.

Microsoft Directory Synchronization Services (MSDSS)

As I mentioned way back in Chapter 1,"Inside Windows 2000 Overview," most of today's directory services are based in some fashion on the X.500 model. Because they have this common base to work from, it has become much easier to synchronize resources between the different NOS environments. In order to achieve this goal between Windows 2000 and the NetWare world, Microsoft has provided the MSDSS tool.

MSDSS provides synchronization with all versions of the NetWare environment. The type of synchronization method that will be employed depends on the version of NetWare involved. For NetWare systems using NDS, MSDSS provides two-way synchronization of the directories. For NetWare systems that are bindery-based, only one-way synchronization is available.

MSDSS is very flexible in terms of allowing you to employ whatever administrative model you want. Perhaps you are primarily a Novell shop, but you have some rogue development groups who went off and created applications using Windows 2000 and the Active Directory. We would assume in this case that the administrative staff involved are probably CNEs rather than MCSEs, and so they probably want to keep the primary administrative authority on the Novell side of the house. Administrators in this situation can choose to consolidate their administrative tasks into a single point using their choice of management interface.

If you would rather divide up the administrative responsibility—perhaps by type of network object, such as users and printers—that's also possible to do with the help of MSDSS. You could manage the users on the Windows 2000 side of the house, and all the printers on the Novell side.

Two other benefits you will receive from the use of MSDSS are automatic password synchronization between Windows 2000 and the NetWare environment, and the ability to do two-way scheduled synchronizations or manual synchronizations when network traffic is low.

Some of the features of MSDSS are illustrated in Table 5.1.

Table 5.1 **Advantages of the Microsoft Directory Synchronization Services Tool**

Feature	**Function**
Object synchronization	Synchronizes all adds, deletes, modifies, renames, and moves at the object level. Synchronizes the modified object and all applicable attributes.
Password synchronization	Allows passwords to be automatically synchronized across platforms. Password synchronization is secure and one-way from Windows 2000 to the NetWare environment.
Multiple instance and session support	Multiple instances of the MSDSS servers are accepted and each server can be operating up to 128 active synchronization sessions simultaneously.

continues

Table 5.1 **Continued**

Feature	Function
Object mapping flexibility	Allows the Active Directory and NDS trees to be configured identically or have different structures. Also allows synchronization to be designated to start at any node in the tree. So, full-tree synchronization is not required.
Built-in access controls	Because the MSDSS is hosted as part of the Active Directory, there are built-in access controls both through the authentication mechanisms of Windows 2000 and through the file system. This guarantees that synchronization information will be securely kept on the system—at least as securely as any other part of your Active Directory

MSDSS's two-way synchronization has two modes: forward and reverse. Forward synchronization refers to the synchronization of changes in the Active Directory to the NetWare environment. This type of synchronization can be accomplished with earlier versions of Novell that used the bindery. In this mode, the Active Directory is searched for modified objects. Then, only the attributes that have been modified are sent to the NDS directory. This type of synchronization can be accomplished without any changes to the schema of the NDS directory.

When doing a reverse synchronization from NDS to the Active Directory, the NDS directory is searched for objects that have been modified, and those objects are written to the Active Directory. To accomplish this reverse synchronization, the schema of the NDS directory must be modified to include a GUID for objects that will be synchronized because tracking of objects in the Active Directory requires a GUID.

Naturally, the interface for the directory synchronization service is an MMC snap-in that also employs a Wizard to help set up the synchronization service settings in the first place. Microsoft wants you to use this tool and be able to meld your environments rather than have to make a decision to go all-Novell!

So what are the drawbacks? Well, obviously, the one thing that has been left out is password synchronization from the Novell environment to the Windows 2000 world. If a user changes his password on the Windows 2000 side, you're okay, but if he does it on the Novell servers, the password change doesn't replicate to Windows 2000. Would anyone care to bet how long it will be before Novell comes out with a tool to do this? Other than that, the only thing to be concerned about is network traffic during synchronizations.

Migrating to Active Directory from NetWare

From Microsoft's standpoint, an even better option than peaceful coexistence with a NetWare environment is migration from Novell land to Windows 2000 land. In legacy NT systems, you had this capability with the NetWare Migration Tool, `nwconv.exe`. This tool allowed you to migrate NDS objects such as users, groups, files, and ACLs into an NT 4 style SAM. You could do a trial migration (highly recommended) and then see how well the Novell information translated to the NT 4 setting.

The addition of a 3D directory service to Windows 2000 has meant that the migration tools for NetWare could be reengineered and improved upon, as the migration was occurring between two systems that had similar levels of sophistication in their directory services platforms. The new tool is called the Directory Service Migration Tool. This tool enables you to migrate both bindery-based and NDS-based objects as well as volumes to the Active Directory. A really neat feature of this new tool is that the migration is first done to an offline database. This gives you the opportunity to reconfigure the container structure should you find it necessary or desirable to do so.

To install the migration tool, you will need to go to Control Panel's Add/Remove Programs and select Add/Remove Windows Components. The tool will be listed under Management and Monitoring tools. Follow the prompts, and you should be just fine. When you install the Directory Service Migration Tool, the system will install Gateway Services for NetWare if they are not already installed. For the sake of minimizing the impact of the migration on the network traffic volume, it is recommended that you perform the migration on a domain controller.

When you migrate a Novell system, there are several steps you must complete:

1. Create a project in the Directory Services Migration Tool
2. Select the NetWare resources to migrate.
3. Model an offline view.
4. Migrate the offline view to the Active Directory.
5. Migrate selected volumes to the Active Directory.

As I said earlier, Microsoft want to make this process as easy as possible for you, so there is a Wizard that walks you through these steps. The Discover Wizard takes you step-by-step through creating the project and selecting the NetWare resources you want to migrate. Once you have selected the objects, you can right-click on any object and modify its attributes. In this way, you can easily change usernames, passwords, whatever you want, and it all happens in the offline model. Once you have the system the way you want it and are happy with the objects, you can migrate the offline view to the Active Directory by right-clicking on an object in the offline view and selecting the Configure to NTDS option. Doing this starts another Wizard, aptly named the Configure to NTDS Wizard. This Wizard is used to migrate nonvolume objects into the Active Directory. First the Wizard will do a preconfigure verification and then ask if you want to continue the migration. If you choose to continue, it begins writing data to the Active Directory.

If you have selected volume objects during the discovery process (selecting the NetWare resources to migrate), you can right-click on the volume objects to start the File Migration Wizard.

Naturally, after you have done all this, you will want to verify that the migration has proceeded as you expected. Open a directory management session and examine the users, OUs, and volumes that you migrated over.

Maintaining User Accounts

Now that you have all these user accounts created, let's look at some of the other settings you might be interested in using to make your administrative tasks just a little easier.

When you create a user account, you aren't allowed to fill in a whole lot of attributes. You first have to access the Properties of your newly created user; then you can fill in all the attributes you want. You can also fill these in through a script that uploads a spreadsheet to fill out the attributes. The Properties for a domain user include all the tabs shown in Figure 5.4.

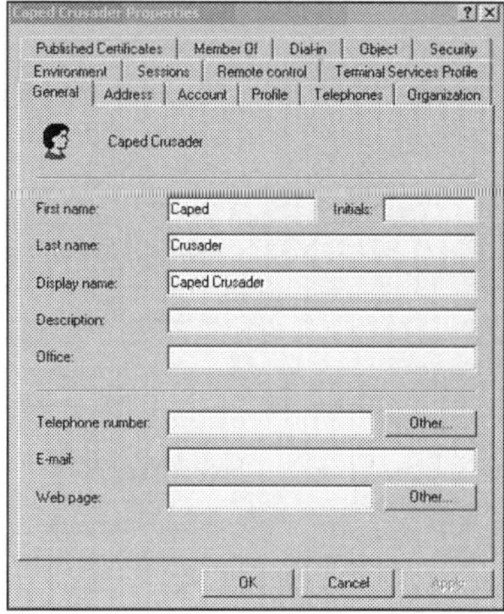

Figure 5.4 User Properties tabs.

As you can see, this front tab lets you have all the information at first glance that you might need to contact Bob. It even lets you specify more than one phone number and Web page to associate with Bob.

I won't bore you with looking at all the tabs, but there are a few that are worth talking about from an administrative standpoint. You can already see that the format of this interface is very different from the Create New User interface. For example, nowhere on all of these tab pages will you see a place to retype a password for your user Bob. In order to do this, you have to right-click on Bob in the Active Directory and select Reset Password from the context menu. The context menu gives several helpful functions, such as reset password, copy a user account, disable, rename, move, or even send the user an email. For everything else, however, you have to access the user's Properties.

Account Tab

The account information for a user includes all his account restrictions and parameters. You can set logon hours, restrictions on the workstations the user may log on from, and account expiration info. You can also reset the password options from this tab. This is where the account's lockout status will be displayed if applicable. Naturally, the defaults are wide open. A user can log on at any time, from any workstation, and his account never expires.

Profile Tab

The Profile tab looks the most like NT 4 to me. This is where you will set the user's profile path if he is using a roaming or mandatory profile. The profile path can be any valid network path, any server, any share. We'll talk more about profiles in Chapter 7, "User Profiles."

Although you can specify a logon script here for a user, it really makes more sense to use your group policy capabilities to set users' logon and logoff scripts, rather than doing it on an individual account basis as you would have to here. One warning about logon scripts if you do decide to fill in a script path here. At the time of this writing, it's not possible to use true scripts in this location, for some reason. You couldn't, for example, use `logon.vbs` as a logon script. The only types of files that can be run as logon scripts are `.cmd`, `.bat`, and `.exe` file types. Does that mean you can't use that really cool script you created? Of course not. You can either use group policies to deploy it or simply put the script call inside a little batch file. Whatever you do, you only need to enter the filename, because the system automatically looks for the script in the NETLOGON share. For domain logons, scripts will be pulled from the network NETLOGON share.

It is also where you can specify a user's home directory. Home directories are the local or network paths that can be set for a user to default to when opening or saving documents or running applications. Of course, if you specify a network path as the home directory, you want to use the FQDN format, such as `\\pc1.usops.pizzaplace.com\sharename`. The problem with network paths is that application-specific settings can override whatever you set in the user account. A good example is the My Documents folder in Microsoft Office. Even if you set this home directory to some network location, Office applications will open and save to the My Documents folder on the hard drive, by default. In order to change that behavior, you have to change it in the application.

Environment Tab

The Environment tab enables you to specify that a certain program starts up automatically when the user logs on. It also lets you specify whether to connect drives and printers when this user logs on. Often, these types of functions were handled through logon scripts in previous versions of NT. Now, you can transfer that task to the Environment tab.

Terminal Services Tabs

Three tabs exist that govern the user's Terminal Services settings if they are needed. They are the Terminal Services Profile, Sessions, and Remote Control tabs.

- **Terminal Services Profile tab.** Enables you to set the terminal services profile that will be used for this user as well as their Terminal Services home directory path that can be either local or remote.
- **Sessions tab.** Enables you to set timeouts for disconnected and idle sessions and specify where reconnection will be allowed to occur from, the originating client or any client.
- **Remote Control tab.** Lets you set up the details of how a remote control Terminal Services session will proceed. The administrator (or anyone allowed to manage this user's attributes) can set up this user so that his or her session can be subject to remote control. Once you have chosen to enable this feature, you can specify whether you want to have the session remotely controlled or merely remotely observed, and whether or not you need the user's permission to do so.

Member Of Tab

I think the Member Of tab is going to be a great help to administrators. In legacy NT systems, there was really no way in the native product to enumerate a user's group memberships. This tab will list all groups that the user is a member of. That will be a timesaver when troubleshooting. Of course, because deep group nesting is allowed, you will still have to figure out what groups those groups are members of. Only first-level membership shows up here. Sorry, couldn't let your world get too rosy! But you can use this interface to add or remove a user from a group. So, that's a nice piece of integration. You can also set the user's group priority with this tab.

Security Tab

The Security tab (which can only be seen if you enable Advanced Features in your Active Directory management session) will give you the DACL and SACL for this user object. In other words, it will tell you who is allowed to manage this user and what type of auditing functionality is set up for this account. Again, very helpful when troubleshooting problems with delegated administration.

Dial-In Tab

Although we had a Dial-In button in NT 4, this interface has much more advanced capabilities than that one did. With this Dial-In tab, you set up whether or not the user is allowed to use RAS and what his callback options will be. Here's where the advanced part comes in: You can also say that rather than manage this function by individual user, you want to use the Remote Access Policy settings. You can also specify that the user has a static IP address and set it here, and/or that the user will use static routing and set the routes. You even have the option to verify the user's caller ID.

Copying User Accounts

Another way to create a new user account is to copy it from an existing account. Not a bad plan as long as you use variables such as `%username%` when specifying home directories that are named after the user. Wherever this variable appears, the system will substitute the new user's name for the name on the account you are copying. You should be aware, though, that not all attributes get copied over to the new account. Terminal Services settings don't seem to make it over, for example. Also, one little detail about the security on copied accounts needs to be mentioned. When you copy an account that has an inherited DACL, the DACL on the new account is the same as the original except that the ACEs show up as explicit rather than inherited. What that means to you is that any inherited permissions you pass to this copied object will be subordinate to these explicit permissions. Because this is a directory object, you will not have the option of erasing the DACL from a higher container and starting over. I'm not saying don't copy accounts because of this. I'm just saying be sure you really like the permissions set before you copy it, because it'll be a small pain to change it on all your copied accounts, one by one.

Deleting User Accounts

I mentioned a little earlier in the chapter that you should always disable a user's account rather than deleting it. I just want to reinforce that statement. Naturally, there will be some of you reading this who are governed by a security policy that demands that all inactive user accounts be deleted. If that's the case, delete away. You have no choice. If you do have a choice, however, keep the account and disable it.

I used to tell my staff that if they'd been to the funeral, they could delete the account. I soon learned the error of my ways when we had to recreate a user's permissions for the new employee who took the dearly departed's place. We didn't get it straight for months. As the new employee would get involved in another aspect of the previous user's job, he would find he had no permissions to do what he needed to. If we had disabled the account and then renamed it for the new employee, the SID would have been preserved and all the DACLs would have still been active and appropriately set for this job position. There is something to be said for role-based security!

I have also learned that people don't just retire and go fishing in Montana for the rest of their lives. Sometimes they retire and come back six months later as consultants! Again, in that case, if we delete the account upon retirement, we would have to rebuild everything from the ground up. If you can put a policy into place that says accounts of users who have retired or left the company will be disabled for six months or a year before they are deleted, you might find you save yourself a whole lot of work.

In Summary

I think we've hit the highlights of creating and managing users. Whenever possible, you want to use group policies to manage a group of users. If you have to manage them individually, this chapter should have helped you figure out how to do that. Don't forget to dig into Appendix A, "Directory Management with Windows Script Host," to have a look at common management tasks using WSH and VBScript.

6

Group Management

As you have already seen in so many areas of user management in Windows 2000, the rules have changed. This holds true for group management as well. There are new categories and types of groups you are allowed to create, as well as new membership and nesting rules. Naturally, all the new features are tied to the native-mode Active Directory operational model. In this chapter, we'll cover all those new capabilities, but in the spirit of cooperation and peaceful coexistence with our legacy NT systems, we'll also cover mixed-mode domains, as well as what happens if you're looking at a native-mode domain from a legacy NT domain.

The first rule of group management is what it has always been: Make groups! I have seen many a novice NT administrator try to set access control lists (ACLs) by just putting individual users on the ACL or granting rights one individual at a time. Although this works just fine if your company is Bill & Ted's Excellent Itty Bitty Adventure Outfitters with three employees, the process doesn't scale well. And trust me, it's a real pain to go back to every resource on the servers and reset permissions. Does that sound like experience talking? Even if you only have one person to put into a group today, create that group and set your DACLs, SACLs, and rights using the group name rather than the individual. After all, individuals leave the company, get hit by buses, and retire every day; groups don't. Now that I have said all I need to about why you need to create groups, regardless of the size of your organization, I can descend from the soapbox and we can get on with the rest of our discussion!

Group Categories

The first thing we're going to have to agree on in this chapter is terminology. Windows 2000 now supports two broad categories of groups within the native-mode Active Directory structure. Within those categories, several types of groups are allowed to exist. Do I have your curiosity piqued?

Those broad categories of groups are called security and distribution groups. Security groups are used to grant rights and set DACLs and SACLs. These are the traditional groups you are used to working with if you have administered previous NT environments.

The second category of groups is distribution groups. If you have been an Exchange or SMS administrator, this group concept will be familiar to you. These groups are not used to set permissions, nor does membership in any distribution group affect your rights on the system. These groups are used more for application environments. For example, you might set up a distribution group for an email list or to distribute software.

Group Types

Within each of the group categories, several types of groups are allowed to exist in the Active Directory in native mode. These group types include the Windows 2000 built-in groups (system-defined groups), which we will talk about a little later in the chapter, as well as any groups you create (user-defined groups) to organize your users and machines. That's right, machines. Don't ever forget that machines can now be assigned to groups. Remembering this fact will really help you out when you filter group policies and apply your software distribution policies.

Each type of group is differentiated by two criteria: scope within the directory and membership eligibility. Some groups can only contain members from within their own domain, whereas others can have members from anywhere in the enterprise. Some groups only have visibility within their own domain, and others can be seen throughout the directory tree or forest. These are the rules you have to memorize to be successful in recreating your legacy group structure to take best advantage of the Active Directory.

You also need to consider the structure of your OUs during this group planning phase. For many of us, a correctly structured OU configuration can go a long way toward easing the burden of defining group membership. Many of the things for which you used to create groups are now bounded by the OU structure. OUs can be used to delegate administration, define organizational boundaries, and deploy policies, but you need to understand the limits of what the OU system can accomplish. One thing the OU structure *cannot* be used for is the assignment of rights and resource permissions. You must still create groups to accomplish those tasks. Novell devotees will give you a hard time over this one (because apparently, with Novell, you can assign permissions using the organization), but be brave, stand tall, and go forth and create those groups!

Domain Local Groups

Domain local groups can be loosely compared to the local groups of NT 4. As with NT 4, they are the most powerful of the groups even though they have the narrowest scope. We say the most powerful because the Administrators group is an example of a local group. Almost all of the built-in groups we will discuss later are domain local groups. It is by being a member of these built-in domain local groups that individuals—and even other groups—get their "powers" in a system. Hence, we tend to think of domain local groups as the real workhorses of a system.

Scope of Domain Local Groups

As the name implies, domain local groups can only be "seen," (that is, used to set permissions and rights) in the local domain. The local domain can be defined as a single machine if the machine is a member server or workstation, or as the domain in which the group was created, if operating in a Windows 2000 native- or mixed-mode domain environment.

In NT 4, the local group was only available on the machine on which it was created. If the machine happened to be the PDC, the group was available for use on the PDC and all BDCs in the domain because they actually shared a copy of the same instance of the SAM database. Other machines, member servers, and workstations, for example, couldn't see the group to add it to their local ACLs. In a Windows 2000 member server or workstation, the scope of a domain local group is still the local machine, regardless of whether the machine is standalone or participates in a domain. These groups are created and kept in the local database.

If the domain local group is created as part of the Active Directory structure, it can theoretically be used throughout the domain to set permissions and rights. In other words, its scope extends beyond the domain controllers. A workstation that is a member of the domain should be able to access the Active Directory, see the domain local group, and use it to make a DACL entry for a local resource. When created as part of the Active Directory, a domain local group is stored on all DCs in that partition as part of the multimaster replication strategy.

Membership Eligibility of Domain Local Groups

Within the domain the group is created in, basically, anybody can be designated as a member of the domain local group. Users, machines, and all other types of groups can belong to a domain local group. We'll discuss group nesting in more detail a little later in this chapter.

When we talk about adding members from outside the domain partition in which the local group resides, the rules are just a little different. Because the scope of a domain local group is its own domain, it can't be seen anywhere else in the forest. So it makes sense that, when it comes to membership in interdomain groups, you can't add domain local groups to groups in other domains. As a result, when you are establishing who can be a member of a domain local group from another domain, you can only add users, machines, global groups, and universal groups ... because you can't "see" the other domain's local groups to add them to the membership lists in this domain. Got it? Logical—in a Microsoft sort of way.

Global Groups

Global groups resemble the functionality of NT 4's global groups with a few small differences. These groups also have a set of scope and membership rules associated with them.

Scope of Global Groups

A global group is hosted in the Active Directory structure in the domain in which it was created. If you create a global group in the `pizzaplace.com` domain, its name and membership list are stored on every DC in the `pizzaplace.com` partition. Its scope, however, is global, meaning that it can be seen and used from any domain in the forest. A user in the `tacogiant.com` domain who wants to allow access to a share on his machine for the `pizzaplace.com` accounting staff can go to the resource, drop down the `pizzaplace.com` domain member list, and select the Accountants global group. It's that simple due to the trust relationships that exist between the domains. The only possible gotcha in this scenario is that the Accountants group must exist for the user to select it. Assuming that it exists, though, the process is pretty simple.

Membership Eligibility for Global Groups

The first rule of global group membership is that global groups can only contain members from their own partition in the Active Directory. They cannot contain members of any kind from other domains. This said, because they are global in nature, it makes sense that when we discuss who can be a member of this type of group, we specifically deny membership to local resources, such as domain local groups. So the resulting membership set for global groups is users, machines, and other global groups from within the domain in which the group is being created. We'll discuss this more in a moment when we talk about universal groups. You also cannot add a universal group to a global group because the universal group's membership list is hosted outside the AD partitions.

Universal Groups

Universal groups are the new addition to the fold and are designed to cover all eventualities not covered by domain local and global groups. Universal groups have very few restrictions on scope and membership and are, therefore, perfect for supporting the enterprise-wide directory structure. On the downside, there might be replication performance issues associated with the use of these groups, and we'll discuss those in the following section, "Replication Considerations in Group Design."

Scope of Universal Groups

The scope statement for a universal group is really pretty simple. A universal group can be seen and used from anywhere in the Active Directory forest. It has the same visibility definition as a global group. The difference between them lies in where the membership list for the group is hosted. As I mentioned in the last section, global group membership lists are hosted and replicated within their own partition of the Active Directory. In contrast, a universal group's membership list is kept in the Global Catalog—technically, a structure outside the individual partitions.

Membership Eligibility for Universal Groups

Again, this can be summed up in a rather simple statement. A universal group can contain any universal security principal from anywhere within the Active Directory tree or forest. A universal security principal would include users, machines, global groups, and universal groups. Again, logically, domain local groups are not eligible for membership.

Replication Considerations in Group Design

When we discussed the types of groups Windows 2000 allows, I made a point of specifying where the group was hosted, either in the local Active Directory partition or the Global Catalog. Regardless of the category of group, security, or distribution, domain local and global groups are hosted in the Active Directory partition in which they were created. Universal groups, on the other hand, are hosted in the Global Catalog. This is a very important difference you need to be aware of so that you can understand how the type of group created can affect replication cycles and, therefore, system performance.

Because domain local and global groups are hosted in the local domain, when a change is made to the membership list of that group, the change is replicated to all DCs within that domain, because a copy of the partition information is kept on every DC. The replication cycle follows the same logic that any change to the Active Directory would employ in that domain, taking into account variables such as site topology and connection speeds.

Unlike those local and global groups, the universal groups are hosted in the Global Catalog. Therefore, any change to the membership list in a universal group would be replicated to all copies of the Global Catalog, wherever they exist throughout the enterprise. Basically, you could theoretically be talking about a replication cycle that has to hit every DC in your whole enterprise. Now, I don't know how you feel about it, but personally, I wouldn't want too many of those cycles happening on my network, unless I had a pretty terrific network!

If you do have a great network and all the connections can be considered well connected by the site info standards, you could use all universal groups for your interdomain access needs. After all, the scope is the same as a global group, and you don't have all the restrictions to membership that a global group has.

If, on the other hand, you do have slower areas of the network (and who doesn't!), you will want to approach your universal groups a little differently. In this networking scenario, create global groups and only allow those global groups to be listed as members of a universal group. Do not allow individual users to be listed as members of a universal group.

Let's walk through an example of exactly what happens when we change the membership lists of each of these groups. If our user Bob's SID is listed as an entry on the universal group Accountants and he quits, when we remove his user SID from the universal group's membership list, that change has to replicate to every copy of the catalog, everywhere. On the other hand, if we listed Bob in a `pizzaplace.com` global group called Pizza Place Accountants, and then added the Pizza Place Accountants group SID to the membership list of the universal Accountants group, there would be no change to the membership list of the universal group Accountants if we remove Bob, because the removal of Bob from the domain global group membership list doesn't alter the universal group's membership list. That means that the replication cycle caused by the removal of Bob is confined to within the DCs of the `pizzaplace.com` domain.

Group Nesting

As you may have gathered from the membership possibilities listed in the last sections, Windows 2000 is a lot more relaxed about allowing you to nest groups within groups than legacy NT systems have been. You can nest many layers of groups. This is sometimes referred to as deep group nesting.

The capability to do deep group nesting gives a flexibility that can be a great benefit to an administrator if it is used in a manner similar to the scenario shown in Figure 6.1. As you can see, the group design of this company is such that the groups with more restrictive membership lists fall through and become members of groups with broader membership bases. Resources within the organization can be hierarchically structured to match the group design. So, as you can see, the most sensitive resources have the smallest access defined, but a resource such as the Cafeteria Suggestion Box would have a single ACL entry that would contain the sum total of the memberships of all the groups that have fallen into that one broad group.

Now, that's a very well-thought-out, well-designed match between the overall group design and resource management. How many organizations would actually go through such an exercise to do that level of planning? Well, if yours is like most real-world organizations, I doubt you could say that such forethought was given to administration of groups and resources. For most of us, groups just seem to appear, and the resources that are shared seem to proliferate like rabbits, with users assigning permissions in many varied and wonderful combinations. Some organizations have responded to the chaos by taking the ACL task away from the users and formalizing the process for adding a new group. That's great in a centralized administrative environment, but might not be feasible in decentralized models. Whatever your decision on an administrative model, you can see from the example how deep group nesting can be used to your advantage.

So what are the disadvantages of nesting groups like this? There are three you should be aware of: a lack of tools to enumerate nested groups, the complexity of the token explosion process, and finally, limitations when accessing these nested groups from downlevel systems. Because of these severe drawbacks, even Microsoft is recommending that group nesting be limited to two levels at the most in the early phases of the Windows 2000 life cycle. Let's talk about each drawback individually.

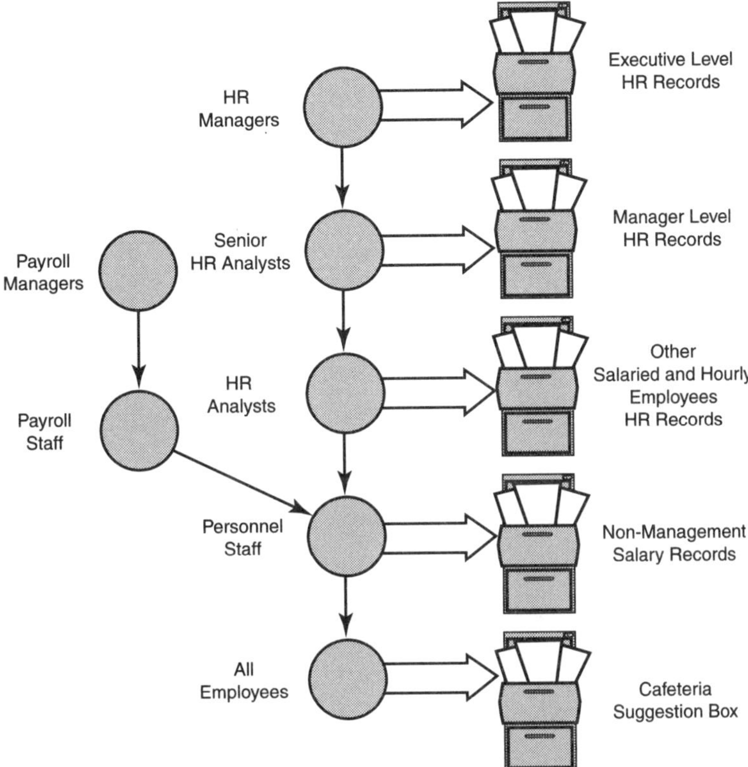

Figure 6.1 Deep group nesting example.

Lack of Enumeration Tools

The first inconvenience you will encounter if you use deep group nesting is that currently there are no tools to assist you in enumerating the groups as they are nested. That means it would be very difficult to track down the effective access in a group structure similar to the one shown in Figure 6.2. Even if each group only has two other groups listed in the DACL, you can see how quickly this becomes a complex troubleshooting problem. When user Mary calls you and says she can't write to a particular share, you have to go through an exercise that expands each group into its member groups, step-by-step, manually. In an organization with a multidomain forest structure and, let's say, 80,000 or so users, I think you can see what a pain this would be without automated tools. It is expected that Microsoft will either develop tools as a part of a resource kit or service pack or that, as usual, third-party software tool vendors will step in and fill the void as they did for NT 4.

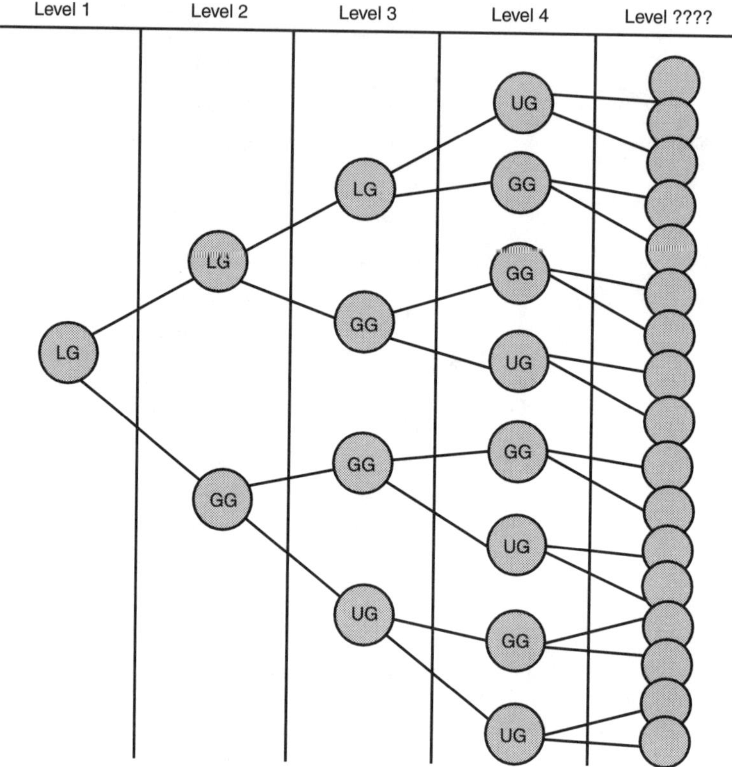

Figure 6.2 Group proliferation with deep group nesting.

Token Explosion

A second disadvantage of using deep group nesting has to do with something we call token explosion. Basically, token explosion is the process of creating and adding SIDs to a user's token as he requests access to a particular resource. When the user logs on, SIDs are added to his access token, as we discussed in Chapter 3. Those SIDs will be the user SID and group SIDs for all groups that their user SID is a member of in the domain they are logging into. That sounds pretty simple, but let's look at our user Bob and see what happens as he logs on to the `pizzaplace.com` domain shown in Figure 6.3.

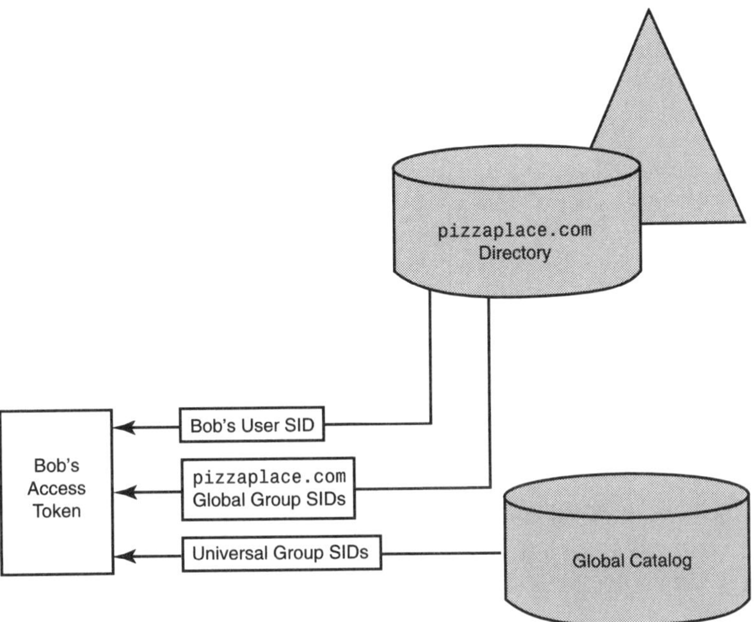

Figure 6.3 Bob's token in his own domain.

When Bob successfully authenticates into the `pizzaplace.com` domain, his token is created, and his user SID is placed on the token. Then the `pizzaplace.com` DC starts to search its group membership lists for instances of Bob's user SID in the membership list. Even if Bob's user SID doesn't appear in the first-level groups, if there are groups that are members of the first-level groups, the second-level groups' membership lists must also be checked for Bob's user SID. This process continues until all groups are exploded and the system is satisfied that it has found all instances of Bob's user SID. After the groups are enumerated, the applicable group SIDS are added to Bob's token.

Finally, based on those SIDs and his user SID, any system rights are placed on the token. This is the token that will follow Bob around the `pizzaplace.com` domain as he accesses resources within that domain. What happens, though, when Bob wants to access a shared volume in the `tacogiant.com` partition of the directory? You can see the result of that access request in Figure 6.4.

In that case, the token explosion process has to be carried to a higher level. When Bob clicks on the share in the `tacogiant.com` domain, his token is expanded to account for any local groups he might have been added to in the `tacogiant.com` domain. For interdomain access requests, Bob's home domain provides his user SID and any `pizzaplace.com` global group SIDs for groups that Bob is a member of, either directly or through nesting. It also checks the Global Catalog for any universal groups that Bob is a member of, again either directly or through group nesting, and if necessary, adds those SIDs to the token. Finally, the DC checks the Global Catalog for universal groups that the global groups previously added that the token are members of, either directly or through nesting, and adds those universal group SIDs to the token.

Now the `pizzaplace.com` DC's job is over and the `tacogiant.com` DCs take over. As you can see from Figure 6.4, the `tacogiant.com` DCs take all the SIDs enumerated by the `pizzaplace.com` DCs and begin searching their domain local groups to see if any of these SIDs are members. Remember that you can nest a domain local group in another domain local group in another domain local group in another...Well, you get the point, I'm sure! When all the `tacogiant.com` domain local groups memberships are enumerated, the `tacogiant.com` DC adds those local group SIDs to Bob's token. As the final step in this token explosion, if Bob is granted any rights in the `tacogiant.com` domain based on those `tacogiant.com` domain local groups, those rights are also added to the token.

When all that is done, the system checks to see if Bob is even allowed to log on over the network, and the DACL on the resource is checked against this meticulously enumerated token to see if Bob has the requested access. Whew! All that just so Bob can check out his friend's newest version of Monster Truck Madness!

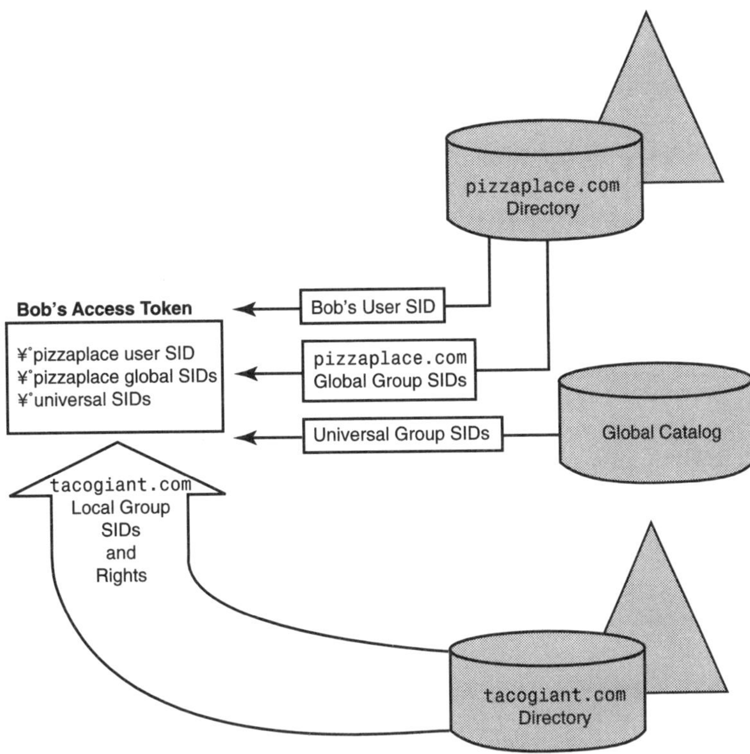

Figure 6.4 Bob's token when he accesses `tacogiant.com`.

Group Memberships as Viewed from Downlevel Systems

The final disadvantage of using deep group nesting might not apply to you if you are planning the big bang approach to your conversion to Windows 2000. If, however, you might have a mixed operating environment for awhile, with some domains and client machines being Windows 2000 and others being NT 4, you should be aware of the level of enumeration that those NT 4 domains will have when accessing your groups to set ACLs or grant permissions.

First, if you have created distribution groups as well as the traditional security groups, the distribution groups will not be seen by the downlevel machines. Second, any local groups will only contain one level of nesting, and so if you have two or three levels, you have effectively lost all those membership enumerations. Third, your universal groups will all look like global groups to the downlevel clients or domains. Finally, any global groups created in the Windows 2000 world will only show the global users who are members. Other members, such as nested global groups or universal groups, will not be listed. I think you can imagine the impact this will have on setting resource permissions.

Mixed-Mode Operations and Groups

While we are on the subject of downlevel clients and domains, let's look at a related topic: what happens to group functionality in the mixed-mode domain. We have already discussed some of the things you will be missing out on if you are not operating your Windows 2000 environment in full native mode. Full group functionality is another one of the advantages you will lose by operating in mixed mode. Remember that mixed mode exists for backward compatibility with legacy NT systems. As a result, you shouldn't be too surprised to find out that the group rules in a mixed-mode environment are basically the NT 4 group rules.

For example, when dealing with security groups, you can only create local and global groups. Universal groups are not allowed. The only type of group nesting that is allowed is for a global group to be a member of a local group. This makes sense because your NT 4 components of the mixed-mode environment wouldn't have a clue about what to do with a universal group or deep group nesting.

Some people are surprised by the fact that although limitations exist when creating security groups, distribution groups can still be created and used. In addition, all three types of groups can be used when creating distribution groups. Why? Simply because these distribution groups are not used by the operating system; they are used by application environments and, as such, have no impact on permissions or system rights.

Built-In Groups

As you might expect, Microsoft has provided several built-in groups to make your life as an administrator easier. These built-in groups are classified as security groups because they are used to assign default permissions and system rights. Groups like these existed in all previous versions of NT. The concepts are the same, but some of the group names have changed. Furthermore, where the system-defined groups are stored has changed with the addition of the Active Directory. When you have an Active Directory structure defined in a domain, the built-in groups are stored in designated Active Directory containers.

As with NT 4, the groups that appear in your directory or user management tool are dependent on the role defined for the machine at installation. Workstations and member servers have different built-in groups than domain controllers. After all, what sense would it make to have a "Domain Administrators" group in the SAM of a standalone Windows 2000 Professional box? In the next section, we'll cover the built-in groups and their storage locations for all Windows 2000 machines in your environment.

Regardless of whether you are talking about a workstation, server, or domain controller, you have the capability to restrict the memberships in these built-in groups through the use of policies. With the group policy editor, you can set local security policies.

Workstation and Member Servers

Workstations and member servers have the same list of built-in groups, just as they did in NT 4. The only type of built-in groups that exist on these machines are local groups. The groups are stored in the local SAM and affect only the local machine rights and permissions.

The different default groups and the default memberships of those groups appear in Table 6.1.

Table 6.1 **Groups and Memberships for Windows 2000 Professional and Windows 2000 Servers Running as Member Servers**

Group Name	Default Members	Powers
Administrators	Administrator	Members of the Administrators group have full control over the computer. It is the only built-in group that is automatically granted every built-in right and capability in the system.
Backup Operators	None	Members of the Backup Operators group can back up and restore files on the computer, regardless of any permissions that protect those files. They can also log on to the computer and shut it down, but they can't change security settings.
Guests	Guest	The Guests group allows occasional or one-time users to log on to a workstation's built-in Guest account and be granted limited abilities. Members of the Guests group can also shut down the system.

continues

Table 6.1 **Continued**

Group Name	Default Members	Powers
Power Users	NT AUTHORITY\ INTERACTIVE	Members of the Power Users group can create user accounts, but can modify and delete only those accounts they create. They can create local groups and remove users from local groups they have created. They can also remove users from the Power Users, Users, and Guests groups. They cannot modify the Administrators or Backup Operators groups, nor can they take ownership of files, back up or restore directories, load or unload device drivers, or manage the security and auditing logs.
Replicators	None	The Replicators group supports directory replication functions. The only member of the Replicators group should be a domain user account used to log on the Replicator services of the domain controller. Do not add the user accounts of actual users to this group.
Users	All users of the computer	Members of the Users group can perform most common tasks, such as running applications, using local and network printers, and shutting down and locking the workstation. Users can create local groups, but can modify only the local groups they created. Users cannot share directories or create local printers.

Naturally, you can add and delete members from these groups. You can even rename the groups. The only thing you can't do is delete these system-created groups. In the workstation and member server world, system rights and capabilities are granted based on membership in these groups, as you might surmise from the last column in Table 6.1. So that you have a quick reference as to the available rights and who is assigned them by default in a vanilla Windows 2000 workstation or member server, I have put them in Table 6.2 for you.

Table 6.2 **Groups and Rights**

Right	Group(s) Granted To
Access this computer from the network	Administrators, Backup Operators, Everyone, Power Users, Users
Act as part of the operating system	Not defined
Add workstations to a domain	Not defined
Backup files and directories	Administrators, Backup Operators
Bypass traverse checking	Administrators, Backup Operators, Everyone, Power Users, Users
Change the system time	Administrators, Power Users
Create a pagefile	Administrators
Create a token object	Not defined
Create permanent shared objects	Not defined
Debug programs	Administrators
Deny access to this computer from the network	Not defined
Deny logon as a batch job	Not defined
Deny logon as a service	Not defined
Deny logon locally	Not defined
Enable computer and user accounts to be trusted for delegation	Not defined
Force shutdown from a remote system	Administrators
Generate security audits	Not defined
Increase quotas	Administrators
Increase scheduling priority	Administrators
Load and unload device drivers	Administrators
Lock pages in memory	Not defined
Log on as a batch job	Not defined
Log on as a service	Not defined
Log on locally	Administrators, Backup Operators, Guest, Power Users, Users
Manage auditing and security log	Administrators
Modify firmware environment variables	Administrators
Profile single process	Administrators, Power Users
Profile system performance	Administrators
Remove computer from docking station	Administrators, Power Users, Users
Replace a process level token	Not defined
Restore files and directories	Administrators, Backup Operators
Shut down the system Power Users, Users	Administrators, Backup Operators
Synchronize directory service data	Not defined
Take ownership of files or other objects	Administrators

You used to be able to change these rights in User Manager, but naturally, that has changed in Windows 2000. To change rights assignments and add or delete new groups or users from the rights list, you must access the Local Group Policy Editor. Go to Computer Configuration | Windows Settings | Security Settings | Local Policies | User Rights Assignment.

Domain Controllers

As you might expect, there are also predefined groups set up on domain controllers. All predefined groups are housed by default either in the Users or Builtin folders in the directory.

The Builtin folder houses all the local groups that will define local rights to administer the domain controller itself, just as these types of groups would on a workstation or member server. The local security groups and their default memberships and rights are listed in Table 6.3. These groups are not considered to be domain local groups, but are actually referred to by Microsoft as Builtin Local groups to differentiate them from domain local groups. As you can see from the table, the group names are different from those for a workstation. For example, you'll notice there is no Power User group. On a DC, the Power User's functionality is divided into three other entities: Server Operators, Print Operators, and Account Operators. The good news is, if you are an NT 4 administrator, you'll recognize these groups because they haven't changed a bit except for the addition of the Pre-Windows 2000 Compatible Access group.

Table 6.3 **Built-In Groups on DCs**

Group Name	Default Members	Powers
Account Operators	None	Members can create and administer user and group accounts.
Administrators	Administrator	Members of the Administrators group have full control over the computer/domain. Because we are talking about built-in groups on domain controllers, controlling the machine is the same as controlling the domain. As with Windows 2000 Professional, this is the only built-in group automatically granted every built-in right and capability in the system.
Backup Operators	None	Members of this group are allowed to back up and restore files on a system regardless of the DACLs set for that file system object. This is a prime example of system rights overriding DACL settings. Remember this for the security implications.

Group Name	Default Members	Powers
Guests	Domain Guests, Guest, `TsInternetUser`	Guests can't do much. They can use the computer, but they can't install software or make system changes.
Pre-Windows 2000 Compatible Access	None	From the name, you can infer that this group is here to achieve backward compatibility with legacy NT systems. Members of the group are allowed Read access to all users and groups in a given domain.
Print Operators	None	Members are allowed to and print queues throughout the domain.
Replicator	None	Supports file replication in a domain. Membership is at the administrators' discretion, but usually includes one or more accounts used by the File and Replication Service in the domain.
Server Operators	None	Members have administrative control over domain controllers.
Users	Authenticated, Users, Domain Users	Just one step above Guests. Users are allowed to use the system and save their documents. They can't, however, install software or devices.

The User folder houses the built-in groups that affect domain administration. These might be domain local, global, or universal group types. Table 6.4 shows you the groups, their type, default membership, and purpose.

Table 6.4 **System-Defined Groups Housed in the Users Container of the Active Directory**

Group Name	Group Type	Default Members	Powers
Cert Publishers	Global	None	Membership consists of enterprise-wide certification and renewal agents and can be used in conjunction with Kerberos interdomain logons and the PKI.
DHCP Administrators	Domain, Local	None	Members have full control over the DHCP servers.

continues

Table 6.4 **Continued**

Group Name	Group Type	Default Members	Powers
DHCP Users	Domain, Local	None	Members are able to view DHCP settings on the DHCP server
DnsAdmins	Domain, Local	None	Members have full control of DNS settings on DNS servers.
DnsUpdateProxy	Global	None	Members are DNS clients who are permitted to act as proxy agents for other clients, dynamically updating the DNS database servers.
Domain Admins	Global	Administrator Account of Domain s Controller	Members are allowed full administrative control of all machines in the domain.
Domain Computers	Global	Any computers that are members of the domain	Member workstations and member servers in a given domain.
Domain Controllers	Global	Domain s Controller	All domain controllers in a given domain.
Domain Guests	Global	Guest	Designed to have members that are infrequent users in a domain.
Domain Users	Global	Administrator, (Domain Controllers), Guest, `krbtgt`, `TsInternetUser`, all other domain user accounts	Domain users have the power to access domain resources to which they have permissions. They do not have the right to log on interactively at domain controllers, or perform any domain administrative functions such as printer administration or adding user accounts to the Active Directory.

Group Name	Group Type	Default Members	Powers
Enterprise Admins	Universal	Administrator account from the domain controller at the root domain in the tree	A group intended to make the cross-domain administration easy to accomplish. You could call this the "super admins" group. This group is automatically added to the local Administrators group on every machine in the forest. Therefore, the members of the group have full administrative privileges everywhere in the enterprise. This is a good thing, just be very careful about whom you add to the group.
Group Policy	Global	Administrator, (Domain Controllers)	Members are allowed to modify domain-level group policy Creator objects.
RAS and IAS Servers	Domain, Local	None	Servers placed in this group have the right to read the RAS properties of domain users.
Schema Admins	Universal	Administrator accounts from domain controllers	Members have full control of the accounts from Active Directory schema and the right to use the Active Directory Schema Manager snap-in. Should be reserved to a very small group of administrators because ill-planned changes to the schema can have a negative affect on all computers and objects within a domain.

Default Permissions of File System and Registry Objects

Naturally, you are interested in the default rights that different groups are assigned, but you might also be interested in the default DACL settings on the vanilla install of the operating system folders and files and the registry hives. These permissions lists are rather lengthy, but they can be very useful when troubleshooting. The permissions tables can be found on the `http://www.microsoft.com` Web site or through TechNet.

Creating Groups

Creating a group can be accomplished in several ways, depending on the role of the machine on which you are attempting to create the group, as well as the scope of the group you are trying to create. For example, if you are on a workstation or member server and are trying to create a group that resides in the local SAM, you use one tool. If you want to create an Active Directory group, you use a different tool. You may even choose to use User Manager for Domains from a downlevel client; that still works. And of course, for those heavy volume tasks, you can always employ scripts to create groups and add users to them. No matter which method you use, they are still all relatively simple and intuitive. Okay, the scripting might be a little tough, but I have given you sample scripts in Appendix A, "Directory Management with Windows Script Host," to help you out there.

Creating Local Groups on Member Servers and Workstations

As you saw earlier in the chapter when we looked at the privileges granted to the User group, anyone who is a user can create a local group on a workstation or member server. Of course, Power Users and Administrators can also create local groups. On these machines, the only type of group that can be created is a local group.

Creating a local group is accomplished by using the Computer Management snap-in. You can access the snap-in by starting an MMC console and adding the snap-in, or by simply right-clicking on the My Computer icon and selecting Manage. Then select the Local Users and Groups node, highlight the Groups folder, and either select New Group from the Action menu bar or go over to the whitespace in the right pane and right-click to bring up the context menu. Select New Group, and you're off and running. Notice that workstations and servers that are members of a domain have the option of choosing members from the local machine's SAM or the domain. Select all the members you want, click the Create button, and voila! A new group is born. That's all there is to it.

Creating Groups on Domain Controllers

As with NT 4, there is really no way to create a truly local group on a domain controller. When you create a "local" group, you are really creating a domain local group that will be replicated out to at least the other domain controllers, and so its scope extends a little further than a truly local group. In Windows 2000, domain local groups are visible throughout the domain.

To create a group of the types we discussed earlier—domain local, global, or universal—you really have only one GUI tool at your disposal: the Active Directory Users and Computers administrative tool. If you start a Computer Management session on a domain controller, you will notice that there is one of those big red Xs over the Local Users and Groups node. If you try clicking on it, Windows 2000 will nicely tell you that you can't use that node on a domain controller. The Active Directory management tool can theoretically be used from any Windows 2000 computer to remotely administer the directory. At the time of writing, however, this tool was not yet available for use on the Windows 2000 Professional product desktop; you could only get it if you were running a Windows 2000 Server product. Personally, I believe Microsoft will have this available by final product release, but if not, you still have other options you can use. For example, from any downlevel system (NT 4 Server, Workstation, Windows 9x box), you can use User Manager for Domains to create new groups on a Windows 2000 domain controller. The only problem is that you can't get the same functionality when it comes to being able to create a group in a particular OU. When you use this method, all groups are created in the Users container of the directory. Another difficulty with this method is that User Manager for Domains only supports local and global groups, not universals.

Remember that if you create a domain local or global group, the group is stored as part of the Active Directory for that domain and replicated to all other domain controllers in the partition. If, on the other hand, you elect to create a universal group, the group and its membership list are stored in the Global Catalog and replicated throughout the forest whenever the catalog is updated.

In addition to the Windows 2000 native tool set, it is possible there will be third-party solutions in the user and group management space, just as there were in NT 4. I personally don't think there is as much need for additional tools in this new product, but I'm sure someone like Hyena will notice something that is missing and fill the gaps with a really spiffy solution.

I'm not going to go into great detail about how to use the interface to create groups because it so simple to use. You select the Active Directory container in which you want to create the group.

As you can see in Figure 6.5, you can specify a security or distribution group category and elect to create any of the three group types. As I said earlier, the interface couldn't be much easier to use. Now that the group is created, all you have to do is go back and put members in it.

Alternatively, you can back into the process by first selecting your users and then creating the group. Figures 6.6 and 6.7 show you that process. Select the members using the multiple object selection key combinations (Shift or Ctrl key plus left mouse click), and then right-click and select Add Members to a Group. Then select the group you want to add those members to from the list provided, and that's it.

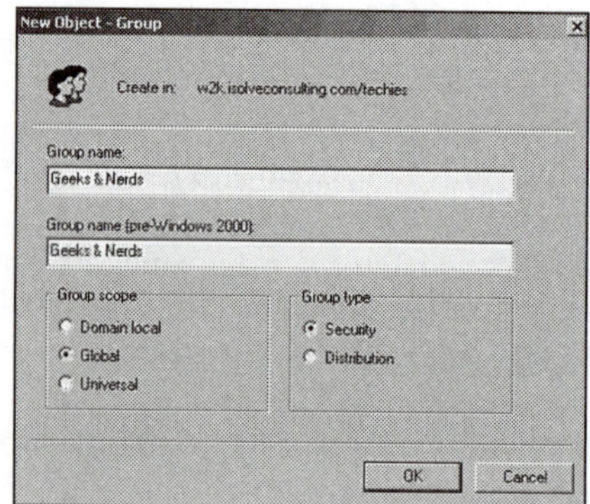

Figure 6.5 Select New Group, and then name the group.

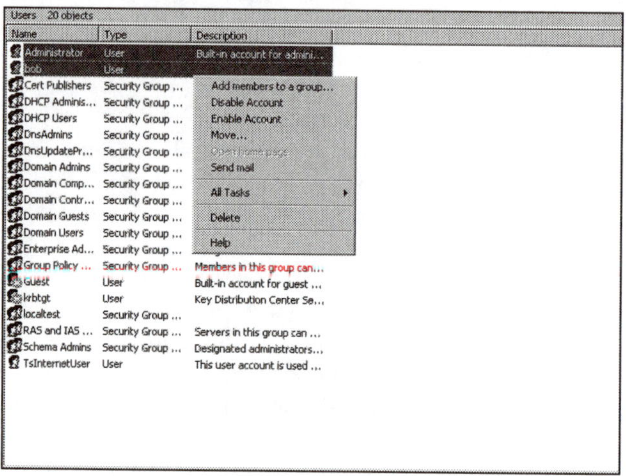

Figure 6.6 Multiple user selection.

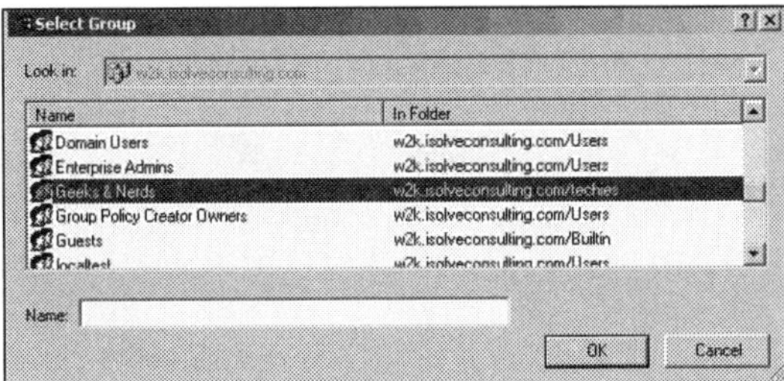

Figure 6.7 Select the group from the list provided.

Remember when I mentioned earlier that the Novell folks were going to give you a hard time about not being able to set permissions based on OU membership? I also said you would have to create a group to reflect that OUs membership and then use the group to set rights and permissions. That sounded like an extra step and kind of a pain to do, but I'm here with good news. Microsoft has made it really easy to create that group. The next two figures show you how to quickly put all the security principals in a certain OU in a group. You simply right-click the OU, as seen in Figure 6.8, select Add Members to Group, and the system will ask you if you want to add all the contents of the container (OU) to the group. If that's what you want, say Yes, and you have a new group that contains all your OUs security principals. This is especially convenient for creating distribution category lists for email and software distribution as shown in Figure 6.9.

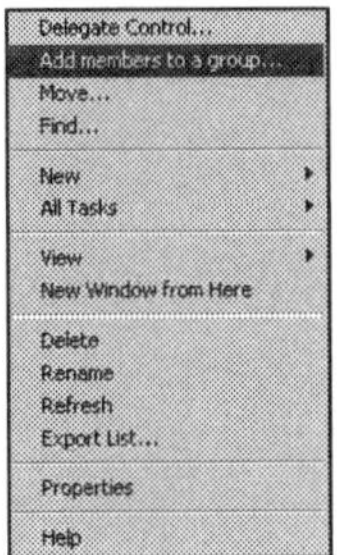

Figure 6.8 A shortcut for creating a group that mirrors an OUs membership.

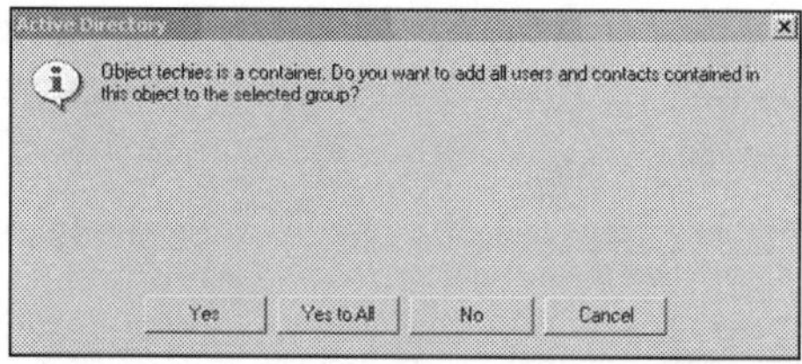

Figure 6.9 Dialog asking your intent.

Adding Users to Groups Through Scripting

GUI tools are all well and good, but sometimes you just need more horsepower for a high-volume job. In Windows 2000, you'll use the Windows Script Host (WSH) to apply those scripts that can create groups and add users to them. Appendix A, has some Visual Basic examples you might use for that purpose. As I mentioned in Chapter 1, "Inside Windows 2000 Overview," any of the supported scripting languages can be used for this purpose. My only advice is to know your LDAP!

You might not ever need to do a lot of high-volume group creation and management because all your NT 4 and Novell groups migrate very nicely to the Windows 2000 environment with membership lists intact. You may have to move them around the tree structure after they come in, but at least they'll be there. About the only time I can see you needing to do some heavy duty scripting for group management is if your current group structure really doesn't match what you have planned for your new Windows 2000 AD structure. If this happens, additional resources for scripting can be found in the Windows 2000 whitepapers at `http://www.microsoft.com` and also in the Microsoft Software Development Kit (SDK).

Planning for Efficient Use of Groups

Now that you know all there is to know about creating groups, you're ready to start throwing them out there, right? Well, many people might do that, but I know you are different (because you bought this book first!). So, I also know that you are going to want to plan your use of groups carefully. To do that, you need to consider why you are forming groups in the first place. As you have already seen, there are several reasons to form groups:

- First, and most obviously, to set permissions on resources and audit access to those resources
- Second, to assign rights and delegate administrative tasks by group membership
- Third, to further refine the filtering of group policy objects in your environment, as you'll see in Chapter 8, "Employing Group Policies."
- Finally, to set up distribution groups to be used by various applications

When you start planning your group design, many factors will come into consideration. As I've already mentioned, one will be your OU structure. Another factor will be the way your shared resources are organized, and a third might be your planned use of group policies and the IntelliMirror features of Windows 2000.

To make the most of your group design, you'll want to take a structured approach to planning this part of your Windows 2000 implementation. The quickest way to accomplish the task would be to just migrate over your existing NT 4 groups, but if you do that, you'll probably end up with a suboptimized Windows 2000 system. It would be like buying a Ferrari and driving it like a '72 Pacer with bad brakes. Get the picture? So, how do you start designing this?

My first bit of advice for a successful effort is to get in synch with other domain and enterprise administrators. I know it doesn't always work politically, but try to keep the lines of communication open between domains. Perhaps you could propose a joint design project, even if people are not going to be migrating over at exactly the same time. This will help a great deal in minimizing duplicate groups and, therefore, improve network response time due to reduced replication traffic. That benefit usually sells most folks on the benefit of cooperation! Nobody wants the boss asking why the network is so *&#%@ slow.

A second bit of advice I can give you is to look at the four reasons for creating groups I mentioned earlier and consider them one at a time. If you focus on one purpose at a time, you often get a clearer picture of what you want to accomplish. Don't be afraid of duplicate groups at this stage. This is just a paper exercise, and you can always reduce the fat before you implement the design. Concentrate, for example, on resource permissions, and then map your resources and OU structure to the group structure. Next, you might want to focus on group policies and again map the planned use of policies to the Active Directory structure. Then look at any additional filtering you might need to do with groups. Continue this way until you have covered all four areas of functionality.

Third, follow the "keep it simple" theory of design here. What I mean is, design for ease of maintenance. Think about what it will be like to troubleshoot problems with the structure you are creating. If you are the one who has to administer the system, you will probably do that automatically. Try to keep group nesting to just a few levels that are easily identified. For example, if you have a group, Novell Access, which is made up of two other groups, Domain Users and Domain Admins, it's very easy to trace the membership of those member groups. You can even logic it out in your head. But what if you have the same Novell Access group, with Bob's Folks as one group listed as a member and MMCG Workgroup as the other member? Now it's not quite as clear cut. A troubleshooter's first question would be, which Bob? It could get confusing very quickly.

In the keep-it-simple vein, you could also lobby hard with the proper authorities to get the OU structure and resources closely aligned—for example, to ensure that the shared resources for the Accountants are in the Accounting OU. Then you can create a group for that OU and set resource permissions and auditing. Life becomes a little better for everyone that way, and you won't be spending as many late nights troubleshooting as you might otherwise.

Keeping it simple will also help achieve that lower total cost of ownerhsip (TCO) you have a good chance of accomplishing with Windows 2000. I can tell you, though, that lower TCO isn't going to happen just because you install a Windows 2000 domain controller. You have to do some planning and then actually use the features of the product that will buy you lower TCO. Good group planning helps.

As usual, you can go to the Microsoft Windows 2000 Server Web site and get help with deployment and migration issues. In addition, the Planning and Deployment Kit that comes with the Corporate Preview Program is a good reference.

Environment Management

7

User Profiles

OFTEN THERE IS A NEED TO CONTROL A USER'S ABILITY TO CHANGE (play or experiment with) his computer's environment. There may be several reasons for this, and not all of them have to do with the administrator being a demented, control freak (as I have heard more than one user describe me).

Sometimes, a requirement exists for a default configuration to be maintained, as would be the case in a training environment or university computer lab. If there were no controls in place, every student who used a machine would be able to configure it to his preferences, and the next user would be stuck with those preferences. I think you can see the obvious problems that would occur. One student could set blinding colors, install personal applications, remove needed applications and shortcuts, as well as destroy network and printer connections. In this case, the administrator needs to decide what the "student" environment should be and then take steps to guarantee, through the use of environmental controls, that each student will get that environment when he logs on.

Another reason to exercise some control over the environment is to simplify the environment for the less sophisticated user. If your organization is composed of computer-literate, relatively high-end users, you may have forgotten that not everyone in the business world is like that. High-level users typically want administrators to have less control and always want to complicate their desktops with new gadgets and applications. The less-literate user, on the other hand, wants simplicity. The user clicks an icon, the machine does what it is supposed to. For these users, the PC is simply a tool to accomplish their real work, and they don't want complicated tools. I compare this idea to what I would do if I were setting up an environment for my Russian grandmother. Find out what she wants to do, get the icons up there, and lock it down so that she couldn't change anything or delete the icons. This is not an insult to her intelligence. I just know that she has better things to do with her considerable brainpower than trying to figure out how to get this "helpful, user-friendly tool" to accomplish what she wants to do without getting very frustrated in the process. I have learned from more than one user that I can't do their jobs, and they don't want to do mine!

With NT and Windows 2000 systems, there are basically two ways to achieve this goal of environmental control. The first and most rudimentary is through the use of user profiles. The second, a more sophisticated and, I believe, preferred method is through the use of system and group policies. Both methods have their place in the administrator's toolkit. We will discuss group policies and their use in Chapter 8, "Employing Group Policies."

In this chapter, I want to focus on the user profile because there is often some confusion surrounding the topic of profiles in Windows 2000. For that matter, the same confusion existed in previous versions of NT. I'd like to use this chapter to make sure that the idea of a user profile is well understood before I start talking about policies. Let's start with the basics.

Defining a Profile

Many people, users, and some administrators, seem to think that a user profile is something the administrators define and then force down to poor, unsuspecting users. Although there is a way for an administrator to use profiles to achieve this objective, it is the exception rather than the norm.

Normally, a user profile is kept by NT and Windows 2000 as part of the everyday operational mode of the machine. What we call a "user profile" is a collection of settings the user can configure to meet his individual preferences. Desktop settings such as wallpaper, screen resolution, applications on the personalized menu bar, and icons that are visible on the desktop can all be part of a particular user profile. These settings are all saved to the individual user's profile folders or the individual's hive file, `ntuser.dat`. Once set, these individual user preferences, along with the universal settings the administrator has defined for all users of a particular machine, combine to create the desktop environment a user sees after he has logged on.

In the default operating mode, these individual preferences are kept in the file system of the local hard drive for each machine to which a user logs on. The universal settings are kept on the hard drive as well. When a user logs on, the registry settings for the environment are set using the information from the hard drive.

Profiles are kept in the local file system, as I mentioned above. In Figure 7.1, I have shown you the structure in a new install of Windows 2000. As you can see, the users' directories, as well as the All Users directory, have been moved out from under `%systemroot%`, and now exist in a directory called Documents and Settings that sits directly off the root of the hard drive where NT is installed (`%systemdrive%`). This change happened in the Beta 3 release of Windows 2000, and it really is a change for the better. One of the complaints about NT 4 was that you couldn't lock down the permissions on the NT system files because of the Profiles directory sitting there that needed all those individual user permissions. This meant you couldn't start at C:\WINNT, for example, and force Read-Only permissions down the tree for the Everyone group. It made life a little interesting to get those profile permissions correct on every single machine and still protect yourself from the user who drags and drops the System32 directory to somewhere else on the hard drive by mistake. With this change in file location in Windows 2000, you can protect all of the `%systemroot%` directory and treat the Profiles directory as a different security entity.

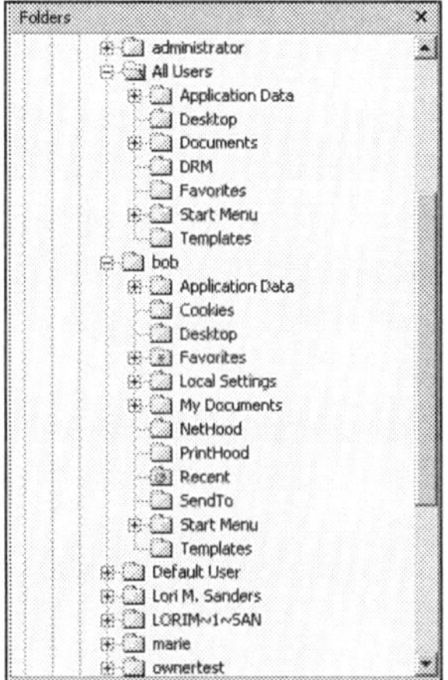

Figure 7.1 File structure showing location of user profile paths in a new Windows 2000 installation.

What about all those scripts you wrote for NT 4 using the Profiles directory naming convention? Well, if you are upgrading NT 4 boxes to Windows 2000, you don't have anything to worry about. In the case of an upgrade, Windows 2000 preserves the location of the Profiles directory for the sake of backward compatibility. If you have a mixture of new machines and upgraded machines, you have a mixture of these two naming conventions by default. If you are planning on using all new machine installs, you might consider using a universal replace on your scripts.

Variables

As we go through this discussion of profiles, I will be making reference to several common variables that are used when creating scripts and profiles intended to run on several machines or are used by many users. Here's a quick list of those you can reference throughout the rest of this chapter if you aren't already familiar with them.

- `%username%` The logon name of the user.
- `%userdomain%` The domain where the user's account resides.
- `%systemdrive%` The drive where NT/Windows 2000 system files are installed, also known as the boot drive in Microsoftese.
- `%systemroot%` The install folder for NT/Windows 2000. By default, this is WINNT, but it can be changed during installation to anything the user wants. This is the reason for the variable; no matter what a user has named his directory, a script written using this variable will find it.
- `%homedrive%` The user's local drive letter connected to his home directory. If you have mapped H: as that drive letter, H becomes the value for the variable.
- `%homepath%` The full path of the user's home directory.
- `%homeshare%` The share name that contains the user's home directory folder.
- `%OS%` The operating system of the user's workstation. Very helpful when creating "If, then, else" type logic in scripts in a mixed OS environment. For example, when distributing batch All User profile updates to your mixed NT 4 and Windows 2000 domain workstations, you can specify the All User directory location based on this variable.
- `%processor%` Allows for designation of processor type (such as 80486 versus Pentium) so you can distribute applications or other elements based on the processing power of the desktop environment.

There are others. Many, many others, actually, but for our purposes, this list will suffice. If you do want to get deeper into writing these scripts and using more of the available variable set, any good book on the NT registry will give you a complete list. One of my favorites for a deep look at this type of stuff is a Macmillan Technical Publishing book, *Windows NT Automated Deployment and Customization*, by Richard Puckett (ISBN: 1578700450).

Elements of the User Profile

As I mentioned earlier, the user's environment is made up of a combination of the All Users and individual user's settings. These are the two basic elements of a user profile. Let's have a look at the types of settings you can control in each of these elements.

Individual User Component

As you can see in Figure 7.1, the individual user profile is actually composed of several folders as well as the `ntuser.dat` file that houses the actual registry settings. Each of these folders houses a specific type of information for the user, so let's look at each one individually.

- **Application Data.** This folder contains application preferences for each user of an application. For example, if we shared a machine and each used the same copy of Word while logged on, this folder would be where Windows 2000 would remember that you liked to run your Word in full-Window mode, while I liked a partial Window. Custom dictionaries and our individual list of recently opened Word documents would also reside in this folder. Be warned, though: the use of this folder is application-specific. That means it's up the software vendor to determine how they want to use this feature.
- **Cookies.** This folder contains the user's Web cookies that have been downloaded as the user accessed Web pages on the Intranet or Internet. These cookies are then used to speed access or change the behavior of a particular Web page when the user next accesses that site. Cookies can be used to provide state information in the stateless HTTP environment.
- **Desktop.** This folder contains any items a user stores on the desktop. These can include files, folders, and shortcuts. My Computer, My Network Places, and Recycle Bin are not included in this folder.
- **Favorites.** Among other things, shortcuts to Web pages you have specified as Favorite sites in Internet Explorer reside in this folder. It can also be used to store other files and folders. In Windows 9x compatible programs, this folder is usually listed as one of the default locations when you select File | Open.
- **Local Settings.** This folder is made up of four subfolders: Application Data (a different one!), History, Temp, and Temporary Internet Files. The difference between this Application Data and the one listed above is that this one is used for Roaming User Profiles.
- **My Documents.** This folder is a place for user documents. This is the folder where most of your Windows compatible applications are going to point for file opens and saves. By default, My Documents contains one subfolder, My Pictures. This is the new default location for any file that is in a recognized graphics format.
- **NetHood.** This folder contains shortcuts to a user's existing network connections that show up when the user opens My Network Places on the desktop.
- **PrintHood.** This folder contains shortcuts to items in the Printer folder.
- **Recent.** This folder contains shortcuts to a user's recently accessed folders and files. When you use the Start | Recent menu, you will see part of this list. Quite honestly, I've not yet figured out what the limits are on this folder, as far as how many shortcuts it will keep. As far as I can tell, it has kept a shortcut for everything my users have opened since we installed Windows 2000 on their systems.

- **SendTo.** This is where you can determine what shows up on a user's Send To menu when they right-click on an object. The defaults, of course, are 3_ Floppy, Desktop (as a shortcut), Mail Recipient, and My Documents.
- **Start Menu.** This folder contains all the information and shortcuts for what the user sees when they access their personal Start menu. You can set these directly by manipulating the user profile or the user can use the Start menu Wizard using Start | Settings | Taskbar | Start Menu. Any items installed in this folder will only show up when that particular user is logged on, so if Bob installs Word and Mary installs Monster Truck Madness, they won't be able to see each other's applications listed on the Start menu. They could still go to the hard drive and start the program that way if the permissions allowed for it. If sharing of programs is required, an administrator should install the program in the All Users Start Menu folder.
- **Templates.** Microsoft says "User template items." What does that mean? When you install a program that includes standard templates (or conversion tools for other applications of a similar nature—such as Excel and Lotus—that require templates), they are stored in this folder. When you install Excel with the Lotus conversion tools, for example, you will see the typical Excel template, an Excel 4.0 template for backward compatibility, a Lotus template, and a Quattro template. Again, these appear for applications installed by a particular user. If the program was installed for All Users, the templates will appear in the All Users/Templates folder.

In addition to these folders, three files appear. `Ntuser.dat` contains the individual user's registry settings, as I mentioned earlier. Examples of these settings would be items that have explicit registry entries, such as the background color of the desktop or the screen resolution. The `ntuser.dat.log` is the log file for `ntuser.dat`. The last file is the `ntuser.ini`. The default security settings for all the folders in a user profile give Full Control to Administrators, the individual user, and the System. No other security entries are defined, but as with all file system objects, new access control entries can be added.

Duplicate User Profiles

Occasionally, you will notice that there are actually two profiles created with the same username. The second has a suffix of .000. I've noticed that sometimes these secondary profiles appear for no apparent reason, and it can be a troubleshooting headache to figure out exactly which profile a user is pulling settings from when he logs on. Of course, the easy thing to do is log on as an administrator and delete the offending .000 profile folder. Okay, that fixes the problem, but inquiring minds (specifically mine) want to know why this happens in the first place. The official Microsoft answer is that the second profile may be created when the system is not sure if this is the same user account or when the original profile is corrupted or unavailable (some helpful person has gone in and changed the DACL!). One support representative told me that, basically, the system gets confused, and this is the way it resolves its dilemma.

One of the nice things that can be done with Windows 2000 is create and run a logoff script that automatically deletes these .000 profile folders whenever they appear.

All Users Component

The folders included in the All Users element of the profile environment include the following:

- Application Data
- Desktop
- Documents
- Favorites
- Start Menu
- Templates

The functionality of each folder is similar to that described above for the individual user. The main difference is that anything put in these folders is available to all users of a particular machine.

Both of these folder sets (All Users and the individual user's folders) are housed in Documents and Settings, or for upgrades, the `%systemroot%\Profiles` folder.

New Users

The individual preferences I have been talking about are all well and good if you have logged on at some time and set them, but what about the new user? A user who has never logged on to a particular machine before has no profile folder to pull settings from, because profile folders are created at first logon. In this case, the user's startup environment is determined by the settings in All Users and the Default User profile folder. When a new user logs on, this Default User profile is copied to the new profile folder that Windows 2000 has created for him with his username. When he logs off, all settings are saved to his local profile folder.

Profile Naming Quirks

Just as with NT 4, the user's profile folder is created from his logon name. If you rename the user account, his profile folder name remains the same. You must manually perform that task on every machine where the user retains a local profile.

Also, post-Beta 3 in Windows 2000 Professional, the system grabs the name the user fills in during the user and company information dialog session of installation and uses that as a logon name. It creates a profile for whoever that is. The first time I installed B3 Professional, I was very surprised to see Lori M. Sanders as my username and profile folder. Just something to be aware of as you roll along.

You'll see in Figure 7.2 that the Default User directory has all the same elements as an individual user profile. An administrator can use the Default User profile as a starting spot for new users on a machine. The administrator can create new folders, shortcuts, basic URL preferences, and set any of the other settings we talked about earlier. This task can also be delegated to nonadministrative users simply by adding them to the ACL for the All User folder tree.

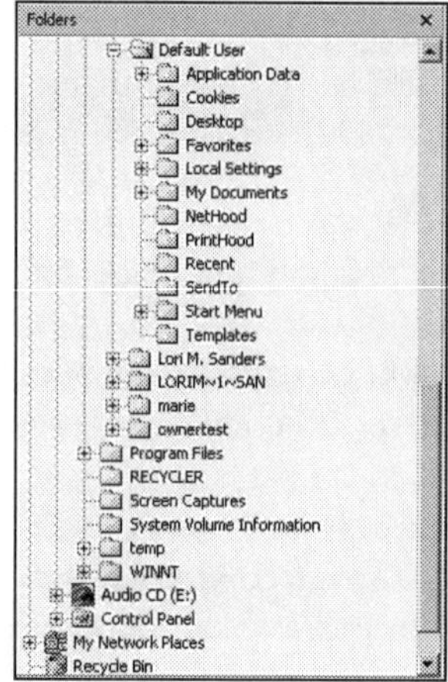

Figure 7.2 The Default User folder structure used to create new user profiles.

An Individual Profile Troubleshooting Tip

If a user has totally messed up his individual profile, simply delete his locally stored profile folders, and he will appear as a new user to the system and receive the Default User profile again.

Applying Profiles

How is this collection of user preferences actually put to use by the system? I've already mentioned how part of the process works in discussing the Default User profile, but let's look at what happens from start to finish.

When a user logs on for the first time, the machine settings have already been set during boot by the hardware profile being loaded. Settings for the pre-logon environment are pulled from the .default registry key. These are the settings for what appears as the desktop when no one is logged on. You can set the company logo as background wallpaper, for example. When a user logs on, the system applies the All User settings to the desktop. Windows 2000 checks to see if the user has ever logged on before by checking for an existing profile folder in his name. If one exists, the user's preferences are pulled from that profile. If not, the system creates a profile folder for the user and copies the contents of the Default User folder into the created folder. The user is then logged on using the contents of the new folder. The settings for All User and the individual user are cumulative. When the user logs off, any changes in settings are saved to his profile folder on the local hard drive. In the "out of the box" Windows 2000 operating mode, this will happen at every machine that a particular user interactively logs on to (profiles are not kept for network logons). Simple, huh? A little later in the chapter when roaming and mandatory profiles are covered, I'll tell you how to change this default modus operandi and some of the reasons it might be necessary or desirable to do so.

What Settings a Profile Can Affect

The folders listed earlier give you an idea of the scope of a user profile and the types of settings that can be changed through the manipulation of the profiles. You will notice that hardware settings are conspicuously absent from the list. That's because you really can't affect machine settings through the use of user profiles. That kind of manipulation is in the realm of hardware profiles and group policies. Sure, you can change things that people think of as "machine" settings, like the appearance of the interface, but those truly are not machine settings, they are software preferences. The difference is hard for some users to keep straight, but from an administrative standpoint, it's pretty simple. If it's in HKEY_USERS, it's a user setting. If the registry setting resides in HKEY_LOCAL_MACHINE, it's a machine setting. Sometimes it's much less confusing to be an administrator!

Default User Versus .default

The .default key is located in the HKEY_USERS hive. As I mentioned, here you can define everything you want to about the appearance a system takes on between logons. Wallpaper, colors, power settings—all kinds of things that you might never even consider can be changed. These settings can be accessed using one of the registry editors.

Logon Scripts and Home Directories

Another point of confusion for some folks is centered around home directories and logon scripts. These are not part of a user profile. Technically, the only thing Microsoft considers "the profile" is the collection of folders and settings contained under the user's folder in the file system.

For more information on logon scripts and home directories, look back to Chapter 5, "Managing User Accounts," under the section, "Creating Users."

Copying Profiles and the Use of Template Accounts

Often, it is convenient to copy a user's account info and profile to a new user who needs a similar environment. If you are planning to do this, be sure and use as many of the system variables I mentioned earlier to make sure that your settings will transfer well to other machines.

One of the most common ways administrators use this idea of copied accounts and profiles is through the use of the template or cookie cutter account. Would you agree that rocket scientists, accountants, and PC support staff probably have different needs as far as their desktop environment is concerned? That they'd want different URLs, network paths, and types of applications? I think the answer would be yes.

One of the things the savvy administrator can do to reduce his or her workload is to determine in advance, and hopefully with the help of the user groups, what exactly each group wants to have on their desktop. Then, once the picture is complete, the administrator creates bogus accounts that can be used as templates for real user accounts as new employees are hired. So we might have accounts named Scientist, Accountant, and PC Support. The administrator logs on with each template account and sets the environments as the user groups requested. Then the administrator logs off, thereby saving the template profile to a hard drive location. Now we have a user account and a predefined environment the user can start to work with. These profiles can be used as starting points that the new employee in a group is free to alter as he desires, or they can be implemented as locked-down desktops for a particular type of user. We'll examine how to accomplish that when we discuss the different types of profiles in the next section.

From our discussion in Chapter 5, you know how to copy a user account, but how do you copy a profile? Well, there is only one recommended way according to Microsoft—by using the User Profiles tab under the System Properties. In reality, there is the old-fashioned DOS-based (Can I say that in a Windows 2000 book?) way as well: Copy the folders and manually change the permissions. I mention this method because if you are using scripts, this command line is the way to go.

There are actually two steps involved in copying a profile for another user to access. The first involves copying the file system object, the template account's profile in this case, to the new user's proper profile location. The second step is to get the file permissions reset so that the new user can access the profile. Let's look at how to accomplish those steps using the Microsoft-approved method, and then let's look at the other way. To copy an existing profile using the graphical interface:

1. Right-click on My Computer and select Properties. One of the tabs you will see is the User Profile tab. (Why this is under system properties rather than the user management node, I have never figured out.)
2. Select the User Profile tab. A list of locally stored profiles will appear.
3. Highlight the profile you want to copy, and click the Copy To button. The dialog shown in Figure 7.3 will appear.
4. In this dialog, type in the target location to which you want this profile to be copied. This can be a local hard drive or network path depending on what type of profile you are implementing for the user.
5. After you have filled in the path, look at the bottom of the dialog and notice the "Permitted to Use" section of the screen. You will see the user who currently has permissions to use the profile. If you simply move this profile to a new location, the DACL remains the same and only that user is able to access the profile. If you copy it to a new location, the folder inherits the permission set of its new parent folder. In order to make sure that your new user has the correct permissions to the profile folder after it is copied, click the Change button and select the user(s) you want added to the DACL for the folder. This action also ensures that the original permission set is removed from the copied folder.
6. Click OK after you have selected the user(s) you want to add.
7. When that window closes, you should see the new DACL entries listed in the "Permitted to Use" box. Click OK again twice to exit the Profiles tab and complete the actions. If you miss any of these OKs, the permissions end up incorrect on the target folder. You can always tell when this happens because the user will get a message about his profile being unavailable or access being denied to his profile. If this happens, simply go directly to the new copy of the profile folder and reset the permissions as needed.

The second way to do this involves old-fashioned DOS batch files using copy commands and a utility to reset the DACL on the folders. Typically you create a batch file using an editor such as Notepad (or if you are a real DOS throwback, `edit.exe`!) to copy the profile folder from one location to another and rename it in the process. After the copy is accomplished, you want to use the `cacls.exe` utility to change the permissions on the folder. For a summary of the `cacls.exe` commands, see Table 7.1. For an example script that copies profiles, renames, and sets permissions, look in Appendix A, "Directory Management with Windows Script Host."

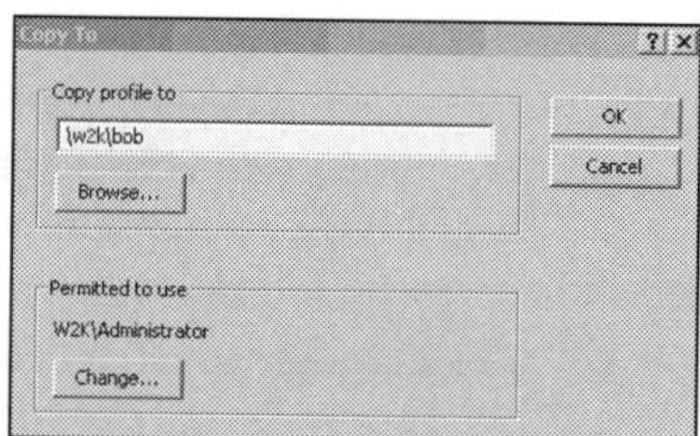

Figure 7.3 Copying profiles with the interface.

The `cacls.exe` utility is a command line utility that allows ACLs to be replaced or altered. These commands can be used when creating batch files to run at logon or during unattended installs. The other uses for it are bounded only by the hacker's imagination. Yes, it can be a security problem if you're not careful. Always remember that every tool you use to make your administrative life easier can also be used by a hacker to make your life miserable. I want to use our powers for good instead of evil, though, so let's look at `cacls.exe` and all the switches and parameters you will need most when accomplishing your administrative work. The format of the `cacls` command line is:

```
cacls.exe filename [options]
```

where *`filename`* is the name of the files or folders that `cacls` is supposed to be applying permissions against.

The available switches for `cacls` are shown in Table 7.1.

Table 7.1 **`cacls` Switches**

Switch	Explanation
/c	Indicates that *`cacls`* should continue to run through the whole file or folder list even if it encounters Access Denied errors.
/e	Probably the most important switch in `cacls`! Indicates that the DACL should be edited, not replaced by the new permissions. The default mode of operation is to replace all permissions in the DACL with the new set specified in the command line, effectively denying access to anyone not specified in your list.
/g user:permission	The grant permission. Permissions that can be granted to a user or group are *r* for Read access, `c` for Change, and *f* for Full Control. *User* is the user or group the access will be granted to.

Switch	Explanation
`/p user:permission`	Replaces a user's existing access control entry with the permissions specified in this line. Rights that can be replaced are `r` (Read), `c` (Change), `f` (Full Control), and `n` (None).
`/r user:permission`	Revokes a permission already granted to the user. Using this switch only makes sense if you are using the `/e` switch, because if you are not using `/e`, all permissions are automatically revoked anyway. Using `/r:username` revokes all permissions granted to a user.
`/t`	Tells `cacls` to search subdirectories for matching files as well.
`/d: user`	Denies access to a user or group.

The `/g`, `/r`, `/p`, and `/d` switches can all take more than one user as arguments so that you can set a whole DACL with one command. Remember that even though I have said `user`, you can specify groups as well as individual users in these command syntaxes.

Static Profiles

Another Microsoftese translation note: The profile model we have been talking about so far in this chapter is sometimes called the static profile model. Not static in the sense that the profile doesn't change, but static referring to the fact that it resides in a static location and doesn't "roam" with the user. It is also sometimes referred to as the local profile. Let's look at some of the other ways we can use profiles in a Windows 2000 domain.

Global Default Profiles

The global default profile allows administrators to configure a new user profile that can be shared by all new domain users and housed in a central location. This makes it much easier to administer and make changes to as the need arises. Doing this allows an administrator to set up needed desktop icons, network connections, commonly used URLs (like the one pointing to the corporate intranet, for example), and any other environmental settings the company wants the new user to have. Imagine how much easier the life of a brand new employee is when all those things are already on the desktop—ready to be used.

To implement this global default profile (sometimes called the network default), the administrator simply creates a profile, sets the environment as desired, saves it, and then copies it to the Default User folder in the NETLOGON share of the domain controllers. This is the only place a global default profile can reside.

When a machine starts up the NETLOGON service, if a Default User profile exists in the NETLOGON share and the domain member machine doesn't have a copy of it on the hard drive, the system logic says to copy that network profile down and store a cached copy of it on the local hard drive. Actually, everything in the NETLOGON share on the server will be copied to the local hard drive at this point if you want to be technically correct. When looking at the local hard drive copies of the profiles, you can always tell the network default from the local default because the folder names are different. The network profile is named Default User (Network), and the local default is simply Default User, either under the `%systemroot%\profiles` directory for upgraded machines or the `%systemdrive%\Documents and Settings` folder for new Windows 2000 installs.

Now that a global default profile has been created and stored when a new user logs on, the system logic says if a network default folder exists on the hard drive, and the network default should be loaded rather than the local Default User profile. The locally cached copy of the network default is compared with the copy in the NETLOGON share. If they are the same, the hard drive cached copy is used. If not, the altered Default User (Network) is downloaded again and overwrites the copy on the local drive.

The only time the local default would not be used is if, when the new user logs on, the locally cached copy of the network profile is corrupted or unusable and the network is unavailable to pull down a good copy. In that particular instance (however unlikely it may be) the system reverts to its standalone profile logic.

After the network default is used to create the user's personal profile and set the initial desktop environment, all the rules are the same as if the user were using a local default. The user can still change settings and save them to his locally stored individual profile, and he will have an individual profile stored on every machine he logs on locally. I stress again that the only thing that changes when global default profiles are used is the location of the new user's initial profile.

NETLOGON Share Replication

Remember that the NETLOGON share path has changed in Windows 2000 to `%systemroot%\sysvol\sysvol\{domainname}\SCRIPTS`. Also, don't make the junior administrator's mistake of assuming that the NETLOGON share is automatically replicated. It isn't. It's not part of the Active Directory. Therefore, automatic replication doesn't happen. This hasn't changed from NT 4. NETLOGON wasn't replicated between the PDC and BDCs there either, but a reminder never hurts!

Roaming Profiles

Another type of profile arrangement you can implement is the idea of roaming profiles. If you're not familiar with these, think of them as a traveling desktop. Instead of being stored on the local hard drive, a user's individual preferences and settings are stored somewhere on the network. Whenever a user logs on to a different machine, the desktop goes with him.

To make any user's profile roaming, you simply enter the path in the user properties using the Profile tab, Profile Path as shown in Figure 7.4. Unlike the global default that must reside in the NETLOGON share, this path can point to any valid UNC path on any server and any share.

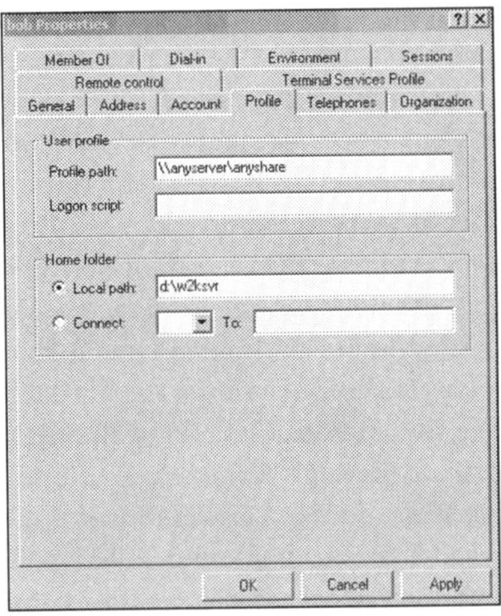

Figure 7.4 Entering the user's profile path to designate the use of a roaming profile.

Configuring Roaming Shortcuts

This "traveling desktop" only works if the shortcuts on the desktop of the roaming profile point to network applications, the network is up and available, and the shortcuts use UNC paths rather than mapped local drive letters. For example, if a shortcut points to `G:\norton\`, that letter may not be available on the client machine and, therefore, the application fails to start. If however, the shortcut points to `\\server1\apps\norton`. As long as the network is up, the shortcut should work. Also logically, if a shortcut points to an application that is installed on the user's local hard drive and he is on another machine, unless the same application is installed in exactly the same place on the machine he's visiting, the shortcut fails.

As a user logs off, his profile is saved to the server location specified in his user properties. A copy is also saved to the local hard drive at logoff. Once a roaming profile path has been specified for a user, regardless of his physical location at logon, the profile will be pulled from the designated UNC path as long as the machine he is logging on to is capable of finding that path. I mentioned earlier that a local copy of the profile is cached. How does the system know which one to use? By default, in an area of good connectivity, the network profile has priority and will be loaded, unless the local profile is newer than the copy saved to the network. In that case, the user is asked which profile he wants to use. The only time this would really happen is if the network connection was down when the user logged off. If the system detects a slow connection, the local profile will be used by default. You can change this behavior using the policy editor. We'll discuss how to do that in more detail in the following section, "Profiles and Slow Network Connections."

You may want to consider limiting the size of a user profile to speed up the desktop load on a machine, as well as optimize network traffic for users with roaming profiles. You might also choose to exclude certain folders from the user profile so that the folders aren't downloading everywhere the user logs on. Both of these tasks can be accomplished on the local machine level using the Local Group Policy (LGPO) Editor. You could also apply the policy at the domain, site, or OU level by invoking the Group Policy Editor using one of the Active Directory management tools.

To edit the LGPO and apply this policy on a local machine, start MMC and add the group policy snap-in to the console. Once it comes up, select the User Configuration node, drill down through Administrative Templates, System, Logon/Logoff. In the right pane, double-click "Limit Profile Size," and you will see the dialog shown in Figure 7.5. If you remember in NT 4, when using the System Policy Editor as you clicked on a check box, it would rotate through the On (checked), Off (cleared check box), and "I don't care, leave it at the Microsoft defaults" (grayed check box) options for each policy setting. In the Group Policy Editor, this same functionality is there, but now there are radio buttons with the choices of Not Configured (meaning Microsoft default mode), Enabled (On), and Disabled (Off). A little less confusing, I think!

To exclude directories, simply double-click the "Exclude directories in roaming profile" icon. You will see the dialog box shown in Figure 7.6. By default, even when this setting is "Not Configured," the Temp and Temporary Internet Files folders are automatically excluded from roaming profile transfers. To specify additional folders, simply enable the setting, and append the folders to the end of the list separated by semicolons.

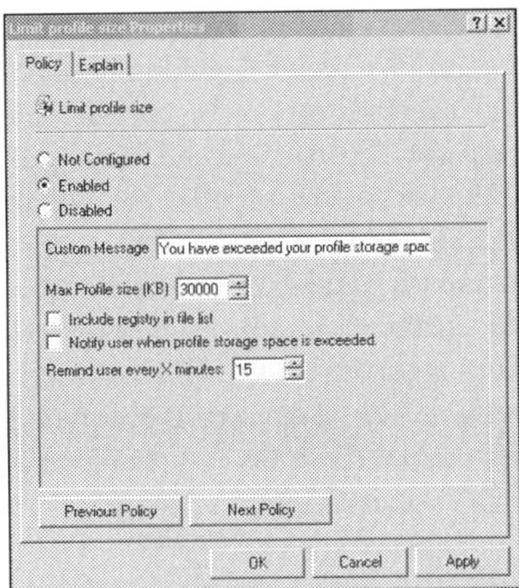

Figure 7.5 Using GPE to limit profile size.

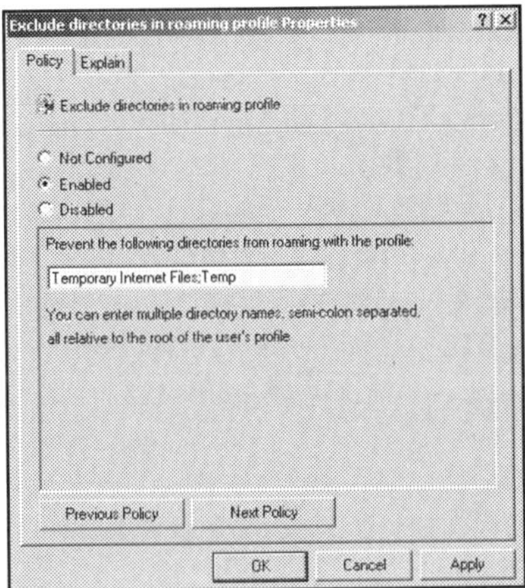

Figure 7.6 Excluding folders from the roaming profile.

To apply a profile size limit at the domain or OU level, use the Active Directory Users and Computers administrative tool, and right-click on the domain or OU to which you want to apply the policy. Select Properties, and then select the Group Policy tab. If you want to apply the policy at a site, select the Active Directory Sites and Services tool instead from the Administrative Tools menu. Right-click on the site, and select Properties and then the Group Policy tab. At this point you can add, edit, or remove policies. Once you have created or selected the policy you want to use, drill down through the Editor just as you would for the local policy (User Configuration, Administrative Templates, System, Logon/Logoff). You will see the same dialog that is pictured in Figure 7.5. (A consistent interface, what a concept!) Apply the "Exclude Directories" settings the same way you did for the LGPO.

If you are using roaming profiles in your environment, one other policy you may want to consider setting on machines is "Delete cached copies of roaming profiles." If this setting is enabled for a particular machine, the local hard drive copy of a user's roaming profile will be deleted as he logs off. Like the policies mentioned above, this policy can be applied at the individual machine, OU, site, or domain level. Often there are "common access" machines in training or conference rooms that people can use to check email or access other corporate resources while away from their usual PCs. In a single day, there may be dozens of different people accessing these workstations. The disk space on these machines quickly disappears if everyone is downloading and storing copies of their roaming profiles there. So, it is something to consider in your policy planning.

Profiles and Slow Network Connections

Windows 2000 has the capability to automatically detect slow network settings. You can set low-end thresholds for acceptable connectivity, which the system will then use to decide if it should try downloading the network default and roaming profiles, or automatically use the locally cached copies instead. This can be helpful for laptop users using a docking station with a 10MB Ethernet card in the office, but using a modem when traveling or working from home.

The policy settings that define a "slow connection," and what action to take if one is detected, are all found in the same place as the setting for deleting local copies of roaming profiles (under Local Computer Policy, Computer Configuration, Administrative Templates, System, Logon). There are four policies that you need to be concerned about.

Changing Profile Types for Road Warriors

These policy settings are nice, but if a user knows that he is going to be on the road for an extended period of time, it might be just as easy to go in and change his profile type on his machine. To do this, bring up the system properties. (Right-click on My Computer, and select Properties.) Select the User Profiles tab, and a list of all the profiles stored on that machine will appear. Select the desired user profile, and click the Change Type button. Finally, select the Local Profile radio button, and click OK. That's all there is to it. You can even get the user to do this before he leaves. Of course, he may decide he wants to keep it this way when he gets back, and you'll have to deal with that!

Automatically Detect Slow Network Connections

This policy is used in conjunction with the "Slow network connection for user profiles" policy. This policy turns on (and off) the capability of the system to automatically detect slow network connections. The "Slow network connection for user profiles" policy sets the thresholds that define what should be considered slow. If this policy is enabled, Windows 2000 will measure the speed of the network connection in kilobits on IP networks. On other types of networks, the system measures the responsiveness of the remote server's file system in milliseconds. If either is slow, the system uses the other policy settings in the Logon/Logoff folder to determine how it should process user profiles.

To use this policy, the "Delete cached copies of roaming profiles" policy must be disabled or not configured.

Slow Network Connection Timeout for User Profiles

This policy allows you to set a threshold that tells Windows 2000 what you consider a slow link. On IP networks, you express the threshold by specifying a minimum transfer rate in kilobits. For other networks, you designate an acceptable response time measured in milliseconds.

For computers connected to IP networks, the system measures the rate at which the remote server returns data in response to an IP ping message. To set a threshold for this test, in the Connection Speed box, type a decimal number between 0 and 4,294,967,200 that represents the minimum acceptable transfer rate in kilobits per second. The default "slow rate" is 500 kbps.

For other networks, the system measures the responsiveness of the remote server's file system. To set a threshold for this test, type a decimal number between 0 and 20,000. This represents the maximum acceptable delay in milliseconds. Here, the default "slow rate" is 120 milliseconds.

Don't Forget About DHCP and RAS Clients!

When setting these thresholds, be sure to consider DHCP clients and machines that may be coming in over dial-up connections. Since you are now able to put computers into groups, you may consider grouping laptops together and applying a separate policy for that group when it comes to network timeouts.

Slow Network Default Profile Operation

If a slow link is detected, the settings in this policy determine whether the default profile is the roaming user profile or the locally cached copy of the roaming user profile. If you disable this policy or do not configure it, the local copy is the default profile. Naturally, you can enable this policy and make the system wait for the roaming profile. Remember, though, that if you have chosen to delete locally cached copies of roaming profiles on exit, your user won't have a locally stored profile to load and will get the Default User profile again. (Funny how all this stuff ties together, isn't it?)

By default, when the system detects a slow roaming user profile connection, it notifies the user and lets him choose whether to wait for the roaming user profile or to immediately load the local copy of the profile saved on his hard drive from the last time he logged off. If the user does not choose within 30 seconds, the system uses the default choice established by this policy.

If you select the "Do not prompt user when slow link is detected" policy, the system selects the default profile whenever it detects a slow connection to the server storing the roaming user profile.

Selecting the roaming profile as the default is appropriate when a user moves between computers frequently and the local copy of his profile is not always current. Using the local copy as the default is desirable when quick logon is the main concern.

This policy is only applied when the "Automatically detect slow network connections" policy is also enabled. Unless you always want the system to use the roaming profile, you shouldn't enable the "Delete cached copies of roaming profiles" policy.

Prompt User When Slow Link Is Detected

This policy enables administrators to choose whether to notify users when the system has detected a slow network connection and asks them if they want to use a local copy of their profile or wait for the roaming user profile. By default, the system lets users choose whether to wait for the roaming user profile or to use a local copy of that profile. If you disable this policy or do not configure it, the system uses the default profile specified in the "Slow network default profile operation" policy without notifying the user.

To adjust the time users have to respond before the default profile is selected, use the "Timeout for dialog boxes" policy. The "Prompt user when slow link is detected" policy is used only when the "Automatically detect slow network connections" policy is enabled.

Well, that pretty much covers what the system will do with profiles when a slow network is a problem. As I mentioned, you want to carefully consider what you set here so that your needs as an administrator, as well as your users' needs, are met. That's the administrators' eternal struggle, isn't it? Good luck resolving it in your organization!

Mandatory Profiles

One last category of profiles we need to discuss is the mandatory profile. A mandatory profile is really nothing more than a roaming profile that is locked down so that a user can't save any changes to the server copy of the profile. Remember the scenarios I mentioned earlier with the training rooms and university computer labs? These are great places to use mandatory profiles. You might also use them in kiosk systems where auto-logon is enabled, or any other system that many users will log on to using the same account.

With a mandatory profile, you must specify the profile path in the user's properties, just as you would for a roaming profile. If the profile doesn't exist on the server, you need to copy the desired profile to the correct place on the server using the methods mentioned earlier in this chapter. After that's done, drill down to the `ntuser.dat` file on the server profile, and rename the file from `ntuser.dat` to `ntuser.man`. In effect, this one step is what makes the profile mandatory because it disables the "save to server" functionality of the roaming profile. Now, when a user who is using this profile logs off, his settings on exit are only saved to the local hard drive. If you have set the system policies to "Delete locally cached copies of roaming profiles," the system will delete this locally stored copy as well.

If you want to take this scenario one step further, you can make sure that a user whose mandatory profile is not available (either because the network or server is down, or because they pulled the network plug to try and get around the profile) is unable to log on at all. To do this, rename the whole profile folder on the server so that it has a `.man` extension. For example, if the profile folder is currently called Bob, rename it `Bob.man`.

Mandatory profiles can be used by a group of users. In our training example, you could store one profile folder called "student" on a server and point all the student accounts to that location as their profile path. As long as the permissions are set accordingly on the profile folders, all the accounts could access the profile. In addition, they could change their environments while they are logged on, but when they logoff, none of those changes are saved to the server copy of the profile.

Disadvantages of Profiles

You can see that profiles can be pretty complicated. No wonder sometimes there is confusion surrounding the topic. Hopefully, I have cleared some of that up for you.

The use of profiles to control users is a topic of hot debate in some circles. (Mostly among people who really need to get out more.) For the rest of us, knowing the disadvantages of using profiles versus using policies is the real issue, and knowing when it is appropriate to use a profile approach instead of a policy.

The main disadvantage of using profiles is that you can only affect the user settings of the registry. In addition, when using mandatory profiles, you have to lock down the whole desktop. You can't be selective about what you want to lock and what you really don't care about. Policies, on the other hand, allow you to give the user some control while keeping control of the things you feel strongly about. Finally, when using roaming profiles, there is the problem of profile size creep. Often uneducated users save documents and other large objects to their desktop. Naturally, this increases the size of the profile and affects the speed at which the desktop environment can be downloaded over the network, not to mention taking up precious server hard drive space. The capability to limit size and exclude directories should overcome this difficulty, however.

The next chapter looks at a way to control users with much more finesse, using group policies. When comparing the profiles versus group policy approaches to user and environment management, you might say it's the difference between painting a canvas with a roller or a small sable brush. The roller will get the job done, in a messy, quick kind of way, but the small brush can let you paint an administrative masterpiece!

8

Employing Group Policies

WITH WINDOWS 2000, AS I HAVE ALREADY MENTIONED several times, you have a much broader range of capabilities than have been available to you in previous NT products for defining settings for your users through group policies. When you create a policy, it is saved as a group policy object and can be applied against Active Directory container objects such as sites, domains, and OUs.

To use domain group policies and apply them against Active Directory objects, you obviously must have at least one Windows 2000 domain controller installed and be using Active Directory. You must also have read/write permission to access the system volume of domain controllers (`sysvol` folder) and Modify rights to the selected directory object. The `sysvol` folder is automatically created when you specify a machine to be configured during installation as a domain controller or when you do a DCPROMO on an existing Windows 2000 member server.

You can also set up local group policy objects (LGPOs) for machines that will function as standalones in your environment. We'll discuss that approach in the section entitled, "Local Group Policy Objects," a little later in this chapter.

Group Policy and Total Cost of Ownership

Why do we want to bother using group policies in the first place? Because we administrators are all irrational, paranoid control freaks who just want to take over everyone's desktop! If you don't believe me, just go ask your users. The real reason, of course, has to do with what this section is all about: lowering the cost of supporting the desktop environment. PC prices may be plunging, but technical support costs aren't.

Recent studies on total cost of ownership (TCO) cite lost productivity at the desktop as one of the major costs for corporations. This loss can be attributed to many factors. It may be a user who, in ignorance, changes his configuration so the PC becomes unusable (also known as the "boat anchor" mode of PC operation). Perhaps he installed a new software package that causes conflicts with the existing desktop environment. To be fair to users, some technical folks, myself included, do the same things to their own machines, or even to users' machines, but we call it troubleshooting. The productivity loss might also be attributed to the fact that a needed application is not available to the user—when a user receives an email with a Visio document attached, for example, and doesn't have Visio installed.

One way to address these issues is for administrators to use group policies to manage desktop environments tailored to their users' job responsibilities and PC literacy levels. With Windows 2000, administrators can manage these desktop environments from a central location using Active Directory group policies. It has been proven that a managed desktop lowers TCO by first reducing user downtime, thereby increasing productivity, and second, by reducing technical support costs for downed PCs.

Applying Group Policies to the Directory Tree

Group policies are created by producing a group policy object that can then be associated with specific Active Directory container objects, such as domains, sites, and OUs. Once assigned to an AD entity, the policy becomes part of a policy chain that is applied down the tree.

Group Policy Hierarchy

Group policies are processed hierarchically in the following order: local policy, site policy, domain policy, and finally, OU policies. Multiple policies are applied from the most distant container within the local domain. Let's say we have a group policy that applies to a user, Bob, and Bob's full LDAP distinguished name is CN = Bob, OU = Catering, OU = Sales, OU = SWOPS, DC = USOPS, DC = pizzaplace, and DC = com. Windows 2000, would start applying Bob's policies by first applying the local group policies, if any, then the site level policies, followed by the USOPS domain level group policies. After that, Windows 2000 would start applying the OU level policies starting at the furthest OU from Bob, SWOPS, and proceeding down through the Sales OU and then the Catering OU. As with NT 4, the system assumes that the policies in closest proximity to the user are the most important.

Policy settings in the Active Directory container closest to the computer or user override group policy set in a higher-level Active Directory container. By default, the group policy settings you define are cumulative and are inherited from parent Active Directory containers. Remember that this is the default behavior. You can use policy, DACL, and registry settings to either force or prevent group policies from affecting particular users or computers in your organization. However, for optimum performance and simplicity, it is best to limit the use of these mechanisms when applying group policy.

Also, you need to keep in mind that the word "cumulative" is a little deceiving when you actually start looking at the behavior of these policies. Although everything is cumulative, some policy settings overwrite others as they are applied over each other and others are indeed cumulative. Let's look at wallpaper and logon scripts as examples. If we set wallpaper for each OU, what wallpaper would our user Bob in the catering OU get? Well, he'd get the Catering wallpaper setting because it's the last to apply and replaces the other OUs wallpaper settings as we get closer to Bob. That's an example of a setting that is overwritten. Logon scripts, on the other hand, will build up and run one after the other as we move down the tree toward Bob. So if we have a domain logon script and a script for every OU, Bob would see four logon scripts process. You can set these scripts to run as visible or invisible (a policy setting, of course!).

Really, what you will need to do is set up a lab and play with these things for awhile to figure out how each policy scenario plays out when applied to your tree.

Applying Multiple Policies

In addition to being able to inherit policies from a higher level container, an Active Directory entity can have more than one GPO associated with it. If this situation occurs, you can specify the order of application of the policies. This is set through the Group Policy tab on the affected Active Directory object. When you right-click on an Active Directory object and select Properties, then the Group Policy tab, the interface will show you all group policies assigned to that object. To change the precedence of the policies, simply use the interface to move the policy closer to the top or bottom of the displayed list. This changes the order in which the policies will be applied.

Conversely, multiple sites, domains, and OUs can use a single group policy object. Although domain policies are not automatically inherited by lower-level domains in a tree or forest, a group policy from one domain can be used within another domain as long as the path to the desired policy is explicitly specified. If you decide to do this, carefully consider (and test) logon performance in the lower-level domains.

Controlling Policy Propagation

By default, policies apply as described in the last section right down the tree within a domain. An administrator can exempt a particular OU from a policy by disabling a policy for an OU. To do this, right-click on the desired AD container, and select the Group Policy tab. Remember, this is the tab that will show you all the group policies applied to the OU. Highlight the offending policy, and set the Disabled flag. Now, unless someone has set the policy for No Override at a higher level, this policy will not apply to this OU. Microsoft recommends that you keep the use of this flag to a minimum because troubleshooting can become a much more complex task as you must look at each OU and decide whether a particular policy is disabled or not.

You can also make sure that no one can override a particular policy, and thus ensure that it will be applied to every OU from the originating container down in the tree. For example, if we set a policy at the SWOPS OU in Figure 8.1, and set the No Override setting in the Policy Properties page, the policy will apply to all OUs below that point, even if an administrator has set the Disable flag on that policy for the Catering OU.

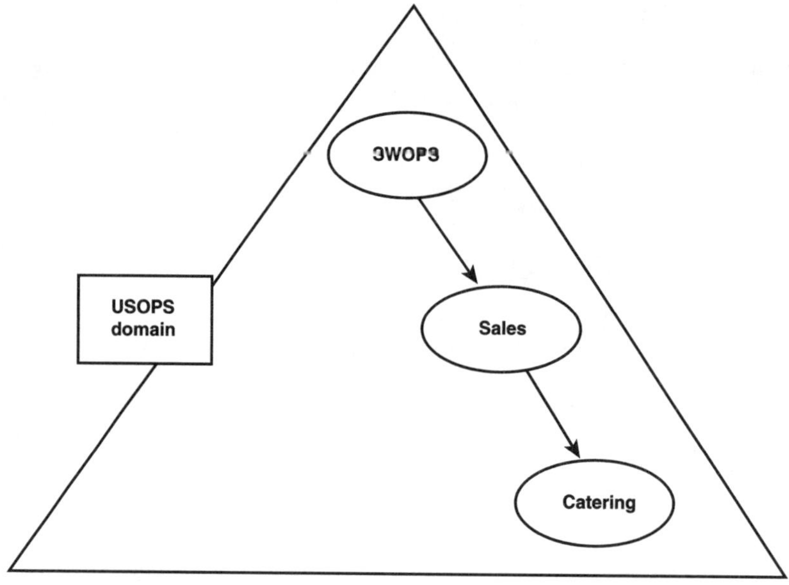

Figure 8.1 Group policy propagation through the USOPS domain.

Administrators can also exempt an individual computer from inheriting policies from their parent site or domain. This is accomplished by setting the following registry switch through either a direct registry edit or by using the local group policy editor on the affected PC:

```
HKEY LOCAL MACHINE\Software\Policies\Microsoft\Windows\System  DisableGPO
Reg_Dword 1,0
```

If you set this switch, the machine will act as if it is a standalone PC rather than a domain member. It will only receive policy from the LGPO and will not inherit any domain or site policies. This would be useful for machines that are remote to the domain: people's home computers, for example, or laptops that are being used on the road. It significantly speeds up the logon time for these users.

Another solution to this dilemma of how to exempt machines from inheriting policies can be achieved by putting all the "on the road" laptops in a single OU or group and then disabling the policy by using the Disable policy option on the OU. You can also filter the use of the policy by setting the Discretionary Access Control List (DACL) so that the group of machines is not given Read access to the policy. In effect, denying Read access means the policy won't apply to a particular user or group. This solution is problematic, though, if there is a higher-level setting of No Override on a policy. In that case, the policy would still apply even though the OU had been exempted. The only way to truly guarantee that a machine is exempted is to use the registry switch mentioned earlier.

Local group policy objects are always processed first, and then the domain policy is processed. If a computer is participating in a domain and a conflict occurs between domain and local computer policy, domain policy prevails. However, if a computer is not a member of a domain (standalones and workgroup machines) the local group policy is applied.

Selectively Applying Policies through DACLs

Even though the OU is technically the smallest unit to which you can assign a group policy object, you can further control the application of policies by using security groups and setting DACLs on your group policy objects. This allows you to apply a policy to certain groups within the OU and also speeds up logon time.

The process for setting permissions on group policy objects is almost identical to file system permission setting, which we talked about earlier in the book. For that reason, I'm not going to drag you through those screens again. The appearance and functioning of the security interface is almost identical.

> **Activating the Local Group Policy Editor**
>
> To activate the local group policy editor, run MMC and select Group Policy from the add-in list. Set the focus to Local Computer, and you now have an MMC console to manage the policies of the local machine. We'll talk more later in the chapter about what policy components are available to you this way when we reach the section, "Local Group Policy Objects."

The first step is to create a group policy object. You can then access the DACL on the group policy by selecting its Properties, and then choosing the Security tab. At this point, you will be able to navigate through the policy's DACL just as you would through a file's DACL. By selecting the Advanced settings option, you can view the DACL, set up an audit list for the policy, and examine the permissions at the most microscopic level. The inheritance settings and rules we talked about for the file system still apply. You will notice that the verbage in the drop-down boxes has changed. For example, you won't see "This folder and subfolders;" you'll see "This object and subobjects."

The default DACL for a policy says that authenticated users have Read permissions, which means that the policy will be applied to all authenticated users. Also by default, domain administrators have full control, as you would expect. This means the administrators can modify the settings contained in the policy. If an administrator wants another group of folks to have the ability to modify the policy, they must be given read/write access to the policy object. This is how delegation of group policies is accomplished. So, the DACL has two purposes. By filtering this way, you can selectively apply policies as well as delegate the responsibility for managing them.

The Group Policy Editor

As we saw in the last chapter, the primary tool for creating, editing, and deploying policies is the Group Policy Editor (GPE), which can be run as an MMC snap-in, or invoked through the Active Directory management console by right-clicking on the Active Directory container object you want to apply the group policy against.

At the root of the GPE namespace are two parent nodes: Computer Configuration and User Configuration. These are the parent nodes whether you are applying a local group policy or distributed group policy as you would if you were going to set policy to a whole domain.

The Computer Configuration node includes policies that specify operating system behavior, desktop appearance, application settings, assigned applications, file deployment options, security settings, and computer startup and shutdown scripts. These are generally applied at system startup.

User Configuration includes all user-specific information such as operating system behavior, desktop settings, application settings, assigned and published applications, file deployment options, security settings, and user logon and logoff scripts. User policies are typically applied at logon.

To change a setting, simply double-click on the policy you want to change in the right pane of the editor. You will see two tabs, Policy and Explain, as shown in Figure 8.2. In NT 4, there were three settings you could set for the policy: on, off, and "I Don't Care." These corresponded to the state of the check box next to the policy in question. If there was a check in the check box, the policy was turned on. The absence of a check meant the policy was turned off, and a grayed-out check box was the "I Don't Care" setting. A good example to use when trying to explain the differences in those settings is the Desktop setting for wallpaper. As an administrator, if you set the Wallpaper setting in a policy to Off, the user can't set any wallpaper. If you turn the setting to On, you specify a path and wallpaper for the user to use (often activated shortly after a general manager has seen a politically incorrect wallpaper on someone's PC). If you select the "I Don't Care" setting, the user can select, change, deactivate, basically do whatever he wants for his wallpaper.

Windows 2000 has the same three choices, but they are expressed a little more eloquently than the NT 4 style check boxes. What you see in the GPE really depends on what node you are examining in the editor. Generally, though, an Off setting will display Disabled. An On setting will either say Enabled or display the actual settings for that node. An "I Don't Care" setting generally shows up as Not Configured or Not Defined. If Not Configured is the option and there is a default value associated with that, the default value may also be displayed. An example of a Not Configured setting defaulting to a value is the Slow Network Connection policy mentioned in the last chapter. If that policy is set to Not Configured, Windows 2000 defaults to 500 Kbps as the minimum acceptable network speed.

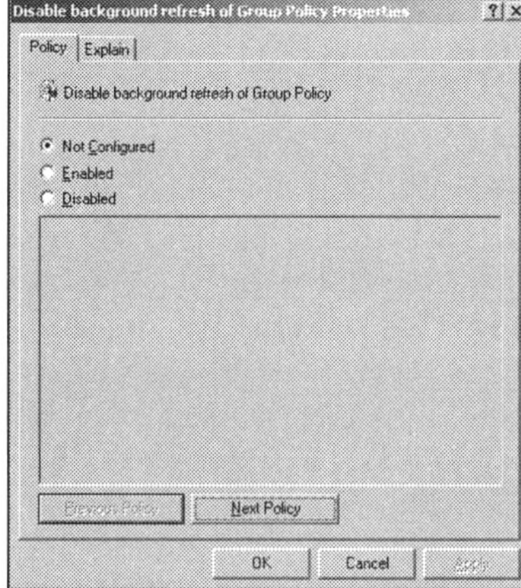

Figure 8.2 Changing the settings on a group policy object.

I do want to talk about the Explain tab for a second. I don't know who programmed this at Microsoft, but they did a heck of a good job on this module. The Explain tab tells you what every policy means and the settings possible, what happens if it's enabled, disabled, or not configured, and the default values if they exist. I've captured one of the screens in Figure 8.3 just so that you can see how much information is there—and this is one of the shorter explanations. Why am I bringing this up? So you'll know it's there and use it!

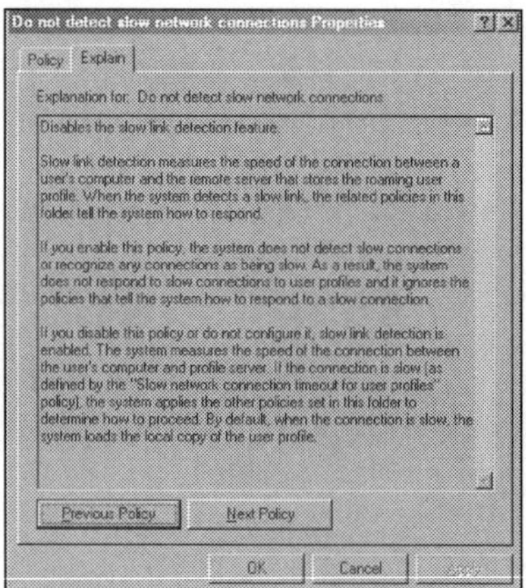

Figure 8.3 A quick look at the Explain tab associated with each group policy.

Administrative Templates (.ADM Files)

The view that is presented to you when you open the GPE for the first time and the options that are available to set at each node are a function of the language in the `.ADM` files shipped with the product. There are five native `.ADM` files shipped with Windows 2000. They are listed in Table 8.1 below. These files are text-based files that specify through the ADM language what registry settings to make available to the editor as well as what parameters may be set and what the acceptable values are for each parameter. For example, if you decide to enable the Wallpaper setting, the .ADM file specifies that a filename is the only acceptable value that can be entered to use as wallpaper. The `.ADM` file would also specify that it must be a graphics file of some kind. In addition to `.ADM` files, the GPE can also use an MMC snap-in extension to the GPE snap-in, but let's concentrate on the `.ADM` template files for now, as you are much more likely to be writing one of those. As with NT 4's System Policy Editor, in addition to the predefined `.ADM` views, savvy administrators can create custom `.ADM` files to extend the capabilities of the GPE.

Table 8.1 Five .ADM Files Shipped with Windows 2000

Filename	Purpose
`System.ADM`	`.ADM` file installed in GPE by default for Windows 2000 clients.
`Inetres.ADM`	Illuminates the Internet Explorer policies for Windows 2000 clients. Installed by default.
`Winnt.ADM`	Included for use with the NT 4 System Policy Editor (`poledit.exe`) to edit settings specific to NT 4 clients.
`Windows.ADM`	Included to illuminate interface options specific to Windows

Filename	Purpose
	9x clients. Meant to be used with System Policy Editor.
Common.ADM	As it was in NT 4, illuminates the settings common to Windows 9x and NT 4 registries.

The .ADM file consists of a hierarchy of categories and subcategories that together define how the options are displayed through the GPE interface. It indicates the registry locations where changes should be made when a particular node is selected. The .ADM file also specifies any options or restrictions (in values) associated with a certain selection. In some cases, it specifies a default value to use when a policy is enabled. For more information on .ADM templates and writing custom .ADM files, see Appendix B, "Custom .ADM Template File Example."

The Role of the Registry

Many people have a misconception about the role of the registry when policies are being applied. They seem to think that a registry is being used from a server somewhere and the local machine's registry is simply ignored. I want to make sure you have a clear understanding of the role of the registry in this process before we start this discussion.

Whether we are discussing NT 4 or Windows 2000 policies, the role of the registry remains the same. The registry holds all the machine and user settings for a particular computer session. As an administrator, you can apply profiles or policies to change the registry settings for a particular machine or user, but the local registry is still the repository for those settings. When a policy is detected and applied, the registry settings of the local machine are changed to reflect the desired state set forth in the policy. I've described the process for you in the next few paragraphs.

How Group Policies Work—The Mechanics

The 10,000-foot level of understanding how group polices work is pretty basic. You create a group policy either by right-clicking on an Active Directory container or by running the MMC group policy snap-in in an MMC console. Then you save the object, set DACLs if necessary to delegate or filter the policy's effects, and sit back and wait for the fun to start. Most administrators want to have just a little more detail than that, however, so let's spend a few minutes exploring exactly what happens in the process from creation of the policy through deployment.

First, all group policy settings are contained in group policy objects that are associated with Active Directory containers (sites, domains, or OUs). Group policy objects store policy information in two locations: a group policy container and a group policy template, which are the topics of the next two sections.

Group Policy Container

The group policy container is an Active Directory object that stores group policy object properties. The object is identified by an English-like name that you specify, like Accountants Policy, as well as a GUID that is used by the system to track the policy. The policy container includes subcontainers for Machine and User group policy information. The group policy container has the following properties:

- **Version information**. Used by the system to synchronize the information in the group policy object with its associated group policy template.
- **Status information**. Indicates whether the group policy object is enabled or disabled.
- **Class Store information**. Used for application deployment.

Group Policy Template

Group policy objects also store group policy information in a file system structure called the group policy template. These folders are located in the System Volume folder of domain controllers (`sysvol`) in the `\Policies` subfolder. The group policy template is the container for all software policy, script, file, and application deployment information.

When you create or modify a group policy object, the directory name given to the group policy template is the globally unique identifier of the group policy object you modified. In other words, the two objects—the Active Directory group policy object and the file system template—share the same GUID. For example, let us assume you have a group policy object associated with our Pizza Place, USOPS domain. The template folder would have the following name:

```
%systemroot%\sysvol\<SYSVOL>\usops.pizzaplace.com\Policies\{Some long GUID
number!}
```

Components of the Group Policy Template

In the root of each group policy Template folder is a file called `Gpt.ini`. This file contains the following information:

```
[General]
Version=0    //Version number of the group policy object
Disabled=0   // 1=disabled - this is only valid for local group policy object
                    (%systemroot%\system32\GroupPolicy)
```

As I mentioned, a local group policy exists on every computer, and by default it contains only security policy. It is stored in `%systemroot%\system32\GroupPolicy`. The `Gpt.ini` file tells us whether the local GPO is disabled or not. For Active Directory group policy objects, this information is stored in the Active Directory.

Group Policy Template Folders and Subfolders

The group policy Template folder contains the following subfolders:

- **Adm**. Contains all the `.ADM` files for this group policy template. How logical!
- **User**. Includes a `registry.pol` file that carries the registry settings applicable to users. When a user logs on to a computer, this file is downloaded and the settings are applied to the HKEY_CURRENT_USER portion of the registry. This User folder can contain different folders depending on the particular machine configuration. Some of the more common ones are listed below:

  Apps. Contains the advertisement files (`.aas` files) used by the Windows installer. These are applied to users.

  Files. Contains the files to be deployed. These are applied to users.

  Scripts. Contains two subfolders. One for Logon scripts and another for Logoff scripts.

- **Machine**. Includes a `registry.pol` file that holds the registry settings that will be applied to computers. When a computer starts up, this file is downloaded and applied to the HKEY_LOCAL_MACHINE portion of the registry. The Machine folder contains the following subfolders:

  Apps. Contains the advertisement files (`.aas` files) used by the Windows installer. These are applied to computers.

  Files. Contains the files to be deployed, and the directory structure matches that of the namespace. These are applied to computers.

  Scripts. Contains two subfolders, Startup and Shutdown, that contain all the startup and shutdown scripts for the machines affected by this group policy template.

- **`\Microsoft\Windows NT\SecEdit`**. Contains the Security Editor file `GPTTmpl.inf`.

The User and Machine folders are created at installation. The other folders are created as needed when policy is set.

registry.pol Files

When information is entered into the GPE, it is saved to the `registry.pol` files. The `registry.pol` files carry the registry settings that will be applied to the Machine (HKLM) or User (HKLU) portion of the registry, as mentioned above when we discussed the group policy template.

> **NT 4 and Windows 2000 Policy Files**
>
> Those of you that are used to NT 4 will notice one major difference between the NT 4 and Windows 2000 policy files. As you'll recall, the NT 4 policy file was binary. In Windows 2000, they're in ASCII text format. You can now (theoretically) use any standard editor and directly examine the contents of your policy file. Won't that be helpful during troubleshooting!

There are actually two `registry.pol` files that are created and stored in the group policy template. One is for Computer Configuration settings. That one is stored in the `\Machine` subfolder. The other is for User Configuration settings and is housed in the `\User` subfolder. The files are created as policies are set, so if you have no policies set other than the defaults, you may not see both files. Once you alter the default policy settings, they will show up.

File Format for the *registry.pol* Files

As you might imagine, given all the changes in the core product and underlying architecture, the format of the `registry.pol` files in the group policy template differs from that of previous versions of Windows NT and Windows 95 operating systems. As you already know if you have administered a mixed-client environment using policy files, policy files created by one operating system cannot be applied to another type of operating system environment. They can *only* be applied to the same type of operating system that was used to create them. The same can be said of the Windows 2000 policy files.

The Windows 2000 `registry.pol` file consists of a header and registry values. One interesting piece of information in the header is version information so that the system can determine the most recent policy if there appears to be a conflict between two stored policy files. For a more complete discussion of the exact formats of the header and these settings, you can refer to the Microsoft whitepaper on Windows 2000 Group Policy at `http://www.microsoft.com/windows2000/library/howitworks/management/grouppolicy.asp`.

How *registry.pol* Files Are Created

When you start the GPE, a temporary registry tree is created with only two nodes: User and Machine. As you wander through the different nodes of the Software Policies section in the GPE, the `.ADM` files associated with a particular node are loaded dynamically when that node is selected, and then the `.ADM` file is cached.

When you expand a policy in the right side of the GPE window, the temporary registry is queried to determine whether the selected policy already has registry values assigned to it; if it does, those values are displayed. If the selected policy does not have a registry value assigned to it, the default value from the `.ADM` file or the associated snap-in extension is used.

> **Using NT 4 Policies with Windows 2000**
>
> Technically, you could use an NT 4 type policy in a Windows 2000 machine, but Microsoft strongly recommends against this. The reason is that Windows 2000 has implemented some intelligence as it relates to the persistence of policies. When a Windows 2000 policy is "unapplied," the settings for that policy return to the previous defaults. With NT 4, once set, they stayed that way, even if the policy was no longer applied to that unit.

After you change a node's settings in the editor, the registry values you specified are written to the temporary registry, in either HKLM (HKEY_LOCAL_MACHINE) or HKLU (HKEY_LOCAL USER). When you close the GPE, the temporary registry is exported to the `registry.pol` files in the appropriate folders of the group policy template. The next time you start the GPE for the same group policy object, even if it's within the same logon session, the registry information from the `registry.pol` files is imported into the temporary registry tree. Therefore, when you view the policies, they will reflect the current state.

Because the GPE stores its information in two locations—the group policy object and the file system—it's possible that policy settings can be overwritten. In the unlikely case where two administrators use the GPE to change the same group policy object at the same time, but are focused on different domain controllers, each administrator can make policy modifications that may end up being overwritten. You should remember that the last policy modifications would be the ones that were saved and are active. This scenario is pretty unlikely if you plan your delegation carefully in a decentralized administrative environment. Keep the number of people allowed to change a particular group policy object to an absolute minimum. In a centralized administrative environment, you will hopefully be communicating with the other administrators on staff so that the right hand knows what the left hand is doing.

Applying Group Policies

When we talk about applying group policies in Windows 2000, there are a few rules (as well as several settings) you should be aware of as an administrator. First, as with NT 4, group policies that affect machine settings are applied at system startup by default. User settings are applied at the start of a logon session by default. This means that when a user logs on, the machine portion of the registry is already set. If settings in either node are changed during a session, they will generally be applied at the start of the next session.

An exception to that refresh model can be set by deciding to apply certain policies periodically. You can set this background refresh rate for computers, users, and domain controllers. Settings for computers and domain controllers are found under the Computer Configuration | Administrative Templates | System | Group Policy node of the GPE. You can set each entity individually (computers or domain controllers). The periodic refresh settings for users are found in the User Configuration | Administrative Templates | System and Group Policy node. In addition, in the Computer Group Policy node, you can also find settings to control the processing of different types of group policies—Security and Software Installation policies, for example. You can also disable background refresh of policies in this same node.

If you choose to apply policies periodically, you can set the periodic refresh interval anywhere from 7 seconds to 45 days (expressed as 64,800 minutes). That gives you a lot of leeway and should cover just about any type of policy you might want to refresh this way. If you select 0 minutes, the computer tries to update the group policy objects every 7 seconds. However, because updates might interfere with users' work and increase network traffic, very short update intervals are not appropriate for most installations. If this setting is enabled, the computer policies are updated in the background every 90 minutes with a random offset of 0 to 30 minutes by default. If you disable this policy, the policy is updated every 90 minutes. Is that insane or what? Even if you disable it, the thing still updates. To make sure that group policies are never updated while the computer is in use, select the "Disable background refresh of Group Policy" policy. For domain controllers, the default refresh rate, if enabled, is 7 seconds, and if disabled, it is 5 minutes. The rules for the user refresh rate are the same as for the computer settings. With the exception of the Application Deployment policies, all group policies can be set to be refreshed periodically.

Why did they leave the Application Deployment settings out? Well, if you think about it for a minute, you can see the logic. Let's say you have decided that users are going to change over to a new word processing software, and so you have unassigned the old word processor and assigned the new one. Keep in mind that if you unassign an application, the system tries to uninstall it when the policy is applied. Now, if this policy were set up to periodically refresh rather than at logon or startup, what do you think would happen if they were using the old word processor when the policy applied? See, it makes sense not to have it refresh except at startup or logon! Especially because you're the one they would call about the documents they lost when you killed their application in the middle of a session.

If you just can't wait, group policies can also be applied on demand. In Windows 2000, there is a `RefreshPolicy ()` API that can be used by applications to apply policy changes immediately. A savvy administrator could also theoretically build a Refresh Now button to force immediate application of a changed policy. This API is also used when a computer changes domain membership. Winlogon will use the `RefreshPolicy ()` API to apply the new domain's policies to the machine without having to reboot.

As with NT 4 logon scripts, you can tell Windows 2000 that you want to process group policies synchronously or asynchronously. You can specify this setting for the user setting or the computer settings. Both of these nodes are found in the Computer Configuration | Administrative Templates | System | Group Policy section of the GPE. The default option is to process group policies asynchronously. (The way logon scripts are processed in Windows NT 4.0 and 2000.)

If you enable the policy to "Apply Group Policy for computers asynchronously during startup," this lets the system display the logon prompt before it finishes updating the computer group policy settings. As a result, the Windows interface might appear to be ready before the computer policies are completely applied. If you disable this policy or don't configure it, users can't log on until the computer group policy is updated. Remember the Microsoft definition of "asynchronous" if you choose to change this setting. Asynchronous in Microsoftese means that things are processed at the same time, and synchronous means serial processing of whatever settings you are referring to.

If you enable the policy to "Apply Group Policy for users asynchronously during logon," this allows the system to display the user's desktop before it finishes loading the user group policy settings into the registry. As a result, the desktop might appear ready for use before the user settings are completely set. If you disable this policy or don't configure it, the desktop is not available to users until the user settings are fully deployed on the machine.

Group Policy and Slow Network Connections

The system's response to a slow connection varies among types of policies. The policy governing how group policies will be deployed over slow network connections actually appears in both the Computer Configuration and User Configuration folders. The policy in Computer Configuration defines a slow link for policies in the Computer Configuration folder. The policy in User Configuration defines a slow link for User Configuration policies.

To use this policy in either node, in the "Connection speed" box, type a decimal number between 0 and 4,294,967,200, indicating a transfer rate in kilobits per second. Any connection slower than this rate is considered to be slow. If you type 0, all connections are considered to be fast. If you disable this policy or do not configure it, the system uses the default value of 500 kilobits per second.

As we discussed in the last chapter when we talked about how profiles behave over slow network links, the policies governing what the system defines as a slow network connection are all contained in "Automatically detect slow network connections" and related policies in the Computer Configuration | Administrative Templates | System | Logon node of the GPE. When Winlogon detects a slow link, it sets the GPO_INFO_FLAG_SLOWLINK flag in the GPO_INFO structure to indicate that policy is being applied across a slow link.

Types of Group Policy Objects in Windows 2000

You can use the GPE to define options for these managed desktop configurations for computers and users. Using group policies, you can define the user's work environment once and rely on the system to enforce your vision. With the GPE you can specify settings for:

- **Software policies**. As I mentioned way back in Chapter 1,. "Inside Windows 2000 Overview," software policies govern the same registry settings that NT system policies affected. Policies affect the client by altering the registry settings of the target machine just as they did in NT 4. Among other things, software policies can be used to configure the desktop for all users of a particular machine, restore settings, set default locations for user directories, and restrict the user's ability to alter the desktop.

- **Security settings**. You can apply security settings in the domain through group policy objects. With the GPE, you can set account policies, local policies (audit, user rights, and other local security options), event log settings, and define the membership of your restricted groups (such as administrators, power users, and server operators). You can also control system settings such as system service configurations, registry hive file security, and file system security.
- **User documents and settings**. You can use these settings to redirect folders to other locations. For example, you could redirect the user's My Documents folder to a network drive to achieve fault tolerance for their files. You could also distribute URLs to all users or a particular group or OU with these policies. You might want to have all the Windows 2000 administrators have a direct link to the Microsoft Knowledge Base or the Windows 2000 Server home page, for example.
- **Application deployment**. Inherited from SMS is the ability to automatically distribute software packages to the desktop. With these deployment policies, you can assign, publish, repair, update, or remove applications for an OU, particular users, or a group of machines. The Microsoft Installer (MSI) tool handles the mechanics of deployment, but the selectivity of deployment is achieved through group policies.
- **Scripts**. In addition to the logon scripting capability that was available in NT 4, with Windows 2000, you can now add logoff scripts for any user, group, or OU. You can also use startup and shutdown scripts for machines, groups of machines, or machines in a particular OU. The Windows Scripting Host (WSH) is fully supported in the deployment of these policies.

Let's go over each of these areas in a little more detail.

Software Policies

The GPEs Software Policies node includes all registry-based group policy information. (This is what the NT 4 system policies controlled.) Software Policies settings include group policy for the Windows 2000 operating system, its components, and applications. These settings are written either to the User or Local Machine portion of the registry database. Policy settings that are specific to a user who logs on to a given workstation or server are written to the registry under HKEY_CURRENT_USER (HKCU), and computer-specific settings are written under HKEY_LOCAL_MACHINE (HKLM).

To generate the namespace under the Software Policies node of the GPE, you use either custom administrative templates (`.ADM` files) or an MMC extension snap-in to the GPE. For more information on administrative templates, see Appendix B.

Security Settings

You use the Security Settings extension to define security configuration for computers within a group policy object. A security configuration consists of settings applied to each security area supported for the Windows NT Workstation or Server. This configuration is included within a group policy object and then applied to computers as part of the group policy enforcement.

The Security Settings extension has been designed to complement existing system security tools such as Access Control List Editor, Local User Manager, and Server Manager. This extension defines an engine that can interpret a standard security configuration and perform the required operations automatically in the background. You can continue to use existing tools to change specific settings whenever necessary.

The security areas that can be configured for computers include:

- **Account Policies.** The term refers to computer security settings for password policy, lockout policy, and Kerberos policy in Windows NT domains.
- **Local Policies.** These include security settings for audit policy, user rights assignment, and security options. Local policy allows you to configure who has local or network access to the computer and whether or how local events are audited.
- **Event Log.** This controls security settings for the application, security, and system event logs. You can access these logs using the Event Viewer.
- **Restricted Groups.** This refers to computer security settings for built-in groups that have certain predefined capabilities. Restricted group policies affect the membership of these groups. Examples of restricted groups are local groups (such as administrators, power users, print operators, and server operators), as well as global groups (such as domain administrators). You can add categories that you consider sensitive or privileged to the Restricted Group Management list, along with their membership information, and then track and manage them. In addition to group membership, Restricted Group Policies track and control reverse membership of each restricted group—the groups to which a selected group belongs. You can use reverse membership to control exactly which groups your restricted members can join, or to limit a selected category of users to one membership group and prevent them from joining any others.
- **System Services.** These control configuration settings and security options (ACLs) for system services such as network services, file and print services, telephone and fax services, Internet/intranet services, and so on. The Security Settings extension directly supports general settings for each system service. This includes startup mode and security on the service. Note that the name of the service must be the same as the one used by the Service Control Manager.

- **Registry.** This is used to configure and analyze settings for security descriptors (including object ownership), the ACL, and auditing information for each registry key. When you apply security on registry keys, the Security Settings extension follows the same inheritance model used for all tree-structured hierarchies in Windows 2000 (such as the Active Directory and NTFS). Microsoft recommends that you use the inheritance capabilities to specify security only at top-level objects and redefine security only for those child objects that require it. This approach greatly simplifies your security structure and will reduce the administrative overhead that would result from a needlessly complex access control structure.
- **File System.** This is used to configure and analyze settings for security descriptors (including object ownership), the ACL, and auditing information for each object (volume, directory, or file) in the local file system.

Microsoft supplies the following set of predefined configuration files for common security scenarios:

- Typical workstation settings (`basicwk.inf`)
- Typical server settings (`basicsv.inf`)
- Typical domain controller settings (`basicdc.inf`)
- Secure workstation settings (`securews.inf`)
- Secure domain controller settings (`securedc.inf`)
- High security workstation settings (`hisecws.inf`)
- High security domain controller settings (`hisecdc.inf`)

By default, these security configuration files are stored in `\%systemroot%\security\templates`. You can use these or other security configurations as the basis for your security settings, and then edit the settings according to your requirements. Security configurations are stored as `.inf` files in a text format. When you create and assign a security configuration or edit an existing security configuration, the Security Settings extension processes the configuration file and makes the corresponding changes to the associated computers as part of group policy.

User Documents and Settings

The User Documents and Settings extension can be used to add files, shortcuts, or folders to special folders that represent the user's desktop. Special folders are those located under `%Windir%\Profiles` or in the Documents and Settings folder in new installs (where `%Windir%` is the Windows NT folder). They include the following folders under the User node:

- Application Data
- Cookies
- Favorites

- Local Settings
- My Documents
- My Pictures
- NetHood
- PrintHood
- Recent
- SendTo
- Start Menu
  - Programs
  - Startup
- Templates

The All Users folder and its subfolders are sometimes referred to in Microsoft's documentation as the Computer Special Folders since the settings contained in those folders will apply to everyone using the computer. Under the All Users folder, you will see the following subfolders:

- Application Data
- Desktop
- Documents
- Favorites
- Start Menu
  - Programs
  - Startup
- Templates

The files you specify are delivered to the user's desktop at either machine startup (if specified under Computer Settings) or upon user logon (if specified under User Settings). The files you place in the Computer Settings node will be available to all users of that computer. The files you place in the User Settings node will be available *only* to the specified user, regardless of which computer the individual logs on to.

Note that you can place any files in the Favorites folder; however, the Favorites menu will *only* display files that are shortcuts—that is, file types that are marked in the registry as "IsShortcut" under the ProgID key. These include `.url`, `.lnk`, `.pif`, and so on.

You can use the User Documents and Settings extension to perform the following tasks:

- Redirect any of the special folders in a user profile to an alternate location (such as a network destination). For example, you could redirect a user's My Documents folder to `\\server\share\%username%`. By redirecting the My Documents folder, you can provide the following advantages:
  - Ensure that the user's documents are available when he roams from one computer to another.
  - Reduce the time it takes to connect to and disconnect from the network. In Windows NT 4.0, the My Documents folder is part of the roaming user profile. This means the My Documents folder and its contents are copied back and forth between the client computer and the server when the user logs on and off. Relocating the My Documents folder outside the user profile can significantly decrease that time.
- Store user data on the network (rather than on the local computer). The data is managed and protected by the information technology department.
- Make users' network-based My Documents available to users when they are disconnected from the corporate network by using the Offline Files technology.
- Publish shortcuts or files in any special folders. For example, you could use this feature to place a URL for a technical support site on administrators' desktops.

Application Deployment

You can use software distribution policies to centrally manage software distribution in your organization. You can install, assign, publish, update, repair, and remove software for groups of users and computers. If you are familiar with the SMS installer capabilities, most of this will be old news to you. The nice part about the Windows 2000 way of doing things is that all this ties into the structure of the Active Directory, and so it becomes very simple to assign an application set to the accountants, for example.

There are two terms you have to become familiar with when discussing the application deployment policies: assigned applications and published applications. You assign applications to groups of users so that all users who require the applications will automatically have the application available to them, without the technical support staff having to set up the application on each machine. When you assign an application to a group of users, you are actually advertising the application on all the users' desktops. The next time a user logs on to Windows 2000, the application is advertised. This means the application shortcut appears on the Start menu, and the registry is updated with information about the application, including the location of the application package and the location of the source files for the installation. The application, however, is not installed at this time. When the user selects the application from the menu for the first time, the setup proceeds and the application opens. This is called "just in time installation," and it's a pretty good idea because it reduces the number of unnecessary applications stored on the users' machines. How? Well, if a user never tries to open the program from the Start menu, the files are never installed. So, if he has no real need for Visio, for example, he won't get stuck with all those files on his hard drive.

The other option for deploying software with group policies is to designate an application as a published application for a group of users. This allows the user to decide whether or not to install such applications. This method can be very helpful when you are trying to move the organization toward a standardized desktop and want the users to be able to install needed applications from a list of approved applications. When you publish an application, no shortcuts to the applications appear on users' desktops and no local registry entries are made. Published applications store their information in the Active Directory.

A published application shows up in the Add/Remove Programs tool, which will include a list of all published applications that are available to the user. If a user tries to open a file that is associated with a published application—an `.mpp` file, for example, that requires Project 98 to open it—the application will install automatically when the user tries to open the file.

Scripts

With the Scripts extensions, you can assign scripts to run when the computer starts or shuts down, or when users log on or off their computers. Using the WSH, you can use either JScripts or VBScripts. Microsoft expects other software vendors to provide scripting engines that will expand the types of scripts that can be sued with Windows 2000.

The names of scripts and their command lines (in the form of registry keys and values) are stored in the `registry.pol` file. For more information about the WSH, check the following Web site: `http://www.microsoft.com/scripting`. You can also see examples of the scripting host in Appendix A, as it is used with VBScript to build Active Directory components.

Local Group Policy Objects

You can set policy for the local machine for any computers that are not members of a domain. To set local policy, use the GPE focused on the local computer. You can access the GPE tool by using the Computer Management MMC snap-in for the local computer.

A local group policy object exists on every computer, and by default it contains *only* security policy. It is stored in `%systemroot%\system32\GroupPolicy`, and it has the following ACL permissions:

```
Administrators: Full Control
System: Full Control
User: Read
```

When focused on a group policy object, the GPE notifies its extensions, and they are loaded based on whether or not they are appropriate for local use. Naturally, when you use the GPE to edit LGPOs, some of the extensions you would see when editing group policy objects are missing. For example, the application and file deployment tools aren't there, which makes sense as it is a standalone machine, and so there is nowhere to deploy them from!

As I mentioned earlier in this chapter, if the computer is not a member of a domain, the GPE will automatically open to the LGPO

Group Policy Design Considerations

One of the things you will want to consider when designing your Active Directory structure is the application of group policies within the tree. Deciding what group policies you want to employ and how you want to apply them may even determine, to some extent, how you end up grouping people and resources. Thinking about the implementation of group policies from the very beginning will help you simplify implementation and reduce administration.

Using the group policy capabilities in various combinations makes group policy very flexible, allowing it to meet a variety of business requirements. Remember the Keep It Simple principle when designing your group policy object deployments. By all means, use the simplest combination possible and test your deployment carefully. The next section lists some very important points to consider when doing group policy planning.

- **Minimize the use of the Block Policy Inheritance feature.** As mentioned previously, you can prevent group policy settings of parent Active Directory containers from affecting users and computers in lower-level Active Directory containers. This is a useful and powerful feature which you should use judiciously and only when a particular situation requires it. Blocking the inheritance of policy from parent Active Directory containers can complicate troubleshooting policy.
- **Minimize the use of the Force Policy Inheritance feature.** You can also ensure that the policy settings you specify in a given group policy object at a higher-level Active Directory container are enforced on lower-level Active Directory containers. Only use this strong and helpful feature when circumstances require it. Overuse of this feature with other related features such as Block Policy Inheritance can complicate troubleshooting policy.

- **Minimize the number of group policy objects associated with users in Active Directory containers.** You can assign more than one group policy object to a particular Active Directory container if your situation requires you to do so; however, you should note that the number of group policy objects you assign can affect logon processing time. During logon time, each group policy object associated with an Active Directory container—and each object the user or computer has Apply group policy ACE access to—is processed, and so the greater the number of associated group policy objects, the longer logon will take to process them.
- **Override user-based group policy with computer-based group policy only when necessary.** You can set user settings per computer and, thus, override user-specific policies with computer-specific policies. This is useful when you want to provide a specific desktop configuration regardless of which users log on to the computer. To set user settings per computer, you would use the Software Policies node under Computer Settings in the GPE console.
- **Avoid using cross-domain group policy objects assignments.** Although you can assign group policy objects from different domains to a single Active Directory container if a particular situation requires it, you should note that in such cases group policy processing would be slower. This is because domain boundaries are crossed.

Administration of Group Policy Objects

Delegation of authority, separation of administrative duties, central versus distributed administration, and design flexibility are important factors you'll need to consider when designing group policy and selecting which scenarios to use for your organization.

Whether or not you implement group policy in a modular fashion (for example, creating a group policy object specifically for software management options, a group policy object specifically for security configuration options, and so on) will be determined by the administrative requirements and roles in your corporation. If administrators are organized according to their duties (such as software management administrators, security administrators, logon administrators, and so on), you may find it useful to define policies in group policy object modules.

Lowering the Number of Group Policy Objects Associated with Users in Active Directory Containers

One way to lower the number of group policy objects affecting users is to use security groups as a way of filtering GPOs. If you apply policy from multiple group policy objects to an Active Directory container and use group policy filtering, making some policies invisible to some users, performance will be significantly improved. This is because fewer group policy objects will be processed.

If your situation requires you to use filtering based on security groups, you should ensure that the users you intend to receive policy from a particular group policy object have Apply group policy ACE access to that group policy object. If the users do not have Apply group policy access to that group policy object, they will not get those policies.

Delegation of authority will depend largely on whether you use centralized or distributed administration in your corporation. Based on their particular corporate requirements, network administrators can use ACL permissions to determine which administrator groups can modify policies in group policy objects. Network administrators can define groups of administrators (for example, software management administrators), and then provide them with read/write access to selected group policy objects, allowing the network administrator to delegate control of the group policy object policies. Administrators who have read/write access to a group policy object can control all aspects of that group policy object. If you are a network administrator who uses centralized administration, you may choose to give other administrators read-only access to group policy objects.

Just remember to plan carefully for your group policy objects. Consider your administrative model as well as your corporate culture, other Active Directory design criteria, and what it is you really want to accomplish with group policies. They're new, they're cool, and they'll make your administrative life a day in paradise if done well. If group policies are deployed badly, however, that paradise evaporates very quickly.

9

IntelliMirror Features for Client Management

WELL, THE FINAL CHAPTER HAS ARRIVED, AND IT IS TIME TO FILL IN THE last few blanks in your Windows 2000 user management toolkit by introducing you to the wonderful world of IntelliMirror. As I mentioned way back in the first chapter, IntelliMirror is not actually one technology, it is a group of technologies that Microsoft is marketing under that trademark. The purpose of the IntelliMirror features are similar to the intent of its predecessors, the Zero Admin initiatives (ZAK and ZAW). All three of these Microsoft efforts have been aimed at reducing the overall total cost of ownership (TCO) for Microsoft desktops by reducing the need for desktop administration. While ZAK and ZAW fell short of the goal in some ways, IntelliMirror has a real chance at achieving a win because it is tightly integrated with the Active Directory structure and other operating system features.

Because this product is an evolution of ZAK and ZAW, you might surmise that many of the underlying technologies were already there. If so, you are correct. In addition to the original functionalities of the Zero Admin products, you will also see capabilities you might recognize from other Microsoft products, such as SMS. For you, this means that IntelliMirror is not bleeding edge at all. Parts of it have already been proven in other products or initiatives. Maybe that's why it works so darn well.

Microsoft has been making some pretty big claims about how Windows 2000 will enable an administrator to remotely restore a user's workstation in a matter of minutes with no loss of user data and without the administrator having to leave his own desk. Sound pretty unbelievable? It sure did to me when I started hearing the first whispers of this capability before the first beta release. Now that I have seen and used these features, I'm a believer. We totally destroyed a user's workstation (short of doing any hardware damage, of course) and were able to recreate his exact environment in a very short time. In addition, while we were working, the user was sitting at his vacationing cubemate's computer, accessing his own data in his own My Documents folder and seeing all his personal applications, favorite URLs, and desktop on his neighbor's machine. Did this happen by magic? No. Did it just appear because we installed Windows 2000? Again, no. It took some planning (There she goes again with the planning stuff!) to accomplish this amazing roaming environment, but overall, it just wasn't that hard to do!

I will warn you that in order to really achieve what Microsoft has promised—and what we did—you will have to use more than just the IntelliMirror technologies. You will also need to use a feature called Remote Operating System Installation (ROSI). IntelliMirror plus ROSI equals total machine replacement, according to Microsoft. The good news is, these are all software modules available in Windows 2000. No extra products to buy!

Remote Operating System Installation

ROSI is a Windows 2000 technology that allows a client machine configured with remote boot capabilities to install an operating system from a remote server onto the local hard drive. To accomplish this, Windows 2000 uses a remote boot technology called Pre-Boot Execution Environment (PXE). This technology is DHCP based. In order to complete such an installation, you must have a remote Windows 2000 server that is running the Remote Installation Services.

The remote server can provide the installation services in one of two ways. It can serve as the host for the Windows 2000 Professional installation source files. This would provide an installation scenario similar to installing Windows 2000 Professional from a CD locally. The difference, of course, being that the files are actually being transferred over the network. This method provides a vanilla installation of the product. Any customizations could then be accomplished using scripts, profiles, or policies.

The other method of accomplishing a remote install is to create and maintain a cloned image of the desired environment on the remote installation server. This environment could include all operating system preferences and services as well as standard application environments for a particular desktop setup. The images are then prepared and replicated to the remote installation server using (what else), a Wizard to walk the administrator through the necessary steps. Now, when a new installation is required, the cloned image can be installed from the remote server onto the local client's hard drive. Microsoft refers to this method as the RIPrep imaging option.

This installation can be accomplished by the user. To start an installation, the user starts a network service boot using the BIOS or a floppy. The user then presses F12. This downloads a Wizard that then walks the user through the available installation options. The user's options are confined by group policy settings that allow an administrator to specify who can install operating systems and what type of installations they will have available to them. The ability to let the user install the operating system frees the tech support group from the rather mundane and time consuming task of installing the operating system and then manually configuring the user's environment. That's the ROSI service from the 10,000 foot level. Naturally, there's a lot more that you will need to know before you run off and attempt to do an install. Fortunately, Microsoft has two good whitepapers on the topic. One is an overview document and the other covers installation. You can find them both listed on the Windows 2000 Server site at: `http://www.microsoft.com/windows2000/library/howitworks/default.asp` under the Management section.

IntelliMirror

The terms Microsoft has been using to describe IntelliMirror have been evolving just like the product has. You may have heard early articles and whitepapers referring to "client-side caching" and "single instance storage," for example. The features are still there, but the terminology has been changed, probably to more clearly reflect what the system really does. Now when Microsoft talks about IntelliMirror, they divide the system into three parts. Those are:

- User Data Management
- Software Installation and Maintenance
- User Settings Management

I mentioned earlier that IntelliMirror wasn't a single technology, but it achieved its goals through a combination of several new Windows 2000 technologies as well as the Zero Admin tools that were already in existence and have found a new home in Windows 2000. You can think of the larger Microsoft categories mentioned above as the goals of IntelliMirror. In the next several paragraphs, we'll look at the combination of technologies required to actually achieve those goals.

Microsoft claims that Windows 2000 will help administrators manage their users' data as they move between workstations in the enterprise. In addition, the fact that this feature can be centrally implemented ultimately lowers TCO. How many hours have you spent trying to retrieve data off a user's damaged hard drive? To accomplish this requires the use of several tools:

1. First, Active Directory so that you can deploy group policy objects.
2. Then the use of Offline Files and the Synchronization Manager so that data is saved in multiple locations in case of network outages.

3. Finally, folder redirection so that a user's data is stored in a secure server location rather than the local hard drive. Disk quotas can be used in conjunction with folder redirection to make sure that one user doesn't end up taking up all your server hard drive space.

The goal of Software Installation and Maintenance is to allow a user to have the software they need to do their jobs and to ensure that it is complete and up to date with established corporate standards. Software packages can be made available to a user or they can be mandated for use by that user. Software is only installed at time of use, minimizing the impact of unneeded software installations. Once the software is installed, it becomes self-repairing. If a discrepancy is noted between the installed package and the server's version, the system automatically reinstalls the missing or damaged components. This is done through the use of group policy objects and Active Directory, as you learned in the last chapter. The actual installation is accomplished through the use of the Microsoft Installer tool (on the administrator's side of the house) and the Add/Remove Programs icon in Control Panel (from the user's standpoint). I think it is obvious how much this automatic repair function could save a company in terms of tech support costs and lost user time.

User Settings Management refers to the ability of the user to have his usual desktop available no matter where he logs on the network. You might also call it the portable desktop environment. A user's desktop settings, such as colors, folders, URLs, printers, and installed software, would all be on the desktop, regardless of what machine he uses to log on. These settings are primarily established through the use of group policy's User Documents and Settings and roaming user profiles. In order to use group policies, obviously, you will have to use Active Directory. Finally, Offline Files can also be employed to make sure that needed user files will be available even if the network is not.

So where do we start? We've already discussed Active Directory, group policy, folder redirection, the Windows Installer, and roaming user profiles in earlier chapters. What's left would be Offline Files and the Synchronization Manager. We'll discuss those in detail in the next section. After that, we'll look at some scenarios where these combinations of technologies can be used in the real world.

Offline Folders and the Synchronization Manager

What Microsoft is now calling Offline Files is the same thing that earlier Beta versions of Windows 2000 called client-side caching. As with many of the tools, it is most useful and effective when used in combination with Active Directory and group policies, but it doesn't have to be used that way. Many of the required settings are local and can be managed through the application of local group policy rather than domain policy. As far as what network folders can be designated for caching, the only requirement is that they reside on an SMB supporting machine on the network. That, of course, means that any other SMB machine can be designated, including your neighbor's Windows for Workgroups peer-to-peer networked machine. So, even if you have a lone Windows 2000 workstation participating in an NT 4 or other type of SMB supporting network, you can still use this feature of Windows 2000.

Exactly what does the tool do for you? Basically, it allows network files and folders to be cached on the user's workstation so that the resources are available during network outages or when the user isn't hooked to the network, as may be the case with many laptop users when they pull the PC out of the docking station and head for the airport. The really neat part is that the user follows the same procedure to access the file that he would if he were connected to the network. If he usually goes to his mapped network drive G: and double-clicks on a document there, that's what he does sitting on the plane as well. From the user's view, the access process is always the same. When the user reconnects, the locally cached copies are synchronized with the network copies on a schedule that can be specified by the user or the machine's administrator.

What about security, you say? Well, the great news is that if the resource is protected by an ACL, the ACL is cached with the resource. I say "if the resource is protected" because some SMB systems may not use ACLs. In that case, you didn't have any security on the file in the first place, so there's nothing to really worry about. In the case of ACL secured resources, I have a suspicion there might be instances where there will be problems with unresolvable ACEs at some point in a large organization, but I haven't been able to effectively prove or disprove that theory. If any of you security gurus find problems with this later, send me an email.

Establishing the Local Cache

There are two modes in which the local cache can be established. One way to set up the cache is by specifying an upper limit on the size of the client-side cache. This size is expressed as a percentage of local hard drive space. If this method is chosen, the system fills the cache with network files until it reaches the upper limit of the cache size. When this happens, it dumps the older files from the cache to allow another requested file to be placed into the cache. If you ever had to suffer through an accounting class or two, you'll recognize its first in, first out (FIFO) method. If you reason this out, you will see that because the system is filling the cache as the user accesses different network files and folders, there is really no way to guarantee what files will be in the cache at any given moment. For example, the document containing today's cafeteria menu might have just been loaded into the cache and caused that critical report you were working on to be dumped. Not exactly the most efficient way to do things, but it would help protect a user if he were working on a particular document and his network went down, as long as the document wasn't bigger than the cache!

The second way to manage this functionality is to "pin" or designate certain network folders for local caching. When this method of cache management is selected, the size of the cache matches the size of the designated network resources and you will always know exactly what is in the local cache. I think you'll find that this is the preferred method of employing the caching functionality for mobile laptop users. That way, when your user heads for the plane, he'll have everything he needs to keep busy on that long flight to London. One example of the things you can accomplish by using these different tools in conjunction is to redirect a user's My Documents folder to the network, give it a disk quota size, and then specify that folder for local caching. When the user unhooks, he has every document that he has saved available to him, and you have the security of knowing there are "safe" copies on your well-pampered and secured servers just in case his laptop gets stolen in London! When the user next hooks up to the network next, the files that have changed will be automatically synchronized. We'll cover the different synchronization options a little later in the chapter.

If you choose to pin folders or files, there is obviously going to be another step to your process after you enable the user of Offline Files on the client machine. You will have to go out to the network resource you want to pin and designate it as such. To do this, simply go to the network share, select the files or folders you want to have available Offline, and right-click. From the context menu, select Make Available Offline. This will activate a Wizard that will walk you through setting the parameters for your Offline access to this resource. Alternatively, as you will see a little later in this discussion, you can designate that certain files be administratively designated for offline use through the use of group policies. Once the designated files or folders are pinned, you're ready for a network outage!

To activate the client-side functionality, you have a choice of tools to use. You can either use the Explorer interface or accomplish the task through the use of policies. We'll look at both methods in the next section.

Setting Up the Client for Offline Files Using the Explorer Interface

In order to start using Offline Files, you must first enable this functionality on the client. You also may be interested in using the local Group Policy Editor to configure additional settings for the local cache. To enable Offline Files, invoke a Windows Explorer window either by double-clicking on My Computer or finding the buried copy under Start, Programs, Accessories, Windows Explorer. Select Tools from the menu bar, and then choose the Offline Files tab. That interface is shown in Figure 9.1 because there a few things I want to point out to you that aren't exactly intuitive.

You can see that much of the interface *is* pretty intuitive. Turning that functionality on and off, for example. How much simpler does it get than a check box? Telling the system to synchronize at logoff ensures that you will have the latest copy possible if the network is not available when you log on the next time, rather than just not being able to work on the documents at all. The reminder balloons are to remind a user that he is working with "stale" or unsynchronized data. You can disable this, and the system becomes a little more invisible to the user if that is your preference.

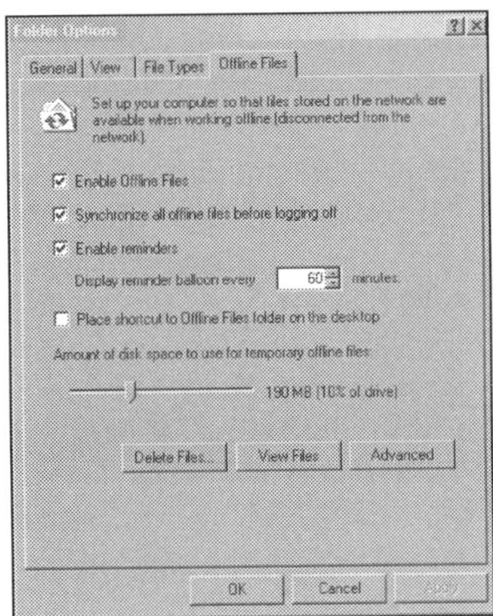

Figure 9.1 The primary Offline Files interface on the client machine.

The part that is not so intuitive is the bar for specifying the amount of disk space to be used. What you see in the figure is the default 10 percent that is set up whenever you enable Offline Files on a Windows 2000 machine. If you do nothing else, the system will fill that 10 percent with the most recently accessed network files until the 190 MB (in this example) is full. If you want to pin certain network resources into the cache, you have to take the further step of going out to the network and designate those resources. What happens then is that the cache becomes self-managing as far as size. Obviously, there must be some consideration given to the available local disk space when selecting network resources. That's why disk quotas are so helpful.

With this same interface, a user can manage his local cache. You can view the contents of the cache and delete files from the cache by using the Delete Files and View Files buttons.

The Advanced button allows you to manage the network connections used in caching by defining what strategy you want the computer to employ should a network connection be lost. Figure 9.2 shows that interface.

I'm showing you this interface because there is another non-intuitive piece here. The top part of this interface specifies the general behavior the machine will employ. You can choose to tell the user what's going on and let him start using the cache, or select the other option, Never Allow My Computer to Go Offline. Now, I don't know about you, but when I first saw this, I wondered what miracle Microsoft had accomplished that allowed a user to exempt himself from network outages because that sure sounds like what the interface is saying. Naturally, that's not what it really means. Selecting this option prevents the user from using the offline cache, so that, for this user, the network resources would be unavailable in the event of a network problem. The exception list lets you designate certain network connections as exceptions to whatever rule you set for the machine in general. Notice, however, that the interface sets this by computer, not by share; so, if all your shares are on the same machine, you've got a small problem.

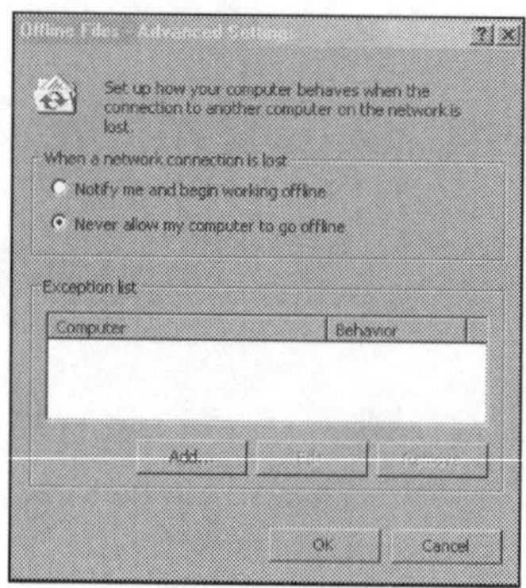

Figure 9.2 The Advanced Offline Files interface.

Setting Up the Client for Offline Files Using Policies

The Advanced interface is all well and good if you are the user sitting at the computer, but what if you want to remotely configure a machine for Offline File use or designate users' Offline File settings for a whole domain. Obviously, you're going to use another method. Are you surprised that you can accomplish this through the use of policies? You can either specify the Offline File settings through the use of the local group policy object on a machine or through the employment of domain group policy objects.

Let's look at the local GPEto show you the actual settings, as they are about the same regardless of which level of editor you are using. There are Offline File settings in both the Computer Configuration and User Configuration nodes of the editor. Both nodes are located under the Administrative Templates/Network node. As a general rule, if the policy appears in both the User and Computer settings, the Computer Configuration settings take precedence. The settings that appear in both nodes are designated in Table 9.2 by an asterisk next to the policy. First, let's look at the Computer Configuration settings. I've shown that interface in Figure 9.3.

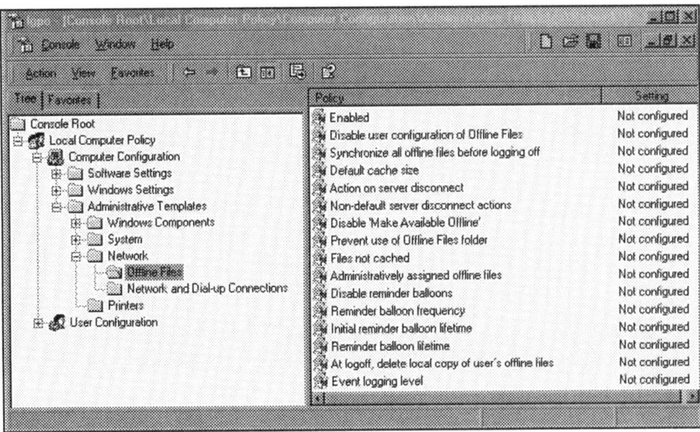

Figure 9.3 The Computer Configuration node settings for Offline Files.

Table 9.2 **The Functionality of Each Setting Under the Computer Node**

Policy	Functionality
Enabled	Establishes the usability of the Offline Files functionality. If enabled, the function is turned on and the user cannot turn it off. If disabled, the use of Offline Files is prohibited and the user can't turn it on. Machine must be rebooted for the policy change to take effect in order to either create or delete the local cache. Default settings: Windows 2000 Professional: Enabled Windows 2000 Server: Disabled
Disable user configuration of Offline Files *	This is an overriding policy setting that quickly locks down the Offline Files function to system defaults or administrative choices. If enabled, users can't affect any of the settings used to configure the Offline Files functionality. Policy disables three functions: the Settings button is removed from the status dialog box, the Offline Files tab is removed from Folder Options, and the Settings entry on the Offline Files right-click menu is removed.

continues

Table 9.2 **Continued**

Policy	Functionality
Synchronize all offline files before logging off *	Enabling this policy means that a full synchronization of files will be performed at logoff. If disabled, only a quick synchronization is performed. If Not Configured, the default is a quick synchronization at logoff, but as with all policies that are not configured, the user can change that option.
Default cache size	If enabled, it allows administrators to set a default size for the local disk cache, rather than leaving it up to the user's whim or the system default of 10 percent. Users can still pin files and folders manually and are not affected by this limit if they are not prevented from using that functionality by another policy setting. A disabled setting defaults the local cache to 10 percent of the hard drive, the same as a Not Configured default size, but if Not Configured, users have the option to change the size of the cache.
Action on server disconnect *	Allows administrators to set what action will occur when a network connection is interrupted. If enabled, action options are Work Offline, meaning the user can use cached copies of the server files, or Never Go Offline, meaning the user will be unable to use the locally cached copies of files from that server. If Not Configured, Work Offline is permitted for all server connections by default, but the user can change these options.
Non-default server disconnect actions *	This policy supercedes the previous policy and allows certain actions to be designated when connections to specified servers are interrupted. An exception list can be created that allows an administrator to specify behavior for certain server connections that is different than whatever the previous policy's default settings mandate. For example, you might have

Policy	Functionality
	redirected a user's My Documents folder to the network and then designated it for offline work. That would be fine because that user is probably the only one using that folder. On the other hand, a project's document share that has shared documents being continually updated might not be a good choice for offline work due to the number of synchronization issues that might come up on reconnect. You could exempt this server from working offline by specifying the server name and a "1" for off. A "0" next to the server indicates that users can use files from this server offline.
Disable "Make Available Offline" *	Enabling this policy stops a user from pinning folders or files by removing the "Make Available Offline" entry from all menus. This does not disable automatic caching of files up to a certain percentage of the disk space either set to the system defaults or administrator's preference.
Prevent use of Offline Files folder *	Enabling this policy turns off the View Files button on the Offline Files tab. Without this button, users can't look at the local cache's contents or use any of the files therein using the Offline Files folder. They could still manually save local copies of server files to their hard drive to use in the event of a network disconnect.
Files not cached	Allows an administrator to specify certain file types as being exempt from caching. File types are designated by their extensions. If more than one file type is selected for exclusion, entries in the list should be separated by a semicolon. Users will receive an error message if they try to pin a file of this type or a folder that contains a file type that is excluded. System must be rebooted for this policy to take effect.

continues

Table 9.2 **Continued**

Policy	Functionality
Administratively assigned Offline Files	This allows an administrator to pin folders or files for the user. For example, an administrator using redirected My Documents folders might pin those network copies for the users. Entries are designated by their UNC paths. Variables such as `%username%` and `%homepath%` might be used to designate network paths and make the policy more generic so that it can be applied to many users.
Disable reminder balloons *	Takes away the prompts telling users they have been disconnected and are working from the local cache rather than the network versions of the files. Prompts are enabled by default when the Offline File functionality is enabled either by user interface or by policy. If this policy is enabled, reminders are turned off and the user can't turn them on. If disabled or Not Configured, the prompts are turned on and the user has the power to disable them.
Reminder balloon frequency *	Determines how often reminder prompts discussed above are displayed to the user. Defaults are: first reminder, 30 second display; subsequent reminders appear every 60 minutes and are displayed for 15 seconds. Enabling the policy allows the administrator to change those Not Configured defaults and also prevents the user from making any changes by removing the option from the Offline Files tab.
Initial reminder balloon lifetime *	Enabling the policy allows an administrator to alter the default display time for the first reminder prompt from the default of 30 seconds to some other value expressed in seconds.
Reminder balloon lifetime *	Enabling the policy allows an administrator to alter the default display time for subsequent reminder prompts from the default of 15 seconds to some other value expressed in seconds.

Policy	Functionality
At logoff, delete local copy of user's Offline Files	Enabling the policy mandates that the system will clear the local cache at user logoff. If files have not been synchronized, changes can be lost as files are not synchronized before being deleted. If disabled or not configured, the cache is retained and available to the user at next logon.
Event logging level *	Allows an administrator to set the detail level of the logging that occurs surrounding Offline File usage events. Events are written to the Application log. By default, an error event is only written to the log if the local cache is corrupted. Additional levels of logging can be established by entering the following numbers into the policy dialog: 0: An event will entered if the offline cache is corrupted. 1: Disconnect events that are server-based will be recorded. 2: Entries will be made for client connect and disconnect events. 3: Server reconnect events will be recorded in the log.

Synchronizing Files

When you synchronize files, the files you opened or updated while disconnected from the network are compared to the versions of the files that are saved on the network. As long as the same files you changed haven't been changed by someone else while you were offline, your changes are copied to the network. There are actually two possible types of synchronization methods that can be specified, full and quick. Full synchronization ensures that Offline Files are complete and current. Quick synchronization ensures that files are complete, but does not ensure that they are current.

Synchronization Manager Tool

Options for how and when locally cached copies of network files will be synchronized are set through the Synchronization Manager. You access this tool by using Start, Programs, Accessories, Synchronize. This tool will show you the files that need to be synchronized as well as synchronize on demand using the Synchronize button.

The Setup button can be used to further refine your synchronization options. By using Setup, you can set up different synchronization schedules and items to be synchronized based on what type of network connection you are using. For example, if you have a laptop that runs through a docking station when you're at your own desk and a nice 100MB Ethernet connection to that docking station, you may choose to synchronize more stuff than when the laptop is undocked and you're using that 56K modem to hook into the corporate net. You can specify the network connection and resources for both the Logon/Logoff and On Idle synchronization schedules.

You can also have Synchronization Manager automatically synchronize the information available to you offline in a number of ways. You can choose to synchronize every time you log on or off your computer, or both, as you can see in Figure 9.4. Notice that you can also specify whether the user will be asked before synchronization occurs.

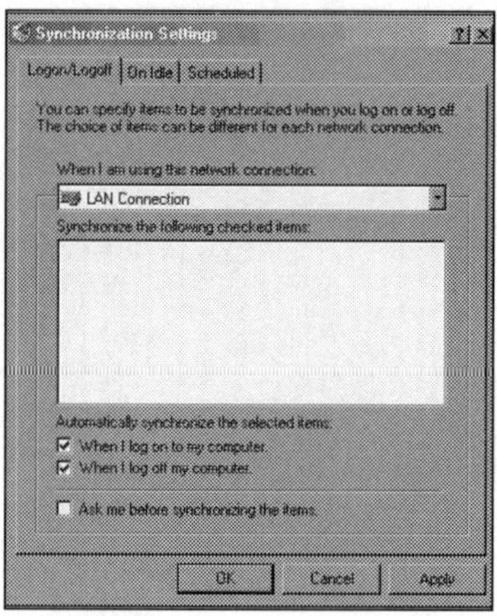

Figure 9.4 Specifying the synchronization or resources at logon or logoff.

You might also specify intervals while your computer is idle, as shown in Figure 9.5. Finally, you can designate a schedule for synchronization. With this option, you can even tell the computer to connect to the desired resource if it is disconnected at the appointed time. Naturally, Microsoft has provided you with another wizard to help walk users through the task.

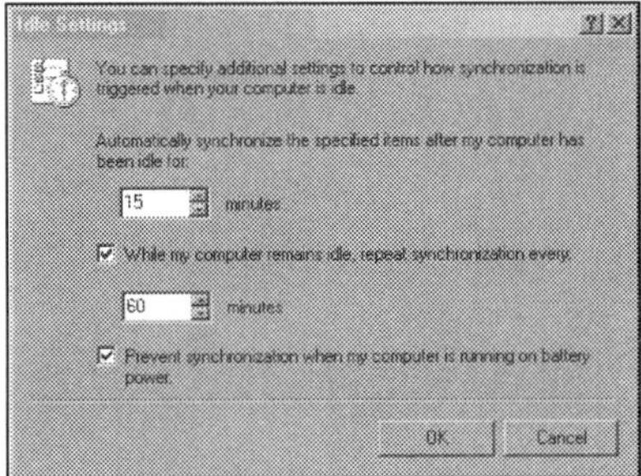

Figure 9.5 Interface for designing On Idle synchronizations and the use of the Advanced button to further refine the On Idle process.

Combinations of these options can be used, and different options can be used for Offline Files from different shared sources. Synchronization Manager compares items on the network to those that you opened or updated while working offline and then makes the most current version available both to your computer and to the network. Among the items you can synchronize are individual files, entire folders, and offline Web pages. Synchronization Manager provides a single location where you can go to synchronize any shared files that have been made available offline, regardless of the type of file or the program used to make the file available offline.

Handling Synchronization Conflicts

If someone else made changes to the same network file you updated offline, you are given a choice of keeping your version, keeping the one on the network, or keeping both. If you choose to save both versions of the file, you will be prompted to give your version of the file a different name. Then both files will appear in both locations. If you delete a network file on your computer while working offline, but someone else on the network makes changes to that file, the file is deleted from your computer but not from the network. If you change a network file while working offline, but someone else on the network deletes that file, you can choose to save your version onto the network or delete it from your computer. If you are disconnected from the network when a new file is added to a shared network folder you have made available offline, that new file will be added to your computer when you reconnect and synchronize. Finally, even if you rename a file while offline, it can still be found on the network. Remember the GUID that we talked about in earlier chapters? That's how the file is identified, so the system will track your renamed file to its network partner just as it tracks shortcuts to renamed executables.

IntelliMirror Scenarios

There are several situations that can be highlighted as great examples of times in your administrative life where IntelliMirror will be a great help to you. It can be used to solve many everyday administrative problems. The following are just some of the scenarios where IntelliMirror can be of assistance:

- Replacing a dead PC
- Coping with the mobile laptop user
- Setting up environments for new employees
- Dealing with the employee who knows just enough to be dangerous

Let's look at how each of these common problems can be solved.

Replacing a Dead PC

In the last chapter, I introduced you to the boat anchor mode of PC operation. In other words, it's not usable for some reason. Let's assume that for a change this situation was not caused by anything the user or an over eager tech support person did, but instead, some critical piece of PC hardware failed. The box has been pronounced deceased by the appropriate corporate staff member, and you are going to plunk down a brand new box for this poor unfortunate user. The only software loaded on the new machine is Windows 2000 Professional. How can IntelliMirror help?

Being a typical user, rather than wait for anyone's help, when the cardboard box with cow spots is delivered to his desk, he rips it open like it's Christmas morning and starts plugging wires into slots until all the little green lights are blinking happily. Then, encouraged by all the cheery little lights, he decides to plug the thing into the network jack and try logging on. Amazingly, he is greeted with a logon prompt. He enters his usual logon credentials and when the desktop appears, everything looks as it did on the boat anchor that just departed in a trashcan. The color scheme, shortcuts, screensaver, applications, and URLs—all of his settings are there. Best of all, when he looks in My Documents, all his files are there safe and sound.

How did we get to this happy state? The IntelliMirror infrastructure, of course. In a disaster recovery scenario, the entire recovery configuration is set up through group policy. Group policy settings follow the user and are applied wherever the user logs on to the network. This gives the appearance of the data following the user because the data location is configured through the group policy objects. This means that wherever the user logs on, the retrieval of the contents appears to be available from the local computer.

This solution isn't limited to the user who gets a new computer. The user could have also moved to another workstation, as all of the data, settings, and environment are mirrored on the network.

I described a case where the new PC came preloaded with the Windows 2000 OS. Remember that even if it had a totally blank hard drive, you could have achieved the same happy ending by using the ROSI facility of Windows 2000.

Coping with the Mobile Laptop User

Another administrative challenge in current environments is the laptop user, often a roaming road warrior who connects anywhere and anytime he wants through a variety of media. He could be at his desk using that docking station with the 100MB 3Com card, or out at a remote office using the slower 10MB PCMCIA card that came with his laptop. He might even be in the hotel suffering a terrible case of insomnia and dialing in over that 56K modem you gave him last week. You never know where, when, or how he will connect, but you know one thing, he always expects his documents to be available and not corrupted.

When this user is working at the office, he might create or edit documents and save them to his My Documents folder. After saving the documents, he logs off, unplugs the PC from the docking station, and takes it home. That night, the troublesome insomnia hits again and he stays up late editing those documents. The next morning, he returns to work and plugs the laptop back into the docking station, powers it up, logs on, and is greeted with a dialog box that tells him his local cache is being synchronized with the network.

To accomplish this miracle, you need to use a combination of folder redirection (group policy) and Offline Files. You use folder redirection to redirect the user's My Documents to a network location. Then you designate the network folder for Offline File usage, and the contents of that folder are copied into the local cache, along with the corresponding security settings. All of this is accomplished transparently to the user.

Redirecting folders has many benefits, including centralized backup and management of user data, access to user data by roaming users from any computer on the network, and protection of data from failure (or loss) of a user's computer. After all, what if our roaming road warrior left his laptop on top of the car when he pulled out of the driveway the next morning on his way to work? It could happen—after all, he didn't get much sleep.

Setting Up Environments for New Employees

Ever get tired of the company hiring new people and making you set up their accounts, access controls, environments, and other stuff? Me too. There are times when I've been thrilled to hear there was a hiring freeze on. IntelliMirror can make this process less painful by letting you configure a standard environment for a certain type of employee and apply it to new hires through the use of group policies. The new hire logs on to a new computer and finds documents and shortcuts already on the desktop. These shortcuts link to common files, URLs, and data that are useful to all employees (for example, helpful sites on the corporate intranet and a link to the electronic

Employee's Handbook might be displayed). The employee will also see all of the applications the corporation uses to do business. All of this is accomplished through the use of group policy objects.

I covered all these functionalities in the last chapter. So, I won't go into them in much detail, but you would use the User Documents and Settings node to set the environment and distribute the URLs, and then configure the Software Distribution node to prepare the list of applications this user will see displayed. When the new hire logs on for the first time and accesses the documents on the desktop, the associated applications needed to open those documents will be automatically installed if they are not already present on the system.

Dealing with the Employee Who Knows Just Enough To Be Dangerous

Sometimes you'll be blessed with a user who thinks he's helping you when he goes in and cleans up all those "extra" files he finds in his application and system directories. Although his heart is in the right place, most of us would prefer that he confine his housekeeping efforts to the My Documents folder. He might even go around helping his neighbors clean up their hard drives. Without IntelliMirror, you would soon be receiving calls as these users try to open PowerPoint and find that "some necessary files are missing to open this application." With IntelliMirror, the users attempt to open PowerPoint, and it opens just fine, even though their helpful neighbor deleted 17 necessary files from their hard drives.

What happened? You just saw the Self Repairing Software functionality of IntelliMirror at work. When they invoked PowerPoint—an application you had assigned to them through group policies—the Installer service automatically checked to make sure the application was installed. Seeing that it was installed already, it then checked to make sure that all the correct files were there and that they matched the version specified by your policy. When Installer discovered the missing files, it simply loaded them onto the machine again and the user was off and running. Much simpler than getting a call, going out to have a look, trying to figure out what's missing, and finally just deciding to reload the whole application—all while daydreaming about creative new ways to maim your helpful user.

Summing Up

As you can see, there is a whole lot of administrative help to be gained by the planned employment of these new IntelliMirror features. With Windows 2000, you do have the ability to rebuild a user's machine without leaving that nice warm cup of coffee sitting on your desk. As a matter of fact, you probably need to be sure to set up some kind of event reporting, or you may never know about the rebuild because the system would detect the problem and fix it without your intervention, based on the group policy settings for that user. What a great time to be an administrator!

So, what are the downfalls of using IntelliMirror? Well, as I have already discussed when talking about some of the technologies involved, many of the tools used to achieve IntelliMirror's functionality carry a network overhead with them. Roaming profiles, for example, will have to be downloaded over the wire whenever a user logs on. Using group policy objects can significantly increase the user's logon time if multiple policies are being used, or if policy objects from another domain are applied. There is the additional training that your administrative staff will have to undergo to learn to use these features. In order to really apply this functionality well, you should do a structure analysis and design before implementing it. Overall, I think you will find that in the long run these tools, carefully applied, will reduce the time and effort you spend trying to keep those workstations online and the users happy.

Speaking of administration, this last chapter brings us to the end of our introductory journey through the wonderful new world of user and desktop management in Windows 2000. I hope you have gleaned a few nuggets of wisdom from this text that you can use and had a few chuckles along the way. I want to wish you the best of luck in this brave new world, and if there is any way I can help you learn more about this system, feel free to email me `LSanders@isolveconsulting.com`. Hope to hear from you.

Directory Management with Windows Script Host

Windows 2000 will include Windows Script Host (WSH) and Active Directory Service Interfaces. With these tools, network administrators have the power to automate repetitive tasks in user and directory management. This appendix describes Active Directory Service Interfaces (ADSIs), and demonstrates how to use WSH to automate these tasks.

ADSI provides a set of interfaces for programmers and network administrators. Programmers can make appropriate calls to ADSI to integrate their applications with Active Directory. Network administrators can use WSH and Visual Basic or JavaScript to send instructions to ADSI. Although ADSI provides connectivity to other directory structures and methods, the focus here is solely on Windows 2000 Active Directory. These examples are included primarily to demonstrate the manner in which a script must be built to navigate the directory structure when creating or altering directory objects. Regardless of the scripting language you choose, the programming logic remains the same. For our examples, Visual Basic Script has been chosen as our language. To use the scripts presented in this appendix, write the code in a standard text editor, such as Notepad. Because these scripts are written in Visual Basic Script, save the files using a `.vbs` extension. The files can then be run by double-clicking on them or by calling them from the command line.

In order to understand the scripts presented here, let's review the structure of Windows 2000 Active Directory. Recall that Active Directory is made up of domain components, organizational units, and objects. An object can be identified by its distinguished name. For example, to identify a user with the user ID, Sophie, in the US Personnel department, you would notate her distinguished name as follows:

```
LDAP://Cn=Sophie, ou=US Personnel, ou=US Headquarters, dc=Us, dc=pizzaplace,
dc=com
```

To manipulate objects using ADSI, simply identify the object using its distinguished name. For common management tasks, identify the container that holds the object(s) you need to work with and then work with the objects in that container. Table A.1 provides a list of standard objects that can be controlled with ADSI.

Table A.1 **Standard Objects**

Standard Leaf Objects	**Standard Container Objects**
Alias	Computer
File Service	Country
File Share	Domain
Group	Locality
Print Device	Name Spaces
Print Job	Organization
Print Queue	Organizational Unit
Resource	
Session	
User	

The OU, computer, and domain container objects will be worked with here. Within these objects, the user, group, print device, and file share leaf objects will be manipulated.

Building the Structure

The first task is to build the OU structure that the directory objects will reside in. In this example, the OU structure shown in Figure A.1 is built. Let's begin by building the U.S. Headquarters structure. To do that, all organizational units down to the Trucking OU in Logistics will be built. Then some objects in the structure will be added and changed.

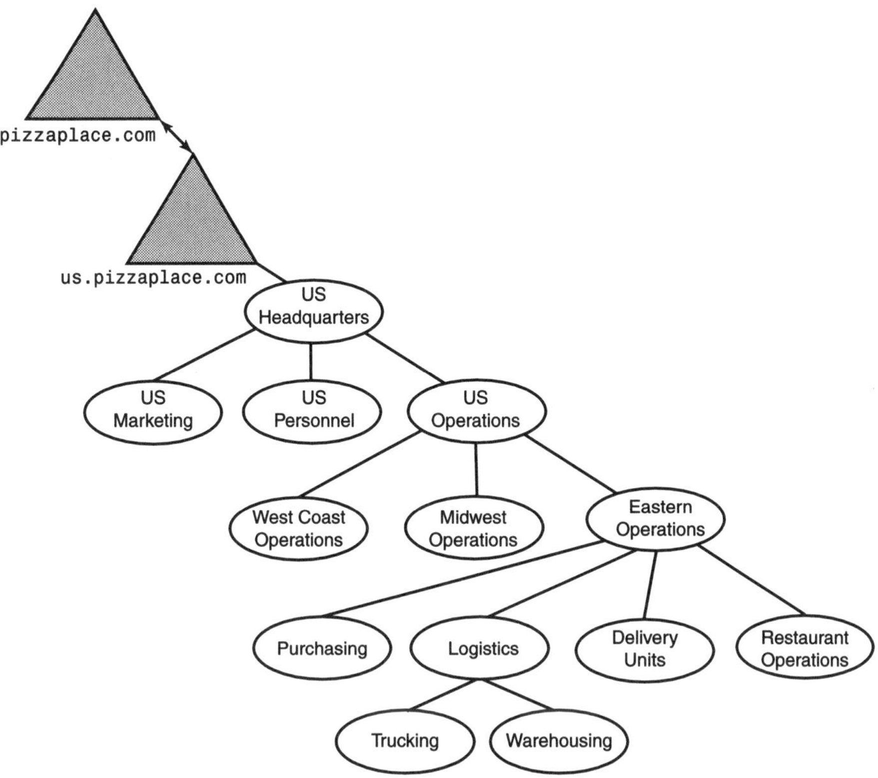

Figure A.1 The proposed OU structure of `us.pizzaplace.com`.

Remember that Active Directory is simply a logical or virtual representation of physical objects. It is important that the objects you create in Active Directory are physically in place before creating them in the Active Directory. In other words, if you are going to create a file share object in the Active Directory that points to `\\SomeServer\Share1`, the share needs to be created ahead of time on the machine SomeServer.

It is my preference to create objects one layer at a time. For example, create US Marketing, US Personnel, and US Operations. Then, step to the next layer, creating West Coast Operations, Midwest Operations, and Eastern Operations.

When using WSH to talk to ADSI, I find it helpful to have the Active Directory User and Computers console open in the background. This way, I can immediately check the results of my scripts and delete or change objects as necessary.

The scripts in this appendix are highly commented. You can use the `wscript.echo` command to notify you of important events in the script. Make sure to turn off word wrap in your text editor. Some of the lines have been wrapped to accommodate the printing of this book. The flow of each script can be summarized in the following steps:

1. Using the `getobject` method, assign the Active Directory component to a variable.
2. Create objects within the component using the *`variable`*`.create` method.
3. Commit the changes to Active Directory using the `setinfo` method.
4. Set the values of the variables to empty. (This is optional, but I think it is a good idea).
5. Repeat as necessary.

If errors occur in your scripts, they will be halted at the point in which the error occurred. You may need to delete some objects, troubleshoot the script, and start again. The error message will indicate the line in which the error occurred. Error messages do not always display. You can use the following script to build the `us.pizzaplace.com` directory:

```
'Load the active directory domain component
set mydirectory=getobject("LDAP://dc=US, dc=pizzaplace, dc=com")

wscript.echo "Create the top level organizational unit (US Headquarters)"
set newOU= mydirectory.Create("OrganizationalUnit", "ou=US Headquarters")
newou.setinfo
set mydirectory=nothing

'Build the next level of OUs
Wscript.echo "Building the ou-s in the US Headquarters OU"
Set mydirectory = GetObject("LDAP://Ou=US
➥Headquarters,dc=us,dc=pizzaplace,dc=com")
set newOU= mydirectory.Create("OrganizationalUnit", "ou=US Marketing")
newou.setinfo

set newOU= mydirectory.Create("OrganizationalUnit", "ou=US Personnel")
newou.setinfo

set newOU= mydirectory.Create("OrganizationalUnit", "ou=US Operations")
newou.setinfo
```

```
'Build the next level of OUs
Wscript.echo "Building the ou-s in the US Operations OU"
Set mydirectory = GetObject("LDAP://Ou=US Operations, Ou=US
➥Headquarters,dc=us,dc=pizzaplace,dc=com")
set newOU= mydirectory.Create("OrganizationalUnit", "ou=West Coast Operations")
newou.setinfo

set newOU= mydirectory.Create("OrganizationalUnit", "ou=Midwest Operations")
newou.setinfo

set newOU= mydirectory.Create("OrganizationalUnit", "ou=Eastern Operations")
newou.setinfo


'Build the next level of OUs
Wscript.echo "Building the ou-s in the Eastern Operations OU"
Set mydirectory = GetObject("LDAP://Ou=Eastern Operations, Ou=US Operations, Ou=US
Headquarters,dc=us,dc=pizzaplace,dc=com")
set newOU= mydirectory.Create("OrganizationalUnit", "ou=Purchasing")
newou.setinfo

set newOU= mydirectory.Create("OrganizationalUnit", "ou=Logistics")
newou.setinfo

set newOU= mydirectory.Create("OrganizationalUnit", "ou=Delivery Units")
newou.setinfo

set newOU= mydirectory.Create("OrganizationalUnit", "ou=Restaurant Operations")
newou.setinfo


'Build the next level of OUs
Wscript.echo "Building the ou-s in the Logistics OU"
Set mydirectory = GetObject("LDAP://Ou=Logistics, Ou=Eastern Operations, Ou=US
Operations, Ou=US Headquarters,dc=us,dc=pizzaplace,dc=com")
set newOU= mydirectory.Create("OrganizationalUnit", "ou=Trucking")
newou.setinfo
set newOU= mydirectory.Create("OrganizationalUnit", "ou=Warehousing")
newou.setinfo

wscript.echo "All OUs Created!"
```

Building the Printers and Shares

Creating printers and shares follows the same five-step procedure as creating OUs. File shares are identified as volumes in ADSI. The following example creates a file share in the Logistics OU that connects to Share1 on the Windows 2000 server:

```
Set myOU = GetObject("LDAP://Ou=Logistics, Ou=Eastern Operations, Ou=US
➥Operations, Ou=US Headquarters,dc=us,dc=pizzaplace,dc=com")
```

```
Set myshare = myou.Create("Volume", "Cn=Logistics-Archive")
Myshare.Put "UNCName", "\\Windows2000.us.pizzaplace.com\Share1"
Myshare.Put "Description", "Plans and Diagrams for Logistics"
Myshare.setinfo
```

Remember that you are simply creating a virtual link to a physical resource. So, you need to physically create the share on the server. This can be done using the Shared Folders MMC snap-in, or by using the net share command.

Here is my opinion on printers. In order to create the printers objects in the directory, the printer must physically exist and be shared on the network. When you create the printer on the print server, there is a check box that says Publish in the Directory. By checking the box, you have accomplished your goal. If you do wish to script this, however, you can follow the standard steps as described for the volumes.

Building the Users

Remember that a user is a leaf object and is placed within a container object. The steps are very similar to the five steps described above. The `variable.create` method is passed the object User and the common name of the user to be created. For example, the command to create a user with the common name, Sophie, would be something like this:

```
Set newuser=mydirectory.create("User", "CN=Sophie")
```

Users have many properties that can be specified. Some properties must be specified in order for the account to be valid. A partial list of standard user properties follows.

- CN (Common Name)
- Userprincipalname
- Samaccountname
- Givenname
- SN (Surname)
- Scriptpath
- Profilepath
- Homedrive
- Homedirectory
- Telephonenumber
- Street
- L (Locality or City)
- St (State)
- Postalcode

There are many, many more properties. See the Active Directory Schema Manager for a complete list.

In order for an account to be functional or usable, you must identify the common name (CN), and the SAM account name (samaccountname). You must also activate the account. This is done by setting the useraccountcontrol to one. In order to set the properties for an object, use the Put method. The following example demonstrates the minimum amount of code needed to create a functional account for Molli Ehling in the Logistics OU.

```
Set mydirectory = GetObject("LDAP://Ou=Logistics, Ou=Eastern Operations, Ou=US
➥Operations, Ou=US Headquarters,dc=us,dc=pizzaplace,dc=com")
set newuser= mydirectory.Create("User", "CN=Molli Ehling")
newuser.put "samaccountname", "MEhling"
newuser.Put "useraccountcontrol",1
newuser.setinfo
```

The next example creates a more thorough account, including address and contact information for Sophie Ehling in the Logistics OU.

```
Set mydirectory = GetObject("LDAP://Ou=Logistics, Ou=Eastern Operations, Ou=US
➥Operations, Ou=US Headquarters,dc=us,dc=pizzaplace,dc=com")
set newuser= mydirectory.Create("User", "CN=Sophie Ehling")
newuser.put "Samaccountname", "SMEhling"
newuser.put "Givenname", "Sophie"
'newuser.put "Middlename", "Marie"
newuser.put "Sn", "Ehling"
newuser.put "streetaddress", "10231 DogsLife Blvd."
newuser.put "L", "Dog Park"
newuser.put "St", "Ohio"
newuser.put "postalcode", "12345-6789"
newuser.put "telephonenumber", "555-555-1234"
newuser.put "mail", "sophie@gsehling.com"
newuser.put "wwwhomepage", "www.gsehling.com"
newuser.put "description", "Garys Yellow Lab"
newuser.put "displayname", "Sophie Marie Ehling"
newuser.Put "userAccountControl",1
newuser.setinfo
```

Modifying the Users

To modify an object once it is created in the directory, simply get the object, and use the Put method to change its properties. To get an object, identify it by the common name. For example:

```
Set myuser = GetObject("LDAP://Cn= Sophie Ehling, Ou=Logistics, Ou=Eastern
➥Operations, Ou=US Operations, Ou=US Headquarters,dc=us,dc=pizzaplace,dc=com")
```

This example will assign Sophie to the `vbscript` variable `myuser`. Now you can use `myuser.put` to change her properties. Let's assign her user profile path and change her address:

```
Set myuser = GetObject("LDAP://Cn= Sophie Ehling, Ou=Logistics, Ou=Eastern
➥Operations, Ou=US Operations, Ou=US Headquarters,dc=us,dc=pizzaplace,dc=com")
Myuser.put "profilepath", "\\Win2000\profiles\Sehling"
Myuser.put "scriptpath", "%logonserver%\scripts\canine.vbs"
myuser.put "streetaddress", "1531 Beggars Lane"
Myuser.setinfo
```

Adding Users to Groups

Once the users are in place, they can be added to groups. Groups can be added anywhere in the directory using the same procedure for adding OUs. The following example adds the user Sophie Ehling to the domain administrative group in the `us.pizzaplace.com` domain:

```
x = "LDAP://cn=users,dc=us,dc=pizzaplace,dc=com"
set groupou = GetObject(x)
y = "LDAP://Ou=Logistics, Ou=Eastern Operations, Ou=US Operations, Ou=US
Headquarters,dc=us,dc=pizzaplace,dc=com"
Set userou = GetObject(y)
Set grp = groupou.GetObject("group", "CN=Domain Admins")
Set usr = userou.GetObject("user",  "CN=Sophie Ehling")
grp.Add usr.AdsPath
```

Enhancing the Scripts

In all of the examples, the names of the users, groups, and OUs are hard-coded. This was done to keep things simple. You can use other techniques to provide input to your scripts so that the scripts can be reused without modification. In the next example, you will use the input box from WSH to provide input for your script. The following script will enable you to change the telephone number for any user in the Logistics OU:

```
x= Inputbox ("Enter the common name for the user")
y= Inputbox ("Enter the new telephone number")
s = "LDAP://cn=" + x + ",Ou=Logistics, Ou=Eastern Operations, Ou=US Operations,
➥Ou=US Headquarters,dc=us,dc=pizzaplace,dc=com"
set u = GetObject(s)
u.put "telephonenumber", y
u.SetInfo
Wscript.echo "Telephone Number for " + X + " has been changed to " + y + "."
```

WSH also provides access to files using the Filesystem object. The use of this object is rather complex. This would enable you to input information from a text file, and populate Active Directory based upon this information. WSH also provides a facility to access databases using ODBC, ADO, and other database techniques. Using one of these two technologies, you could, for example, export your human resources database to a comma-separated value (csv) text file. You can manipulate this file using any spreadsheet or database program. Using WSH with the Filesystem object, you could populate the directory one row at a time. This feature itself will be a tremendous time saver for those who are setting up a new Windows 2000 network.

Summary

The WSH has brought the power and speed of scripting to Windows environments. The scripts can receive input values from the command line, input boxes, and file sources. ADSIs extend this power to Active Directory. Well-designed scripts will enable administrators to automate everyday management tasks and to deploy the Active Directory structure very quickly. Using ADSI, you can deploy your structure and use existing models and resources such as employee databases. By scheduling scripts using the Task Scheduler, daily routines can be run without interaction from the user.

B

Custom .ADM Template File Example

As we discussed in the text, the policy editor, both in NT 4 and Windows 2000, is a tool that lets you see a partial view of the registry in a GUI format. If you want to expand upon the default views given to you by Microsoft in the policy editor, you must add new custom template files to the system. There are several reasons why you may want a custom view. Sometimes .ADM files are sent to you by ISVs to augment the policy editor so that you can configure the ISVs' software settings using the policy editor. You may also decide that you need to use the policy editor to access more of the settings in the registry to more efficiently manage your environment.

Creating your own template files has traditionally required a certain amount of programming knowledge and dedication. This wasn't one of the most fun administrative tasks. Now, however, you have the option of using third-party tools that can accomplish the same purpose and do it without the Extra Strength Tylenol that is required when doing it yourself.

The .ADM file in this appendix was created with just such a tool. It was created with a Simac Software tool called Policy Template Editor version 1.3.1. The tool works against NT 4 and Windows 2000 registries as long as the key specified is a valid registry key. More proof that the registry hasn't changed all that much! To use the tool, you simply identify the registry key you want illuminated in the policy editor and the tool does the rest. Then you add the completed .ADM file to the list of .ADM files in the policy editor, and you're ready to go. If you would like to have a closer look at it, the tool can be downloaded from Simac's Web site, `http://www.spaceguard.com`.

This particular .ADM file opens up the view to the AutoadminLogon key of the registry, which lets a user be automatically logged on with a certain username and password. This capability can be helpful in multiuser environments where security is not a large concern or where convenience is the primary factor. Information kiosks, library catalog terminals, and the kids' PC all qualify for that criteria. Not a really complicated programming problem, but at least you will see the structure of an .ADM file through this example.

```
CLASS MACHINE
   CATEGORY "Automatic Logon"
      KEYNAME "Software\Microsoft\Windows NT\CurrentVersion\WinLogon"
      POLICY "AutoadminLogon"
         VALUENAME "autoadminlogon"
         VALUEON "1"
         ACTIONLISTOFF
            KEYNAME "Software\Microsoft\Windows NT\CurrentVersion\WinLogon"
               VALUENAME "DefaultUserName"
               VALUE ""
         END ACTIONLISTOFF
         PART "Username" EDITTEXT
            VALUENAME "DefaultUserName"
            MAXLEN 255
          REQUIRED
         END PART
         PART "Password" EDITTEXT
            VALUENAME "DefaultPassword"
            MAXLEN 255
            REQUIRED
         END PART
      END POLICY ; AutoadminLogon
   END CATEGORY ; Automatic Logon
```

Glossary

Account lockout A security feature that locks out a user after a designated number of bad logon attempts over a specific period of time. Number of logon failed attempts and time periods can be specified using the policy editor.

ACE (Access Control Entry) An entry in an object's DACL that grants permissions to a user or group. An ACE can also be an entry in the DACL that specifies the security events to be audited for a user or group.

ACPI (Advanced Configuration and Power Interface) Open industry specification that specifies power management on many mobile, desktop and server machines, and peripherals. ACPI support is critical in Windows 2000 to take full advantage of power management and Plug and Play features of Windows 2000.

Active Directory The directory service included with Windows 2000 Server product. Stores information about many types of objects and makes this information available to users and administrators. Gives users network access to authorized resources anywhere in the directory while using a single logon.

Asymmetric encryption Method of encryption that uses two keys to encrypt and decrypt messages. The two keys are mathematically related. One key is termed the public key and is given out to anyone wishing to correspond with a particular user. The second key is a private key and only the intended receiver has the private key. Typically, the public key is used to encrypt messages and the private key is used to decrypt them. Also called Public Key Cryptography.

Backup operator A type of built-in local or global group that allows members to have the necessary level of rights and permissions to back up and restore files and folders. Members of this group can back up files and folders regardless of the permissions, ownership, encryption or auditing restrictions set on the resources being backed up.

Bindery The Novell NetWare 3.x database that contains organizational and security information about users and groups.

Built-in groups Default groups provided for administrative use with the Windows 2000 Server and Professional product lines. Built-in groups have predefined levels of access and privileges associated with them.

CA (certification authority) The entity responsible for establishing and guaranteeing the authenticity of public keys belonging to certificate holders or other certification authorities.

CAPI (CryptoAPI) Provides a set of functions that allow applications to perform the tasks of encrypting or digitally signing data while maintaining the security of a user's private key.

CDP (CRL Distribution Point) Optional extension to a X.509v3 certificate that specifies how information is obtained. Also identifies a directory entry or other source to look for certificate revocation lists.

Certificate A collection of data used for authentication and exchange of data on unsecured networks. Certificates bind the entity that holds the public encryption key to the entity that holds the corresponding private key. Certificates are digitally signed by the certification authority.

Certificate revocation list (CRL) A document listing revoked certificates which is maintained by the certification authority.

Certificate store Usually a permanent storage area where valid certificates, revoked certificate lists, and certificate trust lists are stored.

Certificate template A Windows 2000 construct that specifies the format and content of certificates based on their intended usage. Maintains a variety of certificate types that certificate requestors select from when requesting a certificate for a specific use.

Certificate trust list (CTL) Digitally signed list of root certification authority certificates that an administrator can consider reputable for specific purposes.

Certification hierarchy Web of certification paths that result from the creation of parent/child relationships between certification authorities.

Certification path Unbroken chain of trust between the certification authority and the end user.

Child object Object that resides in another object.

Console tree Left pane in MMC.

Container object An object that can logically contain other objects.

DACL (Discretionary Access Control List) A list that is the part of an object's security descriptor that specifies access permissions to the object by user or group.

Digital signature The process of encoding secret information known only to the originator of data into a tag that is attached to the data and guarantees integrity in a public key environment.

Digital Signature Standard (DSS) Standard that uses the Digital Signature Algorithm for its algorithm and SHA-1 as its message-hashing algorithm. DSA can only be used for generating digital signatures, not for data encryption.

Directory partition A contiguous subtree of the Active Directory that forms a unit of replication; in essence, a single domain.

DLL (dynamic link library) Operating system feature that allows executable routines to be stored separately as files with .dll extensions. DLLs usually accomplish a specific function or set of functions and only run when needed by a particular application.

DNS (Domain Name System) A hierarchically arranged name service for TCP/IP machines.

Domain controller A Windows 2000 Server machine that manages user access to the network, including typical security functions such as authentication and authorization. Also maintains the Active Directory information for the domain.

Domain namespace The namespace defined in the database of the DNS system.

Encrypted passwords Password that is hashed for the purpose of being more secure than a plain text password.

Explicit permissions Permissions on an object that are assigned when the object is created or specifically set at a later time by the object owner.

Full name A user's complete name, usually consisting of first, last, and middle initial. The full name is different from the user's logon name. While there can be duplicate instances of a user's full name within a partition, the logon name must be unique.

Gateway Service for NetWare Service that allows a Windows 2000 Server box to connect to NetWare servers and act as a gateway to client computers on the Microsoft network.

Global group A group that can be created in a domain to grant rights and permissions to a set of users who are members of the group. The scope of a global group is enterprise-wide, but the membership set is made up of accounts from its own domain.

Group A set of users, machines, contacts, and other groups that are collected together for the purpose of security or distribution.

Group policy An MMC snap-in used to define the behavior of users' desktops.

Group policy object A collection of group policy settings that are saved and then applied against users' desktop environments to create a certain look, feel, and mode of operations. Each Windows 2000 computer has a local group policy object that can be overridden by domain-level group policy objects. Domain-level objects are stored as Active Directory objects.

Guest account Built-in account designed to be used when a user doesn't have a valid account on the computer, in the domain, or in any of the domains trusted by the computer.

Hardware profile Profile that describes the hardware configuration and characteristics of a particular computer.

Hash algorithm Mathematical algorithm used to produce a hashed value of some piece of data, such as a password or message.

HCL (Hardware Compatibility List) List of hardware devices supported by Windows 2000. Latest version of the HCL is available at the microsoft.com Web site and should be checked before purchasing any hardware components.

Hive Segment of the registry that appears as a file on the hard drive. Each hive is a specific set of keys, subkeys, and values.

Home directory A folder that can be designated as part of the user's profile that is accessible to the user and stores files for that user.

Interactive logon A network logon by a user sitting at the keyboard of a particular machine. The user fills out the Logon Information screen.

Junction point Physical location on the hard disk that points to data residing in another location, either local or remote.

KDC (Key Distribution Center) A Kerberos V5 service that runs on a domain controller and issues ticket-granting tickets and service tickets used to obtain network authentication within the domain.

Kerberos V5 An Internet Standard authentication protocol that assumes a position of mutual distrust, requiring users and servers to validate their identity in the domain.

Key A folder that appears in the left pane of the Registry Editor. A key can contain subkeys and values.

Local group A group that can be created and has scope in a single domain (a domain being identified as a particular machine or a partition in the Active Directory). All other group types and security principals can be legal members of local groups.

Local user profile The user profile created automatically when a user interactively logs on to a particular machine. Stored on the local hard drive of that machine.

Logon rights Rights assigned to a user that define the methods in which the user is allowed to log on to the system.

Logon script A file assigned to a user account that runs each time a user logs on. Can be used to configure a user's environment at logon, including mapping network drives and assigning printers to the desktop.

Mandatory user profile A type of roaming user profile that is not updated at the server each time the user logs off. Mandatory profiles are typically created by an administrator and assigned to more than one user.

Master domain An NT 4 domain that holds all user accounts for the master domain models of domain trusts.

Member server A computer running Windows 2000 Server product, but that is not running as a domain controller and has no role in the administration of the domain.

MMC (Microsoft Management Console) A framework for hosting administrative tools called consoles. The main MMC window contains commands and tools for creating and authoring consoles.

NDS (Novell Directory Services) A distributed directory database that provides information about every network resource and facilitates access to those resources in a Novell NetWare 4.0 environment.

Node In tree structures, such as MMC, a location on the tree that may have one or more branches below it.

Noncontainer object An object that cannot contain other objects[md]a user, for example.

NTFS file system The file system of choice in NT environments. Provides additional capabilities such as support for long filenames, very large storage media, security, and system recovery.

Object A system entity that can be a directory, file system, or network object that is defined by a set of strictly defined attributes.

Owner The security principal who controls the setting of permissions on a system object.

Parent object The object in which another object resides. A folder, for example, is the parent of a file that resides in that folder.

Permission The level of access granted to a user for a particular system object.

PKI (public key infrastructure) A term that is used to describe the structure of a public key system. Typically, PKI refers to a system of certification authorities, certificates, and public and private key mechanisms.

Policy The mechanism by which desktop settings are automatically configured for users as defined in advance by an administrator.

Predefined key A key that represents one of the major divisions of the registry. HKEY_LOCAL_MACHINE is an example of a predefined key.

Private key The secret half of the cryptographic key pair used in public key infrastructure systems. Private keys are usually used to decrypt data or digitally sign data.

Privileges Also called user rights. Refers to actions a user is allowed to perform on the system or network.

Property A characteristic of an object class.

Public key The nonsecret half of the cryptographic key pair used in public key infrastructure systems. Public keys are typically used to encrypt data that will be decrypted with the corresponding private key. They can also be used to verify a digital signature.

Public key cryptography A method of cryptography in which two different keys are used, a public key and a private key.

Realm In a non-Windows 2000 environment, a set of security principals subject to Kerberos authentication; in other words, a Kerberos realm.

Registry In Microsoft operating environments, a database that contains information about a computer's configuration, such as user profiles, installed programs, installed hardware, and settings and port information. It is organized hierarchically and consulted constantly during a computer's operation.

Remote administration Administration of one computer by an administrator sitting at another location.

Resource domain The flip side of an NT 4 master domain in the Master Domain trust models. The resource domain contains all the resources that will be accessed by the users in the master account domain.

RFC (Request for Comments) Official documents of the IETF that describe specifications for Internet protocols.

Roaming user profile A type of user profile that is based on a server and downloaded to a machine when a user logs on. At logoff, the server profile is updated to reflect any changes the user made to his environment during that logon session. Since it is server-based, the updated profile is available to the user regardless of where he logs on next in the network.

Root authority The certification authority at the very top of a certification hierarchy.

Root certificate A self-signed certification authority certificate issued by the root authority since there is no higher level authority that can sign the certificate for the root.

SACL (System Access Control List) The part of an object's security descriptor that specifies the auditing requirements for that object by user or group.

Scope of influence In the domain environment, a site, domain, or organizational unit.

Secret key encryption Also called symmetric encryption, the same key is used to encrypt and decrypt messages.

Security log An event that captures events specified by the SACL on objects, as well as the audit policy for the computer or domain.

Service ticket A ticket issued by a Kerberos V5 TGS that allows a user to authenticate to a specific service in the domain.

Shared resource Any device, data, or program that is made available to network users.

SID (Security ID) A unique number that identifies security principals and is created at the time the account for the security principal is created. If the account for a security principal is deleted, the SID is destroyed forever.

Single sign-on The concept of allowing a user to log on to one domain in a domain tree and, through that single logon, gain access to all resources within the enterprise that he has permissions to access.

Smart card A credit-card-size device that stores security information for a user, such as public and private keys, passwords, and other personal information. When the smart card is inserted into the smart card reader to initiate the logon process, the card's owner is prompted for a PIN to guarantee that he is indeed the authorized holder of the card.

Snap-in A type of tool that can be added to MMC consoles to achieve added functionality.

Standalone server A Windows 2000 server that doesn't participate in a domain. The server processes logon requests and authenticates users against its local user database.

Subtree Any node in a tree structure and its associated descendent nodes.

Symmetric encryption See *private key encryption*.

System Policy An NT 4-style policy based on registry settings and created using the NT 4 System Policy Editor, resulting in a .pol file that can be saved and applied to domain entities.

Systemroot The path and folder where the Windows 2000 system files are installed. %systemroot% is a variable that can be used to designate this folder regardless of its actual name or path.

TGS (ticket-granting service) A service provided by the Kerberos V5 KDC that issues service tickets that allow users to authenticate to services in a domain.

TGT (ticket-granting ticket) The ticket issued by the Kerberos KDC to enable a user to obtain a service ticket from the Kerberos ticket-granting service.

Trust relationship A virtual relationship established between domains to extend the pass-through authentication channels outside a single domain's security boundary.

UNC (Universal Naming Convention) Sometimes erroneously referred to as NETBIOS names, the UNC naming convention for network resources follows the syntax: *\\servername\sharename\directory…\filename*

User profile The profile that defines a user's operating environment when the user logs on. Encompasses all of the user-specific settings of the Windows 2000 environment.

User rights Tasks a user is permitted to perform on a machine or in a domain. Rights can be granted via membership in groups or individually.

Value entry The entry that appears in the right pane of the Registry Editor when a given key is selected in the left pane. Value entries are composed of the Value Name, Data Type, and the actual Value string.

Workgroup A group of users that are often connected via a local area network, but use a peer-to-peer networking software rather than participating in a domain. Authentication must be performed at every machine as users attempt to access shared resources on different machines.

X.509v3 certificate Stands for Version 3 of the ITU-T recommendation X.509 for syntax and format. An X.509 certificate includes information about the entity to whom the certificate is issued, information about the certificate itself, and optionally, information about the certification authority associated with the certificate.

Zone In the DNS environment, a zone is a subtree of the DNS database that is administered as a separate entity. This entity can consist of a single domain or a domain with subdomains.

Index

A

E

F

G

H-I

J-K

L

M

N

O

P

Q-R

S

V-W

X-Y-Z

Books for Networking Professionals

Windows NT Titles

Windows NT TCP/IP

By Karanjit S. Siyan, Ph.D.
1st Edition
480 pages, $29.99
ISBN: 1-56205-887-8

If you're still looking for good documentation on Microsoft TCP/IP, look no further—this is your book. *Windows NT TCP/IP* cuts through the complexities and provides the most informative and complete reference book on Windows-based TCP/IP. Concepts essential to TCP/IP administration are explained thoroughly and then are related to the practical use of Microsoft TCP/IP in a real-world networking environment. The book begins by covering TCP/IP architecture and advanced installation and configuration issues and then moves on to routing with TCP/IP, DHCP Management, and WINS/DNS Name Resolution.

Windows NT DNS

By Michael Masterson, Herman Knief, Scott Vinick, and Eric Roul
1st Edition
340 pages, $29.99
ISBN: 1-56205-943-2

Have you ever opened a Windows NT book looking for detailed information about DNS only to discover that it doesn't even begin to scratch the surface? DNS is probably one of the most complicated subjects for NT administrators, and there are few books on the market that address it in detail. This book answers your most complex DNS questions, focuses on the implementation of the Domain Name Service within Windows NT, and treats it thoroughly from the viewpoint of an experienced Windows NT professional. Many detailed, real-world examples illustrate the understanding of the material throughout. The book covers the details of how DNS functions within NT and then explores specific interactions with critical network components. Finally, proven procedures to design and set up DNS are demonstrated. You'll also find coverage of related topics, such as maintenance, security, and troubleshooting.

Windows NT Registry: A Settings Reference

By Sandra Osborne
1st Edition
550 pages, $29.99
ISBN: 1-56205-941-6

The NT Registry can be a very powerful tool for those capable of using it wisely. Unfortunately, there is little information regarding the NT Registry due to Microsoft's insistence that their source code be kept secret. If you're looking to optimize your use of the Registry, you're usually forced to search the Web for bits of information. This book is your resource. It covers critical issues and settings used for configuring network protocols, including NWLink, PTP, TCP/IP, and DHCP. This book approaches the material from a unique point of view. It discusses the problems related to a particular component and then discusses settings, which are the actual changes necessary for implementing robust solutions.

Windows NT Performance: Monitoring, Benchmarking and Tuning

By Mark T. Edmead and Paul Hinsberg
1st Edition
288 pages, $29.99
ISBN: 1-56205-942-4

Performance monitoring is a little like preventive medicine for the administrator: No one enjoys a checkup, but it's a good thing to do on a regular basis. This book helps you focus on the critical aspects of improving the performance of your NT system by showing you how to monitor the system, implement benchmarking, and tune your network. The book is organized by resource components, which makes it easy to use as a reference tool.

Windows NT Terminal Server and Citrix MetaFrame

By Ted Harwood
1st Edition
416 pages, $29.99
ISBN: 1-56205-944-0

It's no surprise that most administration headaches revolve around integration with other networks and clients. This book addresses these types of real-world issues on a case-by-case basis, giving tools and advice on solving each problem. The author also offers the real nuts and bolts of thin client administration on multiple systems, covering relevant issues such as installation, configuration, network connection, management, and application distribution.

Windows NT Power Toolkit

By Stu Sjouwerman and Ed Tittel
1st Edition
900 pages, $49.99
ISBN: 0-7357-0922-X

This book covers the analysis, tuning, optimization, automation, enhancement, maintenance, and troubleshooting of Windows NT Server 4.0 and Windows NT Workstation 4.0. In most cases, the two operating systems overlap completely and will be discussed together; in other cases, where the two systems diverge, each platform will be covered separately. This advanced title comprises a task-oriented treatment of the Windows NT 4 environment, including both Windows NT Server 4.0 and Windows NT Workstation 4.0. Thus, this book is aimed squarely at power users to guide them to painless, effective use of Windows NT both inside and outside the workplace. By concentrating on the use of operating system tools and utilities, Resource Kit elements, and selected third-party tuning, analysis, optimization, and productivity tools, this book will show its readers how to carry out everyday and advanced tasks.

Windows NT Network Management: Reducing Total Cost of Ownership

By Anil Desai
1st Edition
400 pages, $34.99
ISBN: 1-56205-946-7

Administering a Windows NT network is kind of like trying to herd cats—an impossible task characterized by constant motion, exhausting labor, and lots of hairballs. Author Anil Desai knows all about it; he's a consulting engineer for Sprint Paranet who specializes in

Windows NT implementation, integration, and management. So, we asked him to put together a concise manual of the best practices—a book of tools and ideas that other administrators can turn to again and again in managing their own NT networks.

Planning for Windows 2000

By Eric K. Cone, Jon Boggs, and Sergio Perez
1st Edition
400 pages, $29.99
ISBN: 0-73570-048-6

Windows 2000 is poised to be one of the largest and most important software releases of the next decade, and you are charged with planning, testing, and deploying it in your enterprise. Are you ready? With this book, you will be. *Planning for Windows 2000* lets you know what the upgrade hurdles will be, informs you how to clear them, guides you through effective Active Directory design, and presents you with detailed rollout procedures. Eric K. Cone, Jon Boggs, and Sergio Perez give you the benefit of their extensive experiences as Windows 2000 Rapid Deployment Program members by sharing problems and solutions they've encountered on the job.

Inside Windows 2000 Server

By William Boswell
1st Edition
1533 pages, $49.99
ISBN: -56205-929-7

Finally, a totally new edition of New Riders' best-selling *Inside Windows NT Server 4*. Taking the author-driven, no-nonsense approach we pioneered with our Windows NT *Landmark* books, New Riders proudly offers something unique for Windows 2000 administrators—an interesting, discriminating book on Windows 2000 Server written by someone who can anticipate your situation and give you workarounds that won't leave a system unstable or sluggish.

BackOffice Titles

Implementing Exchange Server

By Doug Hauger, Marywynne Leon, and William C. Wade III
1st Edition
400 pages, $29.99
ISBN: 1-56205-931-9

If you're interested in connectivity and maintenance issues for Exchange Server, this book is for you. Exchange's power lies in its capability to be connected to multiple email subsystems to create a "universal email backbone." It's not unusual to have several different and complex systems all connected via email gateways, including Lotus Notes or cc:Mail, Microsoft Mail, legacy mainframe systems, and Internet mail. This book covers all of the problems and issues associated with getting an integrated system running smoothly, and it addresses troubleshooting and diagnosis of email problems with an eye toward prevention and best practices.

Exchange System Administration

By Janice Rice Howd
1st Edition
400 pages, $34.99
ISBN: 0-7357-0081-8

Okay, you've got your Exchange Server installed and connected; now what? Email administration is one of the most critical networking jobs, and Exchange can be particularly troublesome in large, heterogeneous environments. Janice Howd, a noted consultant and teacher with over a decade of email administration experience, has put together this advanced, concise handbook for daily, periodic, and emergency administration. With in-depth coverage of topics like managing disk resources, replication, and disaster recovery, this is the one reference book every Exchange administrator needs.

SQL Server System Administration

By Sean Baird, Chris Miller, et al.
1st Edition
352 pages, $29.99
ISBN: 1-56205-955-6

How often does your SQL Server go down during the day when everyone wants to access the data? Do you spend most of your time being a "report monkey" for your coworkers and bosses? *SQL Server System Administration* helps you keep data consistently available to your users. This book omits introductory information. The authors don't spend time explaining queries and how they work. Instead, they focus on the information you can't get anywhere else, like how to choose the correct replication topology and achieve high availability of information.

Internet Information Services Administration

By Kelli Adam, et al.
1st Edition,
300 pages, $29.99
ISBN: 0-7357-0022-2

Are the new Internet technologies in Internet Information Server giving you headaches? Does protecting security on the Web take up all of your time? Then this is the book for you. With hands-on configuration training, advanced study of the new protocols in IIS, and detailed instructions on authenticating users with the new Certificate Server and implementing and managing the new e-commerce features, *Internet Information Services Administration* gives you the real-life solutions you need. This definitive resource also prepares you for the release of Windows 2000 by giving you detailed advice on working with Microsoft Management Console, which was first used by IIS.

SMS 2 Administration

By Michael Lubanski and Darshan Doshi
1st Edition
350 pages, $39.99
ISBN: 0-7357-0082-6

Microsoft's new version of its Systems Management Server (SMS) is starting to turn heads. Although complex, it allows administrators to lower their total cost of ownership and more efficiently manage clients, applications, and support operations. So if your organization is using or implementing SMS, you'll need some expert advice. Darshan Doshi and Michael Lubanski can help you get the most bang for your buck, with insight, expert tips, and real-world examples. Darshan and

Michael are consultants specializing in SMS and have worked with Microsoft on one of the most complex SMS rollouts in the world, involving 32 countries, 15 languages, and thousands of clients.

UNIX/Linux Titles

Solaris Essential Reference

By John P. Mulligan
1st Edition,
350 pages, $24.95
ISBN: 0-7357-0023-0

Looking for the fastest, easiest way to find the Solaris command you need? Need a few pointers on shell scripting? How about advanced administration tips and sound, practical expertise on security issues? Are you looking for trustworthy information about available third-party software packages that will enhance your operating system? Author John Mulligan—creator of the popular Unofficial Guide to Solaris Web site (`sun.icsnet.com`)—delivers all that and more in one attractive, easy-to-use reference book. With clear and concise instructions on how to perform important administration and management tasks and key information on powerful commands and advanced topics, *Solaris Essential Reference* is the book you need when you know what you want to do and only need to know how.

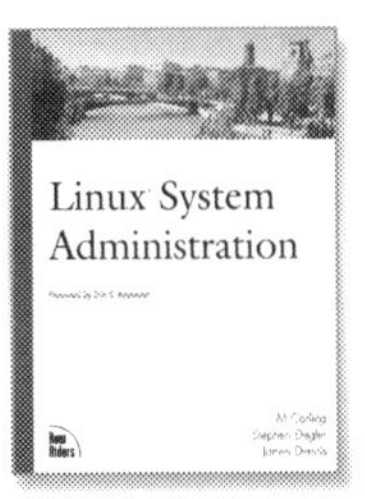

Linux System Administration

By M Carling, et al.
1st Edition
450 pages, $29.99
ISBN: 1-56205-934-3

As an administrator, you probably feel that most of your time and energy is spent in endless firefighting. If your network has become a fragile quilt of temporary patches and work-arounds, this book is for you. For example, have you had trouble sending or receiving email lately? Are you looking for a way to keep your network running smoothly with enhanced performance? Are your users always hankering for more storage, services, and speed? *Linux System Administration* advises you on the many intricacies of maintaining a secure, stable system. In this definitive work, the author addresses all the issues related to system administration from adding users and managing file permissions, to Internet services and Web hosting, to recovery planning and security. This book fulfills the need for expert advice that will ensure a trouble-free Linux environment.

GTK+/Gnome Application Development

By Havoc Pennington
1st Edition
492 pages, $39.99
ISBN: 0-7357-0078-8

This title is for the reader who is conversant with the C programming language and UNIX/Linux development. It provides detailed and solution-oriented information designed to meet the needs of programmers and application developers using the GTK+/Gnome libraries. Coverage complements existing GTK+/Gnome documentation, going into more depth on pivotal issues such as uncovering the GTK+ object system, working with the event loop, managing the Gdk substrate, writing custom widgets, and mastering GnomeCanvas.

Developing Linux Applications with GTK+ and GDK

By Eric Harlow
1st Edition
400 pages, $34.99
ISBN: 0-7357-0021-4

We all know that Linux is one of the most powerful and solid operating systems in existence. And as the success of Linux grows, there is an increasing interest in developing applications with graphical user interfaces that take advantage of the power of Linux. In this book, software developer Eric Harlow gives you an indispensable development handbook focusing on the GTK+ toolkit. More than an overview of the elements of application or GUI design, this is a hands-on book that delves deeply into the technology. With in-depth material on the various GUI programming tools and loads of examples, this book's unique focus will give you the information you need to design and launch professional-quality applications.

Linux Essential Reference

By Ed Petron
1st Edition
400 pages, $24.95
ISBN: 0-7357-0852-5

This book is all about getting things done as quickly and efficiently as possible by providing a structured organization to the plethora of available Linux information. We can sum it up in one word—value. This book has it all: concise instructions on how to perform key administration tasks, advanced information on configuration, shell scripting, hardware management, systems management, data tasks, automation, and tons of other useful information. All of this coupled with an unique navigational structure and a great price. This book truly provides groundbreaking information for the growing community of advanced Linux professionals.

Lotus Notes and Domino Titles

Domino System Administration

By Rob Kirkland, CLP, CLI
1st Edition
850 pages, $49.99
ISBN: 1-56205-948-3

Your boss has just announced that you will be upgrading to the newest version of Notes and Domino when it ships. As a Premium Lotus Business Partner, Lotus has offered a substantial price break to keep your company away from Microsoft's Exchange Server. How are you supposed to get this new system installed, configured, and rolled out to all your end users? You understand how Lotus Notes works—you've been administering it for years. What you need is a concise, practical explanation of the new features and how to make some of the advanced stuff work smoothly. You need answers and solutions from someone like you, who has worked with the product for years and understands what you need to know. *Domino System Administration* is the answer—the first book on Domino that attacks the technology at the professional level with practical, hands-on assistance to get Domino running in your organization.

Lotus Notes and Domino Essential Reference

By Tim Bankes and Dave Hatter
1st Edition
500 pages, $45.00
ISBN: 0-7357-0007-9

You're in a bind because you've been asked to design and program a new database in Notes for an important client that will keep track of and itemize a myriad of inventory and shipping data. The client wants a user-friendly interface without sacrificing speed or functionality. You are experienced (and could develop this application in your sleep) but feel that you need to take your talents to the next level. You need something to facilitate your creative and technical abilities, something to perfect your programming skills. The answer is waiting for you: *Lotus Notes and Domino Essential Reference*. It's compact and simply designed. It's loaded with information. All of the objects, classes, functions, and methods are listed. It shows you the object hierarchy and the relationship between each one. It's perfect for you. Problem solved.

Networking Titles

Cisco Router Configuration & Troubleshooting

By Mark Tripod
1st Edition
300 pages, $34.99
ISBN: 0-7357-0024-9

Want the real story on making your Cisco routers run like a dream? Why not pick up a copy of *Cisco Router Configuration & Troubleshooting* and see what Mark Tripod has to say? They're the folks responsible for making some of the largest sites on the Net scream, like Amazon.com, Hotmail, USAToday, Geocities, and Sony. In this book, they provide advanced configuration issues, sprinkled with advice and preferred practices. You won't see a general overview on TCP/IP. They talk about more meaty issues, like security, monitoring, traffic management, and more. In the troubleshooting section, the authors provide a unique methodology and lots of sample problems to illustrate. By providing real-world insight and examples instead of rehashing Cisco's documentation, Mark gives network administrators information they can start using today.

Network Intrusion Detection: An Analyst's Handbook

By Stephen Northcutt
1st Edition
267 pages, $39.99
ISBN: 0-7357-0868-1

Get answers and solutions from someone who has been in the trenches. Author Stephen Northcutt, original developer of the Shadow intrusion detection system and former Director of the United States Navy's Information System Security Office at the Naval Security Warfare Center, gives his expertise to intrusion detection specialists, security analysts, and consultants responsible for setting up and maintaining an effective defense against network security attacks.

Understanding Data Communications, Sixth Edition

By Gilbert Held

6th Edition

500 pages, $39.99

ISBN: 0-7357-0036-2

Updated from the highly successful Fifth Edition, this book explains how data communications systems and their various hardware and software components work. More than an entry-level book, it approaches the material in textbook format, addressing the complex issues involved in internetworking today. A great reference book for the experienced networking professional and written by the noted networking authority Gilbert Held.

Other Books By New Riders

Windows Technologies

Internet Information Services Administration
0-7357-0022-2
SMS 2 Administration
0-7357-0082-6
Planning for Windows 2000
0-7357-0048-6
Windows NT Network Management: Reducing Total Cost of Ownership
1-56205-946-7
Windows NT DNS
1-56205-943-2
Windows NT Performance Monitoring, Benchmarking, and Tuning
1-56205-942-4
Windows NT Power Toolkit
0-7357-0922-X
Windows NT Registry: A Settings Reference
1-56205-941-6
Windows NT TCP/IP
1-56205-887-8
Windows NT Terminal Server and Citrix MetaFrame
1-56205-944-0
Implementing Exchange Server
1-56205-931-9
Inside Window 2000 Server
1-56205-929-7
Exchange Server Administration
0-7357-0081-8
SQL Server System Administration
1-56205-955-6
Windows 2000 Active Directory
0-7357-0870-3

Networking

Understanding Directory Services
0-7357-0910-6
Understanding the Network
0-7357-0977-7
Domino System Administration
1-56205-948-3
Cisco Router Configuration and Troubleshooting
0-7357-0024-9
Understanding Data Communica-tions, Sixth Edition
0-7357-0036-2
Network Intrusion Detection: An Analyst's Handbook
0-7357-0868-1

Certification

A+ Certification TestPrep
1-56205-892-4
A+ Certification Training Guide, 2E
0-7357-0907-6
A+ Fast Track
0-7357-0028-1
MCSD Fast Track: Visual Basic 6, Exam 70-176
0-7357-0019-2
MCSE Fast Track: Internet Information Server 4
1-56205-936-X
MCSE Fast Track: Networking Essentials
1-56205-939-4
MCSE Fast Track: TCP/IP
1-56205-937-8
MCSD Fast Track: VB 6, Exam 70-175
0-7357-0018-4
MCSE Fast Track: Windows 98
0-7357-0016-8
MCSE Fast Track: Windows NT Server 4
1-56205-935-1
MCSE Fast Track: Windows NT Server 4 Enterprise
1-56205-940-8
MCSE Fast Track: Windows NT Workstation 4
1-56205-938-6
MCSE Simulation Guide: Windows NT Server 4 Enterprise
1-56205-914-9
MCSE Simulation Guide: Windows NT Workstation 4
1-56205-925-4
MCSE TestPrep: Networking Essentials, Second Edition
0-7357-0010-9
MCSE TestPrep: TCP/IP, Second Edition
0-7357-0025-7
MCSE TestPrep: Windows 98
1-56205-922-X
MCSE TestPrep: Windows NT Server 4 Enterprise, Second Edition
0-7357-0009-5
MCSE TestPrep: Windows NT Server 4, Second Edition
0-7357-0012-5
MCSE TestPrep: Windows NT Workstation 4, Second Edition
0-7357-0008-7
MCSD TestPrep: VB 6 Exams
0-7357-0032-X
MCSE Training Guide: Networking Essentials, Second Edition
1-56205-919-X
MCSE Training Guide: TCP/IP, Second Edition
1-56205-920-3
MCSE Training Guide: Windows 98
1-56205-890-8
MCSE Training Guide: Windows NT Server 4, Second Edition
1-56205-916-5
MCSE Training Guide: Windows NT Server Enterprise, Second Edition
1-56205-917-3
MCSE Training Guide: Windows NT Workstation 4, Second Edition
1-56205-918-1
MCSD Training Guide: VB 6 Exams
0-7357-0002-8

Graphics

Inside 3D Studio MAX 2, Volume I
1-56205-857-6
Inside 3D Studio MAX 2, Volume II: Modeling and Materials
1-56205-864-9
Inside 3D Studio MAX 2, Volume III: Animation
1-56205-865-7
Inside 3D Studio MAX 2 Resource Kit
1-56205-953-X
Inside AutoCAD 14, Limited Edition
1-56205-898-3
Inside Softimage 3D
1-56205-885-1
HTML Web Magic, Second Edition
1-56830-475-7
Dynamic HTML Web Magic
1-56830-421-8
Designing Web Graphics.3
1-56205-949-1
Illustrator 8 Magic
1-56205-952-1
Inside trueSpace 4
1-56205-957-2
Inside Adobe Photoshop 5
1-56205-884-3
Inside Adobe Photoshop 5, Limited Edition
1-56205-951-3
Photoshop 5 Artistry
1-56205-895-9
Photoshop 5 Type Magic
1-56830-465-X
Photoshop 5 Web Magic
1-56205-913-0

New Riders

We Want to Know What You Think

To better serve you, we would like your opinion on the content and quality of this book. Please complete this card, and mail it to us or fax it to 317-581-4663.

Name ______________________________

Address ______________________________

City______________ State______________ Zip ______________

Phone ______________________________

Email Address ______________________________

Occupation ______________________________

Operating system(s) that you use ______________________________

What influenced your purchase of this book?

- ❑ Recommendation
- ❑ Cover Design
- ❑ Table of Contents
- ❑ Index
- ❑ Magazine Review
- ❑ Advertisement
- ❑ New Riders' Reputation
- ❑ Author Name

How would you rate the contents of this book?

- ❑ Excellent
- ❑ Very Good
- ❑ Good
- ❑ Fair
- ❑ Below Average
- ❑ Poor

How do you plan to use this book?

- ❑ Quick Reference
- ❑ Self-Training
- ❑ Classroom
- ❑ Other

What do you like most about this book? Check all that apply.

- ❑ Content
- ❑ Writing Style
- ❑ Accuracy
- ❑ Examples
- ❑ Listings
- ❑ Design
- ❑ Index
- ❑ Page Count
- ❑ Price
- ❑ Illustrations

What do you like least about this book? Check all that apply.

- ❑ Content
- ❑ Writing Style
- ❑ Accuracy
- ❑ Examples
- ❑ Listings
- ❑ Design
- ❑ Index
- ❑ Page Count
- ❑ Price
- ❑ Illustrations

What would be a useful follow-up book for you? ______________________________

Where did you purchase this book? ______________________________

____

Can you name a similar book that you like better than this one, or one that is as good? Why?

____

____

How many New Riders books do you own? ______________________________

What are your favorite computer books? ______________________________

____

What other titles would you like to see us develop? ______________________________

____

Any comments for us? ______________________________

____

____

____

Windows 2000 User Management: 1-56205-886-x

Fold here and tape to mail

Place Stamp Here

New Riders Publishing
201 W. 103rd St.
Indianapolis, IN 46290

How to Contact Us

Visit Our Web Site

www.newriders.com

On our Web site you'll find information about our other books, authors, tables of contents, indexes, and book errata.

Email Us

Contact us at this address:

nrfeedback@newriders.com

- If you have comments or questions about this book
- To report errors that you have found in this book
- If you have a book proposal to submit or are interested in writing for New Riders
- If you would like to have an author kit sent to you
- If you are an expert in a computer topic or technology and are interested in being a technical editor who reviews manuscripts for technical accuracy

nrfeedback@newriders.com

- To find a distributor in your area, please contact our international department at this address.

nrmedia@newriders.com

- For instructors from educational institutions who want to preview New Riders books for classroom use. Email should include your name, title, school, department, address, phone number, office days/hours, text in use, and enrollment in the body of your text, along with your request for desk/examination copies and/or additional information.
- For members of the media who are interested in reviewing copies of New Riders books. Send your name, mailing address, and email address, along with the name of the publication or Web site you work for.

Write to Us

New Riders Publishing

201 W. 103rd St.

Indianapolis, IN 46290-1097

Call Us

Toll-free (800) 571-5840 + 9 + 4511

If outside U.S. (317) 581-3500. Ask for New Riders.

Fax Us

(317) 581-4663